Housing, Welfare and the State in Europe

Housing, Welfare and the State in Europe

A Comparative Analysis of Britain, France and Germany

Mark Kleinman
Department of Social Policy and Administration, London School of Economics and Political Science, UK

Edward Elgar
Cheltenham, UK * Brookfield, US

© Mark Kleinman, 1996

Published by
Edward Elgar Publishing Limited
8 Lansdown Place
Cheltenham
Glos GL50 2HU
UK

Edward Elgar Publishing Company
Old Post Road
Brookfield
Vermont 05036
US

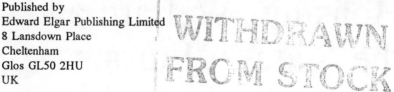

British Library Cataloguing in Publication Data
Kleinman, Mark
   Housing, welfare and the state in Europe: a comparative
analysis of Britain, France and Germany
   1. Public housing – Europe 2. Public welfare – Europe
   I. Title
   363.5'85'094

Library of Congress Cataloguing in Publication Data
Kleinman, Mark
    Housing, welfare, and the state in Europe: a comparative analysis
of Britain, France, and Germany / Mark Kleinman.
    Includes bibliographical references and index.
    1. Housing policy—Europe—Case studies. 2. Public welfare–
–Europe—Case studies. I. Title
   HD7332.A3K55   1996   96–6437
   363.5'094—dc20   CIP

1 85898 451 3

Printed and bound in Great Britain by
Biddles Limited, Guildford and King's Lynn

Contents

Tables

In memory of my parents

Preface

The origins of this book lie in my twin beliefs, first, that the study of housing policy over the last two decades can provide key insights into the fate of the welfare state more generally; and, second, that by looking at housing and welfare comparatively, one can learn about both the differences between countries, rooted in institutional and political specificities, and the common trends which unite them, driven by structural and economic change.

When I began the research on which this book is based, I was not working to any blueprint, and my ideas have evolved considerably over the several years which the research took. Along the way I have benefited from numerous conversations and arguments with, as well as practical help from, academics, researchers and policy makers in several countries. In particular, I would like to thank Laurence Bertrand, Maurice Blanc, Anne-Marie Fribourg, Michael Harloe, Franz Hubert, Volker Kreibich, Peter Malpass, Walter Matznetter, Mark Stephens, Claude Taffin, Bengt Turner, Monique Vervaeke and Christine Whitehead. I would also like to thank the Economic and Social Research Council and the Nuffield Foundation for financing study visits to France and Germany. In addition, I have benefited greatly from the exchange of ideas and information promoted by the European Network for Housing Research through its working groups and international conferences.

Julian Le Grand and David Piachaud provided detailed and helpful comments on sections of the manuscript, as well as invaluable help in defining the focus of my study. I am grateful to Carfax Publishing of Abingdon, Oxfordshire, U.K. for permission to reproduce material previously published in *Housing Studies* Volume 10 Number 1, 1995; and to Prentice Hall, Hemel Hempstead, Hertfordshire, U.K. for permission to use material previously published in *Social Policy in Germany*, edited by J. Clasen and R. Freeman, 1994. I would also like to thank Janice Harrison for assistance in preparing the manuscript for publication.

Finally, above all, I wish to thank my family: Lois, for her support, encouragement and belief in the project; and Sam for his eventual acceptance that a book with neither story nor pictures might nevertheless be of some value!

Mark Kleinman
Cambridge and London

1. Housing, Welfare and the State

1. INTRODUCTION: THE BIFURCATION OF HOUSING POLICY

Housing occupies a unique place in public policy, neither fully part of the welfare state, nor fully part of the free market. Housing was never an integral component of the system of public provision of goods and services which characterized European welfare states in their heyday during the thirty years after 1945. To use Esping-Anderson's (1990) term, housing was never decommodified. In contrast to health, education, social insurance and pensions, housing has always been 'the wobbly pillar under the welfare state' (Harloe 1995).

Nevertheless, housing has been subject to sustained, pervasive and fundamental forms of intervention by the state for well over a hundred years. Today's housing markets and housing outcomes have been decisively shaped by public policy. The physical form of housing, its location, its financing, its social significance and even its personal meaning all bear the imprint of housing legislation and housing administration.

Hence more than any other aspect of the modern welfare state, housing involves a complex mix of state and market activity. As a result, housing *policy* necessarily lies at the intersection of social with economic policy and has therefore always been a *contested* area, provided as a universal service neither by the welfare state nor by a totally free market. The provision of housing has always been characterized by what we now call the mixed economy of welfare. By studying housing policy, one can therefore also discover much about the direction of public policy as a whole, about the balance between economic and social goals in public policy, and about the

1

relative weights given to free markets and state intervention in different countries.

This book is about what has happened to housing policy over the last two decades in Europe, and also about what the study of housing policy can tell us about welfare development more generally over this period. The central argument of the book is that over the last 20 years, housing policy, as traditionally understood, has bifurcated, leading to quite separate policy concerns regarding on the one hand, the middle mass of households, and on the other, the impoverished minority. This process is more advanced in Britain than in France or Germany but the underlying processes are similar. Understanding the causes of this change requires us to look beyond the sphere of housing itself to the pervasive influence of economic orthodoxy over social policy in all three countries and at the European level.

Housing policy has become an ambiguous term. Increasingly to talk about housing policy means to talk about two very different sets of concerns, issues and possible solutions. One set of concerns relates to the circumstances of the majority, who are mainly well housed and can reasonably expect to be better housed in the future. Although these households are mainly in the market rather than the social sector, their housing outcomes are strongly affected by various types of public intervention, those which ensure continuity and reasonable market conditions in the private sector. Ensuring this means that government assumes responsibility for providing a legal framework for the enforcement of contracts; for maintaining the supply of finance; for providing output to some degree, especially counter-cyclically; for defining a land-use planning framework; for maintaining affordability through subsidies, especially to owner-occupiers; and, perhaps most importantly, for ensuring steady economic growth and a reasonably high level of employment.

The second set of concerns relates to the circumstances of the disadvantaged minority, who are badly housed or homeless, whose prospects of future betterment are uncertain, and whose residential segregation, in many cases, compounds social and economic inequality. Moreover, if (as seems likely) economic integration in Europe will lead both to a greater average standard of living and to wider disparities between individual households and between different geographical areas, then there will be a strengthening of such trends.

Whatever the formal appearance, such policies and their associated expenditures are consented to by the majority, not as a type of collective provision, but as a form of altruism (helping the poor); or as an insurance

Conclusion!

payment against riot, theft or social disorder; or as socially necessary expenditure (because low-paid but essential workers need to live somewhere). 'Housing policy', as defined in this narrow way is thus mainly concerned with social housing (including its privatization). As such, it may seem to have little direct influence on the interests of the majority of the population in most Western European countries who do not live in social housing.

This bifurcation of policy can be seen most clearly in the case of Britain. In Britain in the 1980s, elections were won and lost on the level of the mortgage rate rather than the level of housing output, and still less on the level of homelessness. The two constituencies of the well-housed majority and the poorly-housed minority moved considerably further apart during the 1980s and 1990s. Some might argue that the recent slump in the British housing market, and attendant problems of negative equity, mortgage arrears and mortgage possessions (see Chapter 2) demonstrates that there are links between the apparently comfortable many and the deprived few. But this would be to misunderstand the role of mortgage possessions in a mass owner-occupied system. The visible failure of the few ensures compliance by the majority. The crucial political point is that the rise in arrears and possessions does not create a perceived community of interest between the broad mass of owner-occupiers and those living in housing poverty.

In this book, I examine the degree to which this argument can be generalized to two other European countries. Housing policy in Britain over the last two decades has increasingly been characterized by what many European commentators refer to as an extreme neoliberal and pro-market orientation. The differences between housing policies in Britain, and those in the continental European countries are often identified with the distinction between 'Anglo-Saxon' social policy grounded in philosophical notions of liberal individualism, and the more corporatist approach to social policy based around a solidaristic model (Esping-Anderson 1990; Room and Berghman 1990).

How have different welfare states responded to growing affluence, rising expectations and changes in the class structure? Esping-Andersen, in trying to answer this question with regard to social insurance policy, has argued that 'corporatist' welfare states were best equipped to deal with these changes. The Anglo-Saxon countries, faced with an essentially similar choice about the respective roles of market and state in meeting rising expectations, opted for a dualism in two senses: markets for the better off combined with relatively low-level universal benefits; but also preservation of tax expenditures for private welfare coupled with restrictions on direct public expenditure. This description could to a large extent be applied to British housing policy. But as we shall see, even in 'solidaristic' countries such as France and Germany, there have been very similar trends towards a bifurcated housing policy and increasingly polarized housing outcomes.

Moreover, a key factor in promoting these trends has been the pursuit of closer economic integration in Europe, a consistent policy aim of both France and Germany throughout this period. The completion of the internal market and the moves towards economic and monetary union have pushed national housing systems precisely in the direction of greater deregulation and a more individualistic approach. Thus housing policy in France and Germany over the last two decades can be seen as increasingly squeezed between the economic consequences of the single market/monetary union programme on the one hand, and the social imperatives of a broadly corporatist welfare state. In comparing housing policies across countries, we need to be aware not only of the differences in institutions, in ideology and in traditions, which distinguish each country, but also of the similarities between countries which are engendered by cross-national economic forces and by an increasingly similar political outlook which narrowly circumscribes the role of social policy.

1.2 THE BIFURCATION OF HOUSING POLICY

1.2.1 Mass Housing Policy: Supporting the Market

While policy towards social housing, housing needs and multiple deprivation has evolved in the direction of 'holism' (see 1.2.2 below) the strand of policy that affects the majority of households in the countries examined has moved in a very different direction. Policy is no longer mainly (or, in the case of Britain, at all) about quantitative output targets. Instead it is about access to owner-occupation, about asset acquisition, about economic and political stability, about environmental quality and about individual choice.

All three countries in this study have been committed for twenty years or more to promoting owner-occupation, albeit via different mechanisms and with different degrees of fervour. The most extreme case is Britain, where an entire politics of owner-occupation has arisen, based around the notion that to be a home owner is closer to a political right than to an informed consumer choice; that cheaper housing in the form of constant or falling house prices is not only undesirable, but actually a threat to economic growth and political stability; and that government, while it no longer has a duty to maintain full employment, or to meet housing needs, nevertheless has an obligation to promote house-price inflation. In France and Germany, the position is less extreme, but the key aspect is similar - the separation of the policy concerns of the mass from those of the poor and disadvantaged.

The political economy of owner-occupation in Britain, organized as it is around rates of house-price inflation, mortgage interest rates, and competition in finance markets, has little to do with the residualized concerns of sink housing estates, homelessness, social isolation and chronic economic insecurity. This separation follows from the very different political strengths of the two constituencies that are the objects of policy. Housing was a factor in the defeat of the British Labour government in 1979. But it was not the government's record in housebuilding or slum clearance that was under attack, but rather its reluctance to commit resources to giving already well-housed families in the council sector a chance to share in the one-way bet that owner-occupation was then deemed to be. Similarly, as Harloe points out, housing policy became a political issue in West Germany in the 1980s not primarily because of homelessness and housing need among the poorest, but only when shortages began to affect the middle mass of the population:

the [West German] government responded to the shortage of housing and the growing political pressure for action with measures that were mainly directed to sections of the population in housing need which had a strong political voice - such as younger, middle-income white-collar and skilled manual employees who were being priced out of the housing markets of the bigger cities. (Harloe 1995, p. 470)

As Schuler-Wallner and Wullkopf put it (1991, p. 2) 'the propensity to take measures in favour of social groups who possess hardly any lobby has decreased'.

What are the characteristics of this new type of mass housing policy? The starting point is that it is a market-driven system, and hence a key aspect is deregulation and the ending of special circuits of housing finance and specialized actors within the system: *'banalisation'* is the French term. While housing used to occupy a rather unusual locus at the intersection of the welfare state and the market economy, it is now being pushed more firmly into the latter camp. As a consequence, housing finance, and hence housing provision, are now firmly tied into economic conditions and market arrangements.

The key referent for this strand of housing policy is no longer the collective notion of housing need, but the individualized concept of consumer sovereignty. As part of this, housing policy is no longer much about providing a basic human necessity, and more to do with giving the majority of households a 'stake in the country', and maintaining at least the appearance of material progress particularly in the current 'Age of Diminished Expectations' when most Western economies are growing more slowly than in the recent past, and employment becomes both less common and less secure.

1.2.2 Social Polarization and the Emergence of the Holistic Approach

From the mid-1980s on there has been growing academic interest in 'social polarization'. One component of this was the glaring contrasts which could easily be drawn, particularly in the central areas of large cities, between rich and poor, between the new gentrifiers and the older poor tenants, between the 1980s yuppies and the beggars and street homeless over whom they stepped.

Is this anything new? The close proximity of wealth and poverty in big cities has been a source not only of social scientific enquiry but also, of course, of literature and art for centuries. Moreover, one should be wary of accounts of present-day polarization which imply a golden age of greater diversity. As Fainstein puts it in her study of urban change in London and New York, in the past

> people deemed unacceptable by the larger society were kept out of those parts of the city where the upper classes congregated. The enforcement of vagrancy laws and the general lack of restraint on police discretion meant that the least attractive elements of society were simply contained in particular parts of town. ... In addition, the confinement of the mentally ill removed these individuals from the city streets. ... Second, in New York the exclusion of people of color from commercial spaces and housing was a fact of life and not illegal until mid-century. (Fainstein 1994, pp. 229-30)

Furthermore, in the general academic and political consensus that spatial polarization is a bad thing, it is not usually spelt out as to exactly why it is a problem. Why should middle-income groups remain in central city areas? Are they there to act as some kind of 'buffer' between rich and poor? In what ways is the position of poor people improved by having middle-income rather than rich people in close proximity? Are middle-income groups actually disappearing from the income spectrum (bi-modality) or do they continue to exist but live elsewhere? If the latter is the case, are they being 'squeezed out' of the city or are they *choosing* to live elsewhere? In either case, the housing system will be an important intervening variable: problems of housing affordability may be a powerful 'push' factor, while better residential environments outside urban areas can be an important 'pull' factor. Concepts such as social polarization and social exclusion have strong spatial overtones. Yet the 'spatiality' implied by them, and hence the important role of housing markets and housing policy, is often ignored.

At the European Union level, housing policy is mainly addressed in terms of its usefulness as part of a strategy for tackling poverty and social deprivation - or, to use the EU jargon, as part of 'the fight against social exclusion' (see Chapter 5). The emphasis is on multi-dimensional, multi-sectoral policies to attack concentrations of poor housing, unemployment and racial tension. Very often the physical locations of these urban problems are social housing estates, either in the inner city or in peripheral areas. A similar approach has been taken by the Organization for Economic Cooperation and Development. For example, the terms of reference and the work programme of the OECD Project Group on Housing, Social Integration and Livable Environments in Cities advocate a 'holistic sustainable approach' to housing problems. What this appears to mean is that countries must develop more comprehensive, systematic strategies for tackling housing and urban problems. These strategies should relate housing policies to issues such as transport and employment, health care and the environment; they should involve co-ordination between the various levels of government; and they should involve partnership between the private and public sectors (OECD 1990 and 1991a). Housing policies thus become part of a wider strategy for economic growth and social development. The existence of poor housing and homelessness is both a symptom and a key reinforcing factor of the social exclusion of specific groups within a basically affluent society.

While clearly it is important to link housing to broader issues of social exclusion and marginalization, this link brings with it the danger that in doing so, housing policy will be identified as being only about housing for the poor. This obscures the important - but less overt - role which the state plays in supporting the provision of housing for the rest of the population.

In effect, a new orthodoxy has emerged about the place of housing and urban problems in Europe, and the correct policy responses to them. The key elements of this are: a conviction about the importance of dealing with housing and urban problems together; the need to see housing as one element in a complex arrangement of social and economic relationships; the importance of 'community' involvement, often nebulously defined; and the need for partnership between the public and private sectors. Such an approach implies both a rejection of any role for Keynesian type policies of demand management, and the acceptance of the idea that the interests of local actors do not fundamentally conflict. It also implicitly defines housing policy as being about the poor. The majority are assumed to 'house themselves' through the market, ignoring the important role which the state plays in ensuring a functioning market.

The implication of the so-called holistic approach is that the range of problems affecting a local area needs to be tackled through several agencies working together. Moreover, the emphasis is on *local* solutions to local problems. The involvement of the local community and the local business sector is seen as being crucial to the success of urban programmes and housing development. The role of extra-local factors - such as national and international economic restructuring or national macro economic policies, for example - is played down. This policy development follows logically from the retreat from the full employment and welfare goals of the social-democratic state, and the consequent devolution of responsibility on to local communities to effect solutions to problems whose causes are mainly non-local. The true nature of this process has largely been obscured by the attendant rhetoric, which makes plentiful use of ill-defined concepts such as empowerment, community and partnership. There are, of course, real limits to state activity, and there is a vital role for local action in solving social problems. But these facts do not provide a reason for governments to disclaim responsibility, or to retreat behind an ideology in which markets always know best and government intervention is characterized as merely useless when it is not actually dangerous.

1.3 WELFARE-STATE REGIMES

It is important to place a comparative study of housing policies in three countries within a more general context of comparative studies of the welfare state. Several authors have set out broadly similar typologies of welfare-state forms, but the notion of 'welfare-state regime' is most closely associated with Esping-Andersen (1990). He argues that the variations in terms of social rights and welfare-state stratification revealed by international comparative surveys are not linearly distributed but tend to cluster around three models. The first cluster is the liberal welfare state, characterized by means testing and modest universal transfers or social insurance, strict entitlement rules, and state encouragement of the market. Examples include the United States, Canada and Australia. The second cluster comprises conservative-corporatist regimes, in which social rights are deeply enshrined, but in a way which preserves status differences. Private insurance and occupational fringe benefits are marginal; family policy stresses traditional family arrangements and social insurance typically excludes non-working wives. The principle of subsidiarity preserves important roles for the church and the family. Examples include France, Germany, Italy and Austria. The third and smallest cluster comprises the social-democratic regimes in which the principles of universalism and decommodification are extended to the middle classes. Hence services and benefits are 'upgraded to levels commensurate with even the most discriminating tastes of the new middle classes' (Esping-Andersen 1990, p. 27). Family and market hence play more minor roles. These regimes are both committed to the full employment guarantee and in fact are dependent on its attainment. Examples are the Scandinavian welfare states.

Esping-Andersen stresses the relationship between welfare arrangements and the labour market, the extent of decommodification as a classificatory device, and the role of the welfare state as a system of stratification:

> The existence of a social program and the amount of money spent on it may be less important than what it does. We shall devote many pages to arguing that issues of de-commodification, social stratification, and employment are keys to a welfare state's identity. (Esping-Andersen 1990, p. 2)

Esping-Andersen acknowledges the similarities between his typology of welfare-state regimes and Titmuss's classification of residual, industrial-achievement and institutional welfare states (Titmuss 1963). He also admits that in practice the three regimes are ideal types; no nation represents a pure case (Esping-Andersen 1990, p. 49).

In seeking to understand changes in welfare states in general, and in housing policies in particular in the most recent period, Esping-Andersen's account is useful in two ways. First, it emphasizes the range of political and social forces underpinning welfare states. Rather than welfare states arising as a *necessary* consequence of industrialization, or of the growth in power of the working class, they arise in different countries for different reasons (and at different times). Indeed, as Esping-Andersen points out, in every country it was the conservative tradition, rather than emerging radical or socialist groups which first attacked the commodification of labour. The development of welfare states has in some cases been sought explicitly in order to preserve stability and block the socialist threat by rewarding loyalty and discouraging collective action by wage earners (Esping-Andersen and Korpi 1984).

Second, there is the concept of the welfare state as a system of stratification. Each regime type gives rise to a particular form of stratification, which helps us to understand some of the ensuing politics of welfare. As Esping-Andersen puts it, 'in nations with either a social-assistance or a universalistic Beveridge-type system, the option (with post-war prosperity) was whether to allow the market or the state to furnish adequacy and satisfy middle-class aspirations' (Esping-Andersen 1990, pp. 25-6). As we shall see, an essentially similar option faced housing policy in the three countries. In examining each country's response to this challenge, however, we will see important similarities as well as differences between Anglo-Saxon and corporatist policy regimes.

Abrahamson (1992) adopts a similar typology to Esping-Andersen, but with four categories of welfare states in the EU. These comprise: the Scandinavian model, the liberal (UK) model; the corporate model and the Latin model, the latter typified by traditional 'civil society' solutions to welfare - church, family and private charity. Abrahamson argues that discussions about European social policy are about the specific combinations within a welfare mix - that is, all possibilities involve some combination of state and market. Hence the issue is no longer one of state socialism versus market liberalism, but of the form of welfare pluralism. However, the meanings given to welfare pluralism, and whether such developments are seen positively or negatively, will depend on the national context. Abrahamson argues that European welfare systems are converging towards the corporate model, with a dualistic rather than universal welfare state:

> Dualisation in this sense means a bifurcated welfare system where the (labour) market takes care of the 'well-to-do' workers through various corporate arrangements and leaves the less privileged groups in society to predominantly local institutions, either in the form of municipalities or private charity. (Abrahamson, 1992 pp. 10-11)

In terms of housing policy, Abrahamson's characterization of policy development towards a bifurcated or dualized system is, I shall argue, substantially correct. However, it is by no means clear that housing policies are converging towards a corporatist model, or indeed whether the term policy convergence should be used at all.

Esping-Andersen's typology has been criticized on a number of grounds. Lewis (1992) argues that the crucial relationship is not just between work and welfare, but between paid work, unpaid work and welfare. The provision of informal care is an important omission both from Esping-Andersen's typology, and also from Titmuss's (1963) classic division of welfare into state, fiscal and occupational. In Lewis's view, all modern welfare states are, to some degree 'male breadwinner' regimes, and this fact cuts across welfare-state regime typologies. For example, the notion of a 'Scandinavian model' breaks down once gender is considered, as there are major differences on this axis between the Norwegian and Swedish systems.

Taylor-Gooby (1991a) sees Esping-Andersen's classification as being essentially one of ideal types; in practice actual systems combine all elements of all three. Moreover, 'The UK is an anomalous case: elements of social democratic universalism co-exist in unstable combination with the Anglo-Saxon tradition of selectivity and class-divided provision' (Taylor-Gooby 1991a, p. 96). Taylor-Gooby points out that the Marshallian sequence of citizenship rights - civil, political, social - should be seen as specific to the UK rather than universal, a point also made by Leibfried (1993). Like Lewis, Taylor-Gooby also criticizes Esping-Andersen for largely ignoring the issue of unwaged work. Taylor-Gooby identifies four themes which are drawn on in arguments suggesting a less significant future role for government. These are: social changes, such as the burden of welfare spending and the crowding-out of scarce resources by state services; a 'natural' slowdown after four decades of the welfare state (maturity thesis); the impact of new approaches in social science; and a generalized shift in popular values.

The last point is important. Prosperity is accompanied by increases in inequality. This has two effects: first, to increase demands for choice which are better met in the private sector; second

As more and more people exit from mass provision, loyalty becomes the privilege of the poor. In addition, inequality diminishes sympathy between better-off and disadvantaged groups and reduces the grounds for the identification of common interests. Collectivism withers. (Taylor-Gooby 1991a, p. 98)

In conclusion, Taylor-Gooby denies that there is a generalized 'crisis of the welfare state' - the evidence is not conclusive either that demographic changes place an intolerable burden on the welfare state (see also Hills 1993), or that the welfare state undermines economic growth (Pfaller, Gough and Therborn (eds) 1991). He does, however, accept that there will be a diminished role for the state in the new 'mixed economy of welfare' or welfare pluralism.

In Mishra's (1990) view, there are currently three main interpretations of the welfare state. The irreversibility interpretation stresses the resilience of the welfare state in the face of supposed crisis, and the importance for survivability of benefits being enjoyed by middle-class as well as working-class households. Second, the maturity thesis: the welfare state has stopped growing, but this is stability not retrenchment. Third, the growth of welfare pluralism: there is a shift in the distribution of functions within the overall scheme, but this does not imply a reduction in welfare. The state's role becomes that of enabler, financing planning, promoting and regulating, but not producing or delivering. Here, Mishra makes the important point, often missing in the welfare pluralist literature, that different forms of welfare are not functional equivalents. It is important to distinguish ends and means, and *disentitlement* from the privatization of the supply of services. This is close to Self's point that privatization may be pursued by governments for pragmatic, tactical or systemic purposes. While pragmatic purposes are concerned only with the relative efficiency of public and private provision, a systemic approach 'aims at making a "regime change" which will shift the whole system towards a market economy and away from reliance upon government' (Self 1993, p. 60).

Applying a classificatory scheme to actual existing welfare states is always going to be an inexact process. Nevertheless, the sort of typologies set out by Esping-Andersen and Abrahamson are useful in demarcating certain key aspects of welfare-state regimes (although downplaying other aspects such as the relationship between waged and unwaged work). They are an essential part of carrying out any type of comparative study of policy change in a specific area; without an understanding of the institutional, political, historical and ideological factors which are summarized (however crudely) in the concept of welfare-state regime, any empirical comparison will remain rather empty.

Moreover, the discussion of welfare-state regimes and welfare typologies brings out the complex relationship between developments that are common and cross-national (slowing down of growth, shift to welfare pluralism) and the continuing differences between institutional and political arrangements in different countries. This is a key theme of the present study.

In studying the development of housing policies in three countries, the implicit framework used is one in which common forces are mediated through different sets of institutions and practices - welfare-state regimes - producing differentiated patterns of outcomes. In trying to analyse and explain policies and outcomes across three countries, the aim is not only to avoid simplistic convergence ideas, or notions of policy cycles which flatten out the differences in institutions, practices and traditions between countries, but also to avoid producing purely descriptive accounts which provide no general analysis.

1.4 UNDERSTANDING POLICY CHANGE

The analysis of policy and policy change in housing studies is, with some important exceptions, usually poorly theorized (see Ball et al. 1988, Ch. 1 for a discussion). With housing as with other policies, there is often an implicit set of assumptions about the relationship between policy change and system change, which we might term a pseudo-medical model. That is, visible problems arise either in terms of poor housing or of social/economic disadvantage (symptoms). The role of research is to collect information and describe the immediately antecedent causes (diagnosis). Policy makers then prescribe the appropriate remedy for the problem (treatment). Sometimes the treatment may be ineffective; or it may give rise to side-effects; or it may occasionally be catastrophic, leading to even more serious problems arising. But in general scientific knowledge advances, and more is discovered both about the causes and progress of 'diseases' and about the efficacy of different possible remedies. Indeed, some major problems of earlier periods are all but eradicated, allowing attention to be focused on more specific, more localized or rarer conditions.

Policy change is seen from this perspective as resulting from the changing nature of the problem, the object with which policy has to deal. This occurs either because with the disappearance of major problems other issues are revealed, or because the development of society and the economy gives rise to new challenges. Hence, in the housing sphere issues of output and crude deficits give way to concerns about quality, access, affordability and segregation. The main danger is one of inertia, that is, policy change lagging structural change, and hence one of the roles of research is to nudge governments along. The development of housing policies over the last 15-20 years can, on one reading, be fitted into such a framework. Certainly, in housing there has been a movement towards more market-orientated policies, a reduced role for the state in terms of direct provision, deregulation of finance and of rental markets, a shift from supply subsidies to personal subsidies, and a drawing back by the state from national responsibility for housing outcomes.

These policy developments are usually understood within and incorporated into the 'medical' model, that is, within the paradigm of symptom-diagnosis-treatment. So in housing, the story goes that when the major housing problem in advanced industrial nations was the crude deficit of dwellings, the appropriate policy response was large-scale state involvement in the financing and provision of housing. As economies have developed, and the crude shortage has declined or even disappeared, such policies are no longer relevant. Market mechanisms allow greater flexibility and choice, and so policy should appropriately be directed towards enabling markets to function and towards targeting help on the remaining pockets of local or specialized housing needs. Similarly, in terms of urban policy, the implication is one of mis-diagnosis. Policies used to be directed, mistakenly, at trying to prevent structural change and to preserve existing jobs. But with scientific progress, we now understand this to be futile and indeed harmful; the 'correct' policies - which promote adaptation and not resistance to change -are now being applied.

This type of explanation for policy change is superficial: it describes rather than explains. Nevertheless, this type of explanation underlies much of the current policy debate, and moving beyond this framework to a more satisfactory theorizing of the relationship between policy change and structural change presents considerable difficulties.

The approach I use in this study rejects the simplistic medical model. Housing policy is not simply a story about ever more successful attempts by enlightened governments, guided of course by academic and professional researchers, to provide universally satisfactory solutions to changing problems. Equally, however, I reject the determinist view that policies must always necessarily be ineffective in achieving goals, because the system is determined 'in the final analysis' purely by economic structures. I reject this view whether it is expressed in the currently fashionable way by reference to 'market forces' as an Ur-phenomenon, or in the alternative, and now rather nostalgic formulation as the 'logic of capital'. Similarly I reject the view that policies are always, and must always be in the objective interests of the capitalist class, and that apparent gains for the working class, for minority groups, for the poor and the disadvantaged generally are always and necessarily illusory.

Policy comes about through a complex interaction between, yes, deep structural forces, both economic and social; political action by groups, politicians, civil servants and lobbyists; ideological representations by key actors; plus a substantial seasoning of chance, pragmatism, and straightforward error. In particular the relationship between policy change and system change is complex, difficult to tease out, and certainly not reducible to mechanistic formulae, in either direction. Rather than the dualism of the medical model in which the 'magic bullets' of policy cure, or fail to cure the identified tumour, we need to think in terms of a continuing and highly iterative interaction between policy and social reality.

The roots of policy can be found in the processes of economic change and development, and the social forces they give rise to. Politics - both mass and elite - is the key intervening variable, determining the form, scale and content of policy intervention. But equally, policies have real social consequences. The shift in political support away from social housing towards owner-occupation, the 1980s emphasis on urban entrepreneurialism, the greater concern with urban fabric and environmentalism, to take just three policy examples - all of these have 'causes' which can be traced in terms of economic change, the constellation of social forces, and the deployment of political resources. But equally, they have impacts on people and places, and on what becomes defined as the possible.

Furthermore, in understanding the differences between countries, and why and how policy development has varied across countries, I have found the concept of *path dependence* to be useful. This term derives from the work of the economic historian Paul David (David 1986) who showed, using the example of the familiar QWERTY keyboard, how a chance solution to an engineering problem effectively locked in a particular technology for future development. In the early days of the typewriter, the aim was deliberately to slow down typing speeds - the mechanisms could not cope with rapid keystrokes and would jam. Hence the QWERTY arrangement was developed. This system was clearly not the most efficient one, and as the mechanical problems were solved, the underlying need for a QWERTY arrangement disappeared: more efficient keyboard arrangements could be developed. But by this stage typists had become used to QWERTY; effectively the QWERTY system was locked in:

Policy explanations

This, then, was a situation in which the precise details of timing had made it privately profitable in the short run to adapt machines to men (or, as was the case increasingly, to women) rather than the other way around. And the business has continued that way ever since. (David 1986, p. 46)

More recent examples might include VHS videotapes and Windows computer software. Krugman (1991) has extended this idea of path dependence to the study of international trade. Trade arises not only because of some 'fundamental' reason of exogenous differences in resources, but on the basis of arbitrary specializations which then become locked in through the existence of increasing returns to scale and imperfect competition.

We can extend the concept of path dependence further in applying it to the consideration of policy regimes (see also Gotting 1994 and Stark 1992). Countries lock into types of policy regime at a relatively early stage. The reasons for this are likely to be complex - the balance of class interests and forces, inherited tradition and modes of thought, the influence of particular individuals, politicians or reformers, and so forth. But it is important to recognize that they are locked in. This does not mean that it is *impossible* for a country to change from one type of policy regime to another, but rather that the costs of doing so will be high, and so such a change is unlikely to occur.

In carrying out policy analysis, the question then becomes: how do national systems adapt in the face of exogenous and endogenous change? This is a more useful way of formulating the problem than the more usual question: 'which country has the best policies?'. The latter question, which often seems to lurk around the corner in comparative studies (particularly those funded by national governments) is intellectually a dead-end. Trying to determine which country has the 'best' housing policy is an utterly fruitless exercise. The implicit model is that of a race in which everyone starts and finishes at the same place, or perhaps some kind of simplistic perfectly competitive market in which the different countries hawk their wares. Either way it bears no relation to how policies and outcomes are arrived at in advanced industrial countries. Even worse is the practice of identifying some particular aspect of policy in one country and advocating its transplant into another, as if the individual feature could be separated from the organic system of which it forms a part.

Finally, in the analysis of contemporary welfare states, a variety of terminology is employed: quasi-markets, the mixed economy of welfare, welfare pluralism, the welfare triangle, purchaser/provider separation, enabling function, subsidiarity/solidarity, as well as marginalization, polarization, social exclusion and labour-market segmentation. Such terms are often specific to one policy tradition, or one country's literature. As the number of comparative studies multiplies, and under the influence of European integration, there is greater cross-cultural awareness of terminology and concepts. Such terms do not always translate, and national concepts do not easily 'map on to' each other. This should not be seen as a problem to be refined away, but rather as a key tool for investigating comparative social policy. It is through these difficulties and obliqueness that the nature of each welfare regime becomes apparent.

2. Britain: An Anglo-Saxon Housing Policy?

2.1 INTRODUCTION

The bifurcation of British housing policy is a process which begins in the mid-1970s, but accelerates strongly in the 1980s and 1990s. Clearly this process has its roots in earlier phases of housing policy - it was not entirely an invention of Margaret Thatcher or of the International Monetary Fund and Denis Healey. But the late 1970s and early 1980s were a crucial turning point which committed British policy to a particular path.

In seeking reasons for the bifurcation of housing policy in Britain, I reject on principle the search for a single cause. The causes lie in a complex interplay between social and economic changes on the one hand and policy innovations and development on the other. This is a story with a lot of different characters. The growth in owner-occupation has rested on a variety of factors - stable earnings, a well-functioning and accessible housing finance system, favourable tax-and-subsidy frameworks, suburban development, an ideology of home ownership, perhaps a particularly British aversion to renting, and so on. Similarly, in understanding the position of rented housing in Britain in the 1990s, one needs to look at the specific historical and institutional weaknesses of private landlords as a class, the legacy of mass housing built in the 1950s and 1960s, the shift in popular values against collectivism, the failings of public housing management, the assault on local government in the 1980s. Trying to assign primacy to any one of these factors would be entirely arbitrary.

Here, however, the idea of *path dependence* does seem to be helpful (David 1985; Krugman 1991; Stark 1992). The past constrains the present, not by determining outcomes, but by setting limits to what is possible, or perhaps a better way of putting it, by making it easier for the streams of policy to flow one way rather than another. Even Mrs. Thatcher could not make water flow uphill in the sense of being able to re-invent private renting through an act of will. So some aspects of the housing system are, in an important sense, peculiarities of the English; in another country a radical right government would have looked to private renting as well as owner-occupation as a way of cutting down the municipal empire.

In placing housing policy and outcomes in Britain in a comparative context, certain aspects of the tenure structure in Britain are immediately apparent: the very small private rented sector, the large social sector, dominated by local authority landlords, and the large owner-occupied sector - the latter a highly differentiated tenure now catering for a relatively wide group of households.

2.2 POLICY STAGES 1975-1995

A note of caution needs to be sounded about the dangers of dividing history into apparently neat periods. In practice, there are always continuities as well as contrasts between these different periods. Nevertheless, policy over this twenty-year period can usefully be divided into four main stages: the Labour government of 1974-79; the first two Thatcher administrations (1979-87); Thatcher's third term (1987-90); and post-Thatcherism (1990-95).

There are two main themes in the housing policy of the Labour government of 1974-79. First, the explicit acceptance of owner-occupation as the main housing tenure for all; and second the reduction in public expenditure following the 'IMF crisis' in 1976.

Certainly, Labour in the 1960s had not been hostile to the growth of owner-occupation. For example, it introduced the option mortgage subsidy which provided to non-taxpayers a subsidy equivalent to the tax relief enjoyed by taxpayers, thereby encouraging lower-income households into the sector. Moreover, in its 1965 White Paper, the Labour government declared that 'the expansion of building for owner-occupation ... is normal; it reflects a long-term social advance which should generally pervade every region'. This was contrasted with the role of public housebuilding which was to meet 'exceptional' needs (Malpass and Murie 1994, p. 70).

Nevertheless, there was still the sense that Labour's primary commitment was to a large public sector housebuilding programme. By the mid-1970s things were different. Labour's housing policy review in 1977 famously declared that 'For most people owning one's home is a basic and natural desire, which for more and more people is becoming attainable' (Department of the Environment 1977, para. 7.03). Elsewhere, the document argued that

> Home ownership now crosses social boundaries; for example more skilled manual workers are home owners than local authority tenants. ... The Government welcome this trend towards home ownership, which gives many people the kind of home they want. ... The Government will therefore promote measures to widen still further the opportunities for home ownership, including a special scheme of Government assistance for first-time buyers. (Department of the Environment 1977, paras 6.21-6.23)

But in addition to this, by the mid-1970s, Labour had also embraced a major change in its approach to economic policy and the role of public spending. This change in economic thinking was spelled out by Prime Minister Jim Callaghan in his speech to the Labour Party Conference in September 1976:

> We used to think that you could just spend your way out of a recession, and increase employment, by cutting taxes and boosting government spending. I tell you in all candour that the option no longer exists, and in so far as it ever did exist, it worked by injecting inflation into the economy. (Quoted in Smith 1987, p. 65)

The mid-1970s can be seen as the crucial turning point in the fortunes of the council housing sector. According to one study of the period, 'With the benefit of hindsight, the Labour Party let the best opportunity for achieving equity (between tenures) slip by in 1977' (Cooper 1985, p. 159).

The point is not whether or not such equity *would* in practice have been achieved, nor whether Labour was, by the mid-1970s, any longer genuinely committed to council housing. Rather, the point is that subsequently tenure equity was no longer politically feasible. From then on, inequity between the two main tenures and the residualization of the public housing sector become mutually reinforcing. The more council housing moved into a residual or welfare role the less attractive it became for the mass of households. Colin Ward, writing in the mid-1980s, put it as follows:

> There is a grotesque disparity between the two main sectors of the housing market. ... At the end of their working lives, as they join the inevitable queue for housing

benefit, (council tenants) have nothing at all to show for their lifetime investment in their own homes, except a full rent book. (Ward 1985, p. 52)

While the turning point can be identified as being in the mid-1970s, the decisive break with the post-war consensus came in 1979, when Labour's 'reluctant monetarists' were succeeded by a radical Conservative administration which embraced monetary control and reductions in public expenditure not as unfortunate necessities, but as articles of faith. Subsequent election victories for the Conservatives in 1983, 1987 and 1992 reinforced this shift to the right. In the 1980s, there was growing acceptance of the idea that inequality is a necessary prerequisite for growth. At the same time, growth in GDP, and in particular, growth in real incomes for those in work coupled with tax cuts, meant that increases in the size of the owner-occupied sector could be supported. As we shall see below, the situation changed somewhat in the 1990s.

In the 1980s also, the notion that state provision had *failed* became more widespread - not just in relation to council housing, but also in many other areas of the welfare state, and particularly in the nationalized industries. What is meant by 'failure', and whether or not the description is accurate, are less important here than the *perception* of failure. It was this perception which underpinned the political success of the Conservatives in transferring provision from the public to the private sector. Similarly, the fact that in practice there has been a *restructuring* rather than an *abandonment* of state intervention in the housing market was largely irrelevant to the success of an ideology which proclaimed 'rolling back the state' as the key to both economic success and social well-being.

In the general elections of 1979 and 1983, as in those of 1945 and 1964, housing was an important factor in the success of the winning party. However, unlike those earlier elections, the housing issue did not work to the benefit of the Labour vote, but to that of the Conservatives. The Conservatives projected a powerful image of a property-owning democracy and the release of council tenants from 'municipal serfdom' through the creation of a right to buy. Labour's response, by contrast, often appeared defensive and contradictory, without a coherent and positive alternative. In the 1987 election, the Conservatives audaciously stole one of Labour's themes and promised a 'right to rent', referring to plans to revive the private rented sector. Housing was a less salient issue in that election - ironically the legislation passed subsequently (the 1988 Housing Act and the 1989 Local Government and Housing Act) arguably had a far greater impact on social housing in Britain than any other measure since 1945, including the introduction of the right to buy.

In 1992, the Conservatives won despite rather than because of the housing issue. But the relevant housing issues were not the collapse of local authority house-building or the doubling of homeless families acceptances in ten years - these struggled for attention in the media. Rather it was the continuing depression in the owner-occupied market, and the effect of falling house prices on the so-called 'feelgood factor' which received attention.

In terms of housing policy it is important to distinguish between the first two terms of the Thatcher government, and the period after 1987. The 1979-87 period was characterized by an essentially pragmatic ideology based around the achievement of specific policy goals, such as reducing public expenditure on housing, and encouraging growth in home ownership. In Thatcher's third term, by contrast, there is evidence of a more thorough-going ideological approach which embraced both the owner-occupied and the rented sectors. The post-Thatcher period, despite some appearances to the contrary, does not represent a move back towards a more consensual approach to housing policy. Indeed, it is only in the 1990s that the consequences of much of the radical legislation passed in the later 1980s began to take effect. At the same time, a rather different approach to the owner-occupied sector, related to a changed set of economic priorities, also becomes apparent.

The ideology of the New Right, with its emphasis on individual freedom and consumer choice was expressed in housing policy in two main ways. First, home ownership was encouraged and supported and, second, spending on council housing was reduced. New investment was to come primarily from the private sector. The growth of council housing was to be halted and then reversed, and its future role was to become more of a welfare tenure, providing a housing safety net for the poor. Public expenditure on housing, as well as being reduced in overall terms, was to be shifted from general subsidies towards means-tested, personal support, and from new construction to repair and renewal of the existing stock.

The rationale for these policies was both economic and political. The economic argument for the switch from state provision to private provision was the belief that free markets are more efficient than central planning. The operation of the price mechanism in bringing together demand and supply in the housing market will lead to greater total social benefits than the administrative allocation of housing. Some problems of market failure and externalities do exist, but these imply relatively discrete, small-scale government responses. Similarly, issues of equity and need are best dealt with through means-tested personal subsidies, and through the social security system.

But home ownership was promoted for other reasons as well. Michael Heseltine, Secretary of State for the Environment, said in Parliament in 1980:

There is in this country a deeply ingrained desire for home ownership. The Government believe that this spirit should be fostered. It reflects the wishes of the people, ensures the wide spread of wealth through society, encourages a personal desire to improve and modernise one's home, enables people to accrue wealth for their children and stimulated the attitudes of independence and self-reliance that are the bedrock of a free society.

The extension of owner-occupation was seen as a crucial element in the making of a property-owning democracy. Mass home ownership (and, later, mass share ownership) would help to legitimize the more general notion of the private ownership of property.

Cuts in public expenditure on housing were an inevitable consequence of macroeconomic strategy which, particularly in the early period, emphasized the necessity of controlling the public sector borrowing requirement (PSBR) as part of the fight against inflation (Heald 1983). Given the difficulty of reducing central government expenditures, much of the burden necessarily fell on local authority expenditure. Furthermore, capital expenditure is somewhat less difficult to cut back than current expenditure, and the major item of local authority capital expenditure in the late 1970s was the housing programme (Hepworth 1984, p. 34).

Hence, several different strands in the ideology - a belief in the superiority of the market rather than the plan, a belief in the link between individual home ownership and political values, and a macroeconomic policy aim of reducing public expenditure - led to the same conclusion. No more new council houses were to be built, except to meet the special needs of particular groups such as the elderly; and as much as possible of the existing council stock should be transferred into private ownership.

After Thatcher's third election victory in 1987, a more comprehensive housing ideology emerged with the publication of a White Paper, *Housing: The Government's Proposals* (Department of the Environment 1987). This dealt with the rented sectors as well as with owner-occupation. It reflected the government's acceptance of the fact that there is an upper limit to the spread of owner-occupation among the population: probably at least 25-30 per cent of households will be tenants at any one time.

In the White Paper, the government set out four main objectives for its future housing policy. The first objective remained to continue the expansion of home ownership, meaning, among other things, the retention of tax relief on mortgage interest. The second objective was to 'put new life into the independent rented sector' with the term 'independent' covering both private landlords and housing associations. Third, the role of local authorities was to be altered, away from direct provision and towards the encouragement of other forms of tenure. Councils were encouraged to see themselves as 'enablers' (a key new term) 'who ensure that everyone in their area is adequately housed, but not necessarily by them'. Finally, the government intended to 'focus the use of scarce public money more effectively' by developing a new 'businesslike' financial framework for local authorities and by setting up housing action trusts (HATs) to lever private sector money into areas of public housing.

This critique of the role of the public sector in housing rests on two sorts of arguments - one economic, the other more sociological. The first line of attack rests on a neoclassical economic view about *efficiency*. In a market system, the price mechanism ensures that producers respond to market signals and hence ultimately to consumer preferences. In a non-market system, consumer choice is met by administrative, or bureaucratic procedures. While in principle these can be based on the disinterested attainment of social or welfare goals, in practice public sector management tends to respond to the interests of producers (elected councillors, trade unions, bureaucrats) rather than consumers. Public sector management, unlike the private sector, is not subject to the discipline of the market, with its ultimate sanction that inefficiency will eventually lead to bankruptcy. Therefore, breaking up public sector monopolies, introducing private competition and opening up public authorities to competitive tendering will lead to greater efficiency and greater responsiveness to consumer choice.

The second argument is very different. The abstract world of public choice theory is left behind. Public housing is seen as symptomatic of a wider malaise of dependence on the welfare state: William Waldegrave, the housing minister at the time, referred to the difficulties of getting people off 'the drug of dependence', and the White Paper referred to 'whole communities [which] have slipped into a permanent dependence on the welfare system from which it is extremely difficult for people to escape'. Of course, such arguments were not applied to home owners. Apparently, paying housing benefit to working families on below-average incomes or to occupational pensioners was likely to sap the moral fibre of the nation, while the provision of mortgage interest relief, at source and with no means test, was still, at this stage at least, taken to promote a healthy yeoman independence.

The exchequer cost of mortgage interest tax relief rose from £1.96 billion in 1980-81 to £4.67 billion in 1986-87, and to £7.7 billion in 1990-91 (Wilcox 1994, Table 87). This inconsistency between middle-class and working-class subsidies formed part of a more general pattern in which tax breaks which benefited the middle and upper classes, such as company cars and pension schemes, were not made the object of a morality campaign, and aspects of the welfare state which benefited predominantly middle-class households proved to be somewhat less vulnerable to attack from new right ideologies than those where the majority of recipients and employees were working class (Le Grand and Winter 1987).

The fourth period, since 1990, is characterized by a curious combination of less stridency in terms of expressed philosophy, but in fact more radical changes on the ground. While it may be accurate to describe this phase of housing policy as one of 'consolidation and retrenchment', as do Cole and Furbey (1994, p. 204), it is consolidation around the radical changes effected in the 1980s.

In particular, the legacy of the poll tax débâcle was not a retreat from a supposedly 'extreme' example of Thatcherism into a kinder and gentler fiscal and political relationship between central and local government, but rather the acceptance that local *government* was no longer necessary and could be replaced by a combination of local administration in the town halls and the creation of a range of centrally appointed, non-elected bodies with responsibilities for both policy making and service delivery. With more than four-fifths of local expenditure met by central government funding, and with the spending decisions of all councils in effect determined by the Secretary of State, the local state in Britain now comes close to fulfilling Trotsky's dream in which the government of persons is replaced by the administration of things.

Direct government attempts to extend the privatization of local authority housing beyond the successful right-to-buy programme, through innovations such as housing action trusts and tenants' choice, met with only very limited success. But more importantly, the general climate moved remarkably rapidly towards a consensus that the era of council housing was coming to an end. Partly, this came about through the success of some councils in voluntarily privatizing their rented stock through large-scale voluntary transfer - a policy generated by the local authorities themselves as an essentially defensive measure to forestall further financial and legal restrictions on their ability to deliver a social housing service locally (Kleinman 1993). But there were wider political and cultural changes involved also. By the mid-1990s, council housing was seen as a discrete service, to be provided to 'customers', rather than as part of the local state, still less as a component of the social wage, or as an example of 'decommodification'. In part, this resulted from specific legislation, such as the 1989 Local Government and Housing Act, which 'ring-fenced' local authority housing accounts, making them more similar to private sector trading accounts, and through the extension of compulsory competitive tendering to housing management in the early 1990s. These legal changes took place in a climate which was already hostile to the idea that council housing should be provided as anything other than a customer-driven service, and in which was implicit the idea that there was little wrong with council housing which a dose of market forces and healthy competition could not put right.

Furthermore, while in 1979 the introduction of a right to buy for council tenants seemed a bold radical move against a background of continuity in the welfare state, by the early 1990s, the marketization of the welfare state had become a commonplace. The internal market in the NHS, with hospital trusts and fund-holding general practitioners acting as cost centres, opted-out schools and free-standing further education colleges, the huge resources channelled through new quangos such as the Training and Enterprise Councils (TECs) and the large profits and salaries generated by the newly privatized utilities, now made the limited devolution of public housing to some rather similar-looking housing associations and a few trusts and co-operatives look rather tame. Suddenly, it was the continued *existence* of large-scale council housing rather than its disappearance which began to look unlikely. For Cole and Furbey (1994) it was only the timing, and not the fact, of this process which remained in doubt:

> The principle of moving to a more diverse network of social landlords, coupled with the slow but steady development of housing co-operatives, has received broad support ... it seems increasingly certain that the combination of financial pressures, stock transfers and diversification of management will bring to an end the era of municipal landlordism in Britain. (Cole and Furbey, 1994 p. 206)

The playing out of the endgame for council housing - possibly a lengthy process, possibly not - has important consequences for the other rented sectors. Housing associations enjoyed a honeymoon period between 1988 and 1993 in which they benefited from Conservative support in possessing the supreme virtue of not being local authorities, and from support elsewhere as being the only viable form of continued social housing development. However, after 1993 this began to unravel, for a number of reasons: public expenditure cutbacks, internal tensions, loss of Conservative backbench support. As housing associations began slowly to displace local authorities as suppliers of social housing, they found that part of their inheritance was declining popularity with policy makers.

Despite deregulation of rents in the private rented sector in the 1988 Housing Act, and the innovation of a temporary (five-year) tax subsidy through the business expansion scheme, there was no attempt at reviving the sector at anything other than the margins. Indeed, the largest boost to the private rented sector came as a result of the prolonged slump in the owner-occupied market, rather than through any specific legislation in regard to private renting.

In the owner-occupied sector, policy could again be described as consolidating rather than innovative, but nevertheless the effects were fairly radical. The covert policy of the Treasury in the 1980s in reducing the tax expenditures on the sector through lack of indexation and changes at the margin became overt in the 1990s with reductions in the rate of mortgage tax relief (see section 6.3.1). Significantly, it was not any desire to pursue a tenure-neutral housing policy nor a more equitable taxation policy which precipitated this, but the pressure on the government's own balance sheet, reinforced by the specific commitments on fiscal rectitude entered into by John Major in signing the Maastricht Treaty.

Overall, what was noticeable was the increased *external* influence on housing markets and housing policy, in terms of both the overriding needs of budgetary policy, and the greater impact of monetary conditions on a deregulated housing market. In many ways the most significant policy development of the early 1990s was what the government did *not* do: between 1990 and 1995 it did very little to bail out the depressed owner-occupier market. It appeared prepared to follow its free-market rhetoric at least some of the way in standing back and watching repossessions and mortgage arrears mount, and building societies' balance sheets deteriorate. Such measures as it did take were cosmetic bordering on the imaginary (the

almost invisible 'mortgage-to-rent' scheme) or based on bringing forward
committed spending from future years (the housing market package).

2.3 POLICY DEVELOPMENTS IN THE 1980s AND 1990s

In describing policy developments in the 1980s and 1990s, it is useful to
structure the exercise by looking at policy towards the three main tenures
separately. This is a reflection of the form that housing policy has in fact
taken rather than a comment on the underlying significance of classification
by tenure as opposed to other schema.

2.3.1 Owner-Occupation

Owner-occupation has grown throughout the twentieth century in Britain.
The first, largely unsubsidized boom took place in the 1930s, during which
time low wage and materials costs, together with the growth of transport
networks, led to a rapid increase in the suburban, home-owning population.
Owner-occupation rose from 10 per cent of the stock in 1914 (800,000
dwellings) to 32 per cent of the stock in 1938 (3.7 million dwellings). The
expansion continued in the post-war period, to 6.4 million dwellings in
1960, or 44 per cent of the stock. In the 1970s and 1980s, there has of
course been an increased policy emphasis on increasing owner-occupation
so that today more than two-thirds of households in Britain are owner-
occupiers. There is hence a long-term secular trend towards greater owner-
occupation.

This trend is partly a result of deliberate policy, partly a result of
structural factors. Indeed, the relative importance of policy and non-policy
factors, or, to put it another way, whether the growth of the sector has been
demand or supply led, has been fiercely debated in the literature (see for
example, Saunders 1990; Forrest, Murie and Williams 1990). Before
examining the contribution of policy, it is necessary therefore to set out
briefly the key non-policy factors. We can divide these into three broad
groups: intrinsic tenure attributes, economic factors and social factors.

By intrinsic attributes of tenure, I mean those features of owner-occupation
which relate solely to the characteristics of tenure, and not to the relative
financial returns from different tenures, or to the associated political and
ideological aspects. The distinction is thus between owning and renting,
rather than any particular kind of renting (private or public) (see also

Whitehead and Kleinman 1986). Included in this category are: the jointness of ownership and occupation, which avoids difficulties in the landlord/tenant contractual relationship; control over the dwelling, in terms of its use, modification and sale; independence - the absence of petty restrictions; freedom from arbitrary changes in legislation, such as that relating to landlord/tenant relationships; ownership of an asset which can be borrowed against (this aspect - giving greater access to credit - can be distinguished from the actual economic return on home ownership); and lastly, as argued by some, the ontological security provided by owner-occupation. This concept is defined by Giddens as 'Confidence or trust that the natural or social worlds are as they appear to be, including the basic existential parameters of self and social identity' (Giddens 1984, p. 375). Saunders suggests that home ownership can be seen as

one expression of the search for ontological security, for a home of one's own offers both a physical (hence spatially rooted) and permanent (hence temporally rooted) location in the world. Our own home is unambiguously a place where we belong. (Saunders 1990, p. 293)

Second, there are economic factors which have supported a rise in owner-occupation. On the demand side the most important of these have been full employment, at least in the first three decades after 1945, and growth in real wages over almost all the post-war period. This has meant that the ability to take on long-term debt has been extended to a wider group of households. On the supply side, the key factor has been the growth of a national capital market, including in particular the long-term development of the building societies from a temporary means of artisanal self-help to major financial institutions. Building societies, together with domestic and foreign banks now comprise a very effective system of financial intermediation by which savings are channelled into loans to owner-occupiers.

Finally, social and occupational changes have played a role: the break-up of traditional working-class communities, de-industrialization, the move to a service economy, suburbanization, the revolution in aspirations and expectations, and a loss of deference are all factors which might be expected to be supportive of increased owner-occupation.

In addition to these 'intrinsic' aspects of tenure and structural economic and social factors, policy has of course played an important role in the expansion of owner-occupation. The origins of fiscal support for owner-occupation in the post-war period were almost accidental - when Schedule A tax on the imputed rental value of owner-occupied housing was abolished in 1963, while leaving the offsetting tax relief on mortgage interest in place, it was scarcely envisaged that mortgage interest tax relief would, twenty years later become a multi-billion pound housing subsidy, and a Thatcherite totem. But support for owner-occupation rapidly became bipartisan, and governments of both parties shied away from any reforms which could be construed as an attack on owner-occupiers.

The 1980s are sometimes portrayed as a decade of increasing and unchecked support for owner-occupation. In fact, this is only partly true. The major policy innovation was, of course, the introduction of the right to buy for council tenants in the 1980 Housing Act. Over the next 15 years, more than 1.5 million council properties were sold to their tenants. In 1983, the ceiling on the size of loan that qualifies for mortgage interest tax relief was raised from £25,000 to £30,000. Government rhetoric remained firmly in favour of the continuing expansion of owner-occupation; for example, the 1987 White Paper, which dealt mainly with the rented sectors, made it clear that the first objective of housing policy was the continuing commitment to expansion of owner-occupation.

Behind the rhetoric, the reality was rather different. The Treasury was known to be hostile to mortgage tax relief, which it saw as an open-ended and expensive subsidy. Over the decade, the real value of mortgage interest relief at source (MIRAS) as a subsidy was eroded, through a number of indirect and marginal changes, the cumulative effect of which was considerable. First, the ceiling on qualifying loans remained unchanged after 1983, at £30,000, despite the fact that average house prices had more than doubled by the end of the decade, and the average UK house price in 1994 was over £60,000 (over £40,000 for first-time buyers) (Halifax Building Society data). Tax relief on home improvement loans was removed in 1988. In the same year, tax relief was limited to one claim per property; previously joint borrowers (except for married couples) could each claim relief, up to the £30,000 ceiling. There was a three-month delay before this provision was implemented, adding to the demand pressures at the height of the 1980s boom, as multi-person households sought to complete transactions before the August 1988 deadline. In 1991-92 relief was limited to the standard rate of tax; previously higher-rate taxpayers could claim at their marginal rate. Finally, the government's policy of lower rates of income tax reduced the value of the subsidy, while its indexation of capital gains tax reduced the effective value of the exemption of owner-occupied housing from this tax.

As a result, by the beginning of the 1990s, tax relief had become in effect, a flat-rate subsidy to owner-occupiers, capped in nominal terms. The switch to MIRAS (i.e. tax relief deduction at source) and the limitation to the standard rate of tax had the psychologically important effect of making fiscal support for mortgagors look less like a fuzzy tax exemption and more like a straightforward exchequer subsidy. This then paved the way for a more direct assault on MIRAS in the 1990s as part of the strategy to bring the ballooning UK budget deficit under control. The rate of MIRAS was limited to 20 per cent (from 25 per cent) in 1994, and reduced further to 15 per cent in 1995. The cost of tax relief rose from £1.96 billion in 1980-81 to £7.7 billion in 1990-91, before falling to £3.5 billion in 1994-95 (Wilcox 1994, Table 87).

So with hindsight, we can see a gradual but continuing process of reduced government support to owner-occupation after about 1983. Yet the 1980s were characterized by an owner-occupier housing boom. How can this apparent paradox be explained? Three main factors are relevant: rises in real income, the deregulation of the mortgage market, and the lack of rental alternatives. In the UK, real earnings rose by 21 per cent between 1980 and 1989 (compared, for example, with a rise of only 8 per cent in real earnings in France) (Eurostat 1991). Demographic factors also played a part: household growth per annum peaked at 180,000 in England in the 1986-91 period (Department of the Environment 1991). Deregulation brought competition into the UK mortgage market, leading to much easier availability of housing credit compared with the rationed mortgage markets of the 1960s and 1970s and hence a sharp rise in loan-to-value and loan-to-income ratios. At the same time, social housing output fell rapidly, and the private rented sector continued to decline.

The result was an unsustainable boom in the second half of the decade. Average UK house prices rose by 126 per cent in the six years between 1983 and 1989 - in London they rose by 178 per cent, and in East Anglia by 191 per cent. Thereafter there was a dramatic turnaround in the fortunes of the sector. Nationally, prices fell by 16 per cent between the first quarter of 1989 and the first quarter of 1993; in London they fell by 30 per cent and in East Anglia by 35per cent, according to mix-adjusted data from the Nationwide Building Society. The slump continued to the mid-1990s.

Transactions fell considerably from a peak of 600,000 in one three-month period in 1988 to under 250,000 in the first quarter of 1992 (Halifax Building Society, *Viewpoint*, Autumn 1992). In London, transactions fell precipitously from 68,000 in the second half of 1988 to 34,000 in the first half of 1989, and have remained at about 40,000 per half year since then (Bank of England 1992b).

The legacy of the 1980s housing boom has been a major problem of over-indebtedness, negative equity, mortgage arrears and repossessions. Two-thirds of first-time buyers in 1989 borrowed more than 90 per cent of the purchase price of the dwelling, and one-third borrowed more than 100 per cent (Bank of England 1992a). This high level of gearing, together with falls in house prices, the huge rise in unemployment and high real interest rates related to exchange rate mechanism (ERM) membership between 1990 and 1992, led to a disastrous situation in which more than one million home owners have negative equity (outstanding debt exceeds current market value). According to Bank of England calculations, negative equity in the first half of 1992 amounted to a national total of about £6 billion, equivalent to about 14 per cent of personal sector saving in 1991 (Bank of England 1992b). Over one billion pounds was in Greater London. Those with negative equity in Greater London had, on average, £5,500 per household of unsecured mortgage debt (Dorling et al. 1992). Mortgage arrears peaked in 1993, with over 600,000 households more than three months behind with payments. By June 1994, this had fallen to 485,000. Possessions peaked at 75,000 per annum in 1991, and were running at an annual rate of about 50,000 in the first half of 1994 (Ford, 1994).

The most interesting policy aspect of the depressed owner-occupier market of the 1990s was what the government did not do, rather than what it did. The actions it did take were extremely limited. A so-called 'mortgage rescue package', introduced with considerable publicity, included an ambitious mortgage-to-rent plan involving the purchase of properties whose mortgagors were in arrears by housing associations, the owner continuing to live in the same house as a tenant. In practice, the number of properties 'rescued' in this way was extremely small. More importantly, the package also included provision for the Department of Social Security to pay income support covering interest directly to lenders, which may have had some effect in slowing down the number of repossessions. However, a survey of 47 households in arrears by Ford found that

> Only a minority of borrowers in default were eligible for the 'safety net' and the payment of mortgage interest through Income Support. This study supports earlier research, confirming that the majority of home owners in arrears face their payment difficulties without any support akin to that available to low-income renters via Housing Benefit. (Ford 1994)

The housing market package (HMP), introduced a year later, enabled housing associations to buy owner-occupied dwellings. But the majority of purchases were empty units from developers, rather than houses occupied by households in arrears. Finance for the HMP was not new money, but involved bringing forward allocations from the housing association investment programme from future years.

More significantly, the government did not respond to the cries of distress from lenders, builders, the housing lobby and elsewhere by increasing its support to owner-occupation, either through extending mortgage interest relief or introducing mortgage benefit. Rather surprisingly, the government stuck by and large to the implications of its own rhetoric: a market system means that individuals make and live by their own decisions. Significantly, the 1995 White Paper contains no specific proposals addressing problems of mortgage arrears, negative equity or repossessions (Malpass 1995).

The deregulatory reforms of the 1980s and the expansion of owner-occupation had led to a 'marketization' of housing policy. Outcomes and operation were now far more dependent on market processes and housing was less sheltered from the general play of market forces. In the mid-1980s, this had led to easier access to owner-occupation, to house-price gains and to a seemingly endless increase in housing wealth. In the 1990s, it meant negative equity, price falls, arrears and repossessions. But in both cases, in the government's view, the active agent is market forces not political will. In such circumstances, there is relatively little for the government to do. In the 1970s, a combination of high (unanticipated) inflation, negative real interest rates and real capital gains made owner-occupation an extremely attractive investment. In the 1980s, inflation was lower, real interest rates positive and mortgage rates moved closer to market rates. But easier availability of mortgage finance coupled with real income growth, the deregulatory/privatizing atmosphere of the so-called 'enterprise culture' and the lack of housing alternatives, temporarily offset this underlying less favourable position and enabled another house-price boom to occur.

In the 1990s, the situation is different again: inflation is lower, earnings growth is lower, *real* interest rates (even in the post-ERM period) are high. There is the suspicion that, inside or outside the ERM the British government may be serious about an anti-inflationary policy, no longer prepared to tolerate house-price inflation as somehow different from (and morally superior to) other sorts of inflation. Related to this is a greater awareness in policy-making and academic circles of the relationships between the housing market and economic performance. In particular, there is greater concern about the inflationary consequences of house-price booms, operating through increased consumer expenditure via equity withdrawal and wealth effects: and about the effects on labour-market rigidity of the dominance of owner-occupation over private renting.

The shift in policy became clear by the Budget of 1994, which as well as confirming the reduction in mortgage tax relief, also limited income support mortgage payments both for new and (to a lesser extent) for existing borrowers. New borrowers were now expected to take out private insurance to cover the risks of unemployment or other interruptions of earnings.

The 1995 White Paper on housing re-affirmed the government's support for 'sustainable' home ownership. In it, the government stated its intention to increase the number of home owners in England by 1.5 million over the next ten years. The main policy innovation proposed was the extension of the right to buy to all housing association tenants.[1]

2.3.2 Social Housing

The way in which social housing is provided in Britain underwent a radical and substantial transformation in the decade from 1980 to 1990. There were a succession of major pieces of legislation, from the 1980 Housing Act which gave every council tenant the right to buy, to the 1988 Housing Act and the 1989 Local Government and Housing Act which initiated the transformation of local authorities from providers to 'enablers'. This has led to the most important change in the way social housing is provided in Britain since large-scale public housing began in 1919. The nature of this transformation is reflected in, and reinforced by, the change in the language of housing, from a discourse of public provision to one more akin to that of a service industry. Housing organizations now have customers rather than tenants, provide social not public housing, and at 'affordable' rather than low rents. In providing homes to meet needs, the rhetoric is no longer that of output targets, housebuilding programmes and government responsibility; instead, concepts such as asset backing, cash-flow projections and market forces hold centre stage.

Considered in a European context, social housing in Britain has always been an anomaly. Elsewhere, social housing has been provided through a mixture of state support and voluntary or private sector provision. However, in Britain, the vast majority of social housing units have been both built and managed by the local authorities. Even after a decade in which new public housing starts were cut by 83 per cent (from 80,100 in 1979 to 13,700 in

1989) and the right to buy and stock transfer reduced the size of the local authority stock considerably, local authorities still dominated the social rented sector, and indeed the rented sector as a whole (Table 2.1): even in 1993, six out of ten rented dwellings were owned by local authorities.

In Britain, the growth of council housing is sometimes seen as an inevitable consequence of the squalor, disease and sheer human misery associated with the Victorian private landlord system, and the failure of the various nineteenth-century philanthropic and charitable movements to provide a viable alternative. But, as the experience of other European countries has shown, while these factors provide a reason for increased state

Table 2.1 Rented housing, Britain (households, thousands)

	1981 (N)	1981 (%)	1993 (N)	1993 (%)
Local authority	6,447	69.7	4,726	60.0
Housing association	453	4.9	874	11.1
Private rented	2,353	25.4	2,278	28.9
Total	9,253	100.0	7,878	100.0

Source: Department of Environment, Housing and Construction Statistics.

intervention they cannot provide an explanation of the specific historical outcome of British reliance on council housing to the exclusion of other arrangements. The reasons why Britain, by the beginning of the third decade of the twentieth century, had entered on the path of municipal housing rather than subsidized private provision, are complex. Daunton (1987) has suggested two factors: the need on the part of industry to have a well but cheaply housed workforce in order for Britain to compete in an increasingly internationalized economy; and the relative political weakness and social isolation of the landlord class. Whatever the causes, it is clear that the emergence of local authorities as the major suppliers of rented housing has been a contingent rather than an inevitable development.

From the mid-1980s this began to change. The Conservative government signalled its clear intention that after 70 years of large-scale municipal housing the pre-eminence of the local authorities in the rented sector should come to an end. In future, local authorities were to be enablers, facilitating and co-ordinating the provision of housing by others, rather than being direct providers of housing themselves (Department of the Environment 1987). While government wished to see provision by as wide a range of organizations as possible (including private landlords), in practice, the gap left by the local authorities was filled by housing associations (HAs) rather than private activity.

Policy towards local authority housing over the last 20 years has reinforced and intensified trends towards the residualization of the sector. In the 1980s, there was a huge reduction in new building activity, and a partial switch to rehabilitation of the existing stock. General subsidies were reduced, and more tenants dependent on means-tested housing benefit to help pay their rent. After 1989, these trends were strengthened. Ring-fencing of the housing revenue account, greater financial transparency, and a rhetorical emphasis on tenants as 'customers' gave the impression of modernization of council housing, bringing it into line with best practice in service industries in the private sector. But such changes have to be seen in context. Three factors are particularly important: first, the relentless pauperization of the sector, as better-off tenants either moved away or bought their dwelling, and new lettings became concentrated on the poorest and most disadvantaged; second, the incentives to tenants and managers to transfer away from the local council: and third, the enfeebled position of local government generally.

By the mid-1990s, council housing had become a partly self-financing workhouse economy in which surpluses earned on the stock contributed to the housing benefit costs of the majority of tenants who required means-tested support. The income and expenditure levels of individual councils are in effect determined by the Secretary of State, and an increasing proportion of capital resources are both allocated to individual projects by central government officials and also subject to a competitive bidding process.

The prospect of complete demunicipalization, that is, the end of public housing, has become more and more realistic. In order to further its aim of moving local authorities away from provision of housing, the government introduced provisions in the Housing Act 1988 to transfer existing council stock to new landlords. Under 'tenants' choice', potential new landlords can bid for individual estates, subject to a ballot of tenants. In addition, the government sought to establish, in several specific locations, a new type of landlord organization, the housing action trust (HAT) in order 'to take over responsibility for local authority housing, renovate it, and pass it on to different forms of management' (Department of the Environment 1987). The management boards of HATs would be appointed by the Secretary of State, effectively by-passing the elected local authority, somewhat along the lines of the already established urban development corporations (Parkinson 1989).

However, neither of these initiatives met with much success. All of the government's original proposed HATs were subsequently abandoned, usually in the face of determined tenant opposition (Woodward 1991). More recently, six other HATs have been established. But these 'second generation' HATs are very different creatures from the original proposals, with a much higher degree of participation by both the local community and the local authority.

Interest in tenants' choice has been extremely low. Ironically, the first such transfer to go ahead was that of the tenant-controlled Walterton and Elgin Community Homes who took control of two estates from the City of Westminster, one of the Conservatives' 'flagship' local authorities.

However, although tenants' choice and the HAT programme had a negligible impact on the size of the local authority sector, several local authorities themselves decided to transfer the whole of their housing stock to a new landlord - almost always to a newly established housing association registered with the Housing Corporation - through a process known as 'voluntary transfer'. The term 'voluntary' refers to the fact that in these cases it is the local authority itself which initiates the process rather than its being triggered by a potential new landlord (tenants' choice) or by central government (HATs). Large-scale voluntary transfers (LSVTs) take place not under the 1988 Act, but using powers available under previous legislation.

By June 1995, 185,000 homes in England had been transferred from 41 local authorities to 45 new housing association landlords. The total number of housing association units in England in 1995 was 862,000, so the transferred stock amounted to more than one in five of all housing association homes. Voluntary transfer had developed not as a conscious government policy, but rather as a by-product of the housing legislation of the late 1980s, and the desire of senior local authority housing managers in particular to escape the restrictive framework imposed by that legislation. Nevertheless, they became an important component of the restructuring of social housing in Britain: numerically they account for a larger proportion of the local authority stock than any other process apart from the right to buy.

LSVT, in its original form, posed certain problems from the government's point of view. First, in every case, the stock was transferred to a single new housing association landlord, in effect, the former local authority housing department was re-created outside the council structure. A local public monopoly (or near-monopoly) over rental housing had been replaced by a local semi-private monopoly. Second, the Treasury was worried about the financial effects of LSVT. The 1989 Act had enabled the Treasury effectively to claw back surpluses earned on local authority housing. This was not possible if the stock was transferred into housing association ownership. The Treasury was faced with the possibility of a growing proportion of the public stock moving outside its fiscal reach, while an ever-increasing proportion of social tenants claimed housing benefit, which by the early 1990s was not only the largest, but also the fastest-growing component of the housing budget. In 1993, the government changed the rules on LSVT: authorities transferring stock now had to pay a levy to the Treasury of 20 per cent of the excess of the sale price over the outstanding debt; no more than 5,000 dwellings could be transferred to a single landlord; the government made clear its wish to see stock transferred to existing associations and not just specially created ones; and the numbers transferred in any one year were to be limited to 25,000 dwellings in total. These reforms had the effect of slowing down, but by no means stopping, the LSVT programme.

Most importantly, LSVT prompted local authorities to start thinking about a future in which council housing would no longer exist. The financial arithmetic involved in LSVT meant that usually it is feasible only for smaller, non-urban authorities. Its attraction was in the capital value of the stock, which would enable the authority to pay off outstanding debt (including in some cases non-housing debt) and also to provide new capital resources to the new housing association. For urban authorities, the value of the stock was much lower in relation to outstanding debt, and in many cases was actually negative, once the appalling backlog of repairs and modernization was taken into account. In 1993 the Joseph Rowntree Foundation (JRF) put forward the concept of arm's-length local housing companies, into which the local authority stock could be transferred, without being sold (Wilcox et al. 1993). The authors claimed that

The LSVT guidelines, limiting council membership to only 20 per cent of the new landlord committees, are more restrictive than the 1989 local Government and Housing Act requires. ... It would ... be possible, even within the Act's constraints, to transfer council housing to a local housing company where the council retained anything less than majority control. (Wilcox et al. 1993, p. 4)

Furthermore, the authors claimed that there would be Treasury *savings* from the transfer of ownership in most urban areas (i.e. where conventional LSVT is non-viable) through a combination of debt redemption, reduced future public sector capital provision, and income from VAT (Wilcox et al. 1993, p. 87). Importantly, as the authors acknowledge

This is only partly, however, a question of finances. It is also inevitably a question of politics, not just in the sense of party politics but more fundamentally in the sense of deep-rooted local cultural attachments to the tradition, achievements and security of council housing. (Wilcox et al. 1993, p. 87)

Following the JRF report, the Department of the Environment in 1994 commissioned a research study into the feasibility of local housing companies, and in 1995 the Chartered Institute of Housing, the professional body of housing managers, endorsed the principle of establishing local housing companies. In its 1995 White Paper on housing, the government restated its aim of continuing the diversification of council housing through transfers to new landlords, including local housing companies as one option. However, it insisted that local authority representatives should be in the minority on the boards of such companies, and the companies should be clearly in the private sector.

Whatever the viability of local housing companies in practice, the main point is that increasingly professionals and policy makers saw the future of the housing system without the existence of council housing. Also, all three political parties gave cautious acceptance to the idea of establishing local housing companies. These trends were reinforced by the extension of the principle of compulsory competitive tendering to council housing management in the 1990s, leading to a range of organizations, private, semi-private and public, being involved in the delivery of housing management services.

Housing associations enjoyed a brief golden period between 1988 and 1993, benefiting from the fact that by the end of the 1980s, the government had reluctantly accepted that some form of continuing social rented provision was necessary. Housing associations possessed the supreme virtue of not being local authorities. The 1988 Housing Act radically changed the framework under which associations had operated since 1974. Rents were deregulated; instead of having 'fair rents' set by independent rent officers, associations would determine their own 'assured' rents for new schemes and on re-lettings of existing dwellings. Whereas between 1974 and 1988, associations had operated with 100 per cent public finance, they now use a mixture of public grant (Housing Association Grant) and private loans. The proportion of public grant to private finance varies by area and by type of scheme, and average grant rates have been progressively lowered, so that by 1994, on average more than two-fifths of the finance for new investment was provided privately.

The 1988 Act has had several major consequences. First, rents have risen sharply, leading to a prolonged debate about the 'affordability' of new housing association lettings. Government, while stating that rents must be within the reach of people in low-paid employment, has refused to become drawn into the definition of what an affordable or social rent actually is (unlikely in other countries - see Chapters 3 and 4). Average weekly fair rents in England rose from £22.86 in 1987 to £38.42 in 1993, while assured rents rose from £24.50 in 1989 to £46.14 (Wilcox 1994, Table 57). The proportion of housing association tenants on housing benefit had by May 1995 risen to 63 per cent, including 83 per cent of new tenants. As a consequence, association tenants are often caught in a poverty trap in which moving off benefit to take a low-paid job will make them worse off.

Output by associations increased, peaking in 1992-93. Planned modest increases in the Approved Development Programme (ADP) (central government's contribution) were boosted by the addition of private finance, and in 1992-93, additionally by the housing market package (see above). However, output declined sharply thereafter, with cuts in the ADP in the budgets of both 1993 and 1994. There were changes in the composition of output, too. The new financial arrangements made associations more entrepreneurial, more aware of and responsible for, risk, and more finance and development driven. As a result there was a shift away from inner-city rehabilitation work to new building, particularly on greenfield sites; an emphasis on volume building, with standardized products and lower space and other standards; and a move in some cases towards large-scale development.

The more competitive regime and the need for asset backing to secure private finance led to concentration in the sector, with mergers and consortium arrangements, and faster growth by the larger associations (including the new LSVT associations). The nature of associations as organizations changed. Their *raison d'être* was no longer the management of housing but the management of assets (Pryke and Whitehead 1991). Their greater risk-bearing function increased the importance of financial control and management and called into question their governance structure, based around unpaid voluntary committee members.

Many of the larger housing associations responded vigorously to the new opportunities being offered to them. The 'brave new world' of private finance and risk-bearing also led, however, to tensions within the HA movement. Smaller associations catering for special needs or run by and for ethnic minorities felt squeezed out of programmes. More widely there are criticisms that associations are sacrificing their traditional role of meeting housing needs for the sake of faster growth. Undoubtedly, there was a considerable culture change within the sector between 1988 and 1993.

From 1993 onwards, however, the position deteriorated, with substantial cuts in the Housing Corporation's Approved Development Programme. In part this reflected government's determination to limit public expenditure in order to bring down the public deficit, in part it reflected specific circumstances in which, as housing associations took on more of the social role from local authorities, they became less popular politically, particularly with backbench Conservative MPs who viewed the construction of social housing estates in their constituencies with no more favour if the developer was a housing association than if the developer were a local authority.

Finally, the transformation of social housing in the 1980s and 1990s can only be understood in the context of the radical transformation of the role of local government generally over this period. The change from provider to enabler could in principle have strengthened local authorities' strategic role. But in practice the change took place within a framework characterized by the enfeeblement of local government and local accountability, the centralization of control at national government level, and the removal of a whole range of local authority powers and responsibilities to non-elected and appointed bodies. By the 1990s the basis for pretending that local authorities were independent government rather than administrative agents seemed unclear.

2.3.3 Private Renting

Private renting in Britain has been in almost continuous decline for fifty years. The British private rented sector is far smaller than in other comparable countries, and is generally acknowledged to be well below the optimum size for a well-functioning housing system. One of the government's stated aims in the 1980s was to stimulate the independent rented sector, by which they meant both housing associations and private landlords. The 1988 Act deregulated new private lettings, allowing landlords to charge market rents, while tenants continued to have a considerable degree of security of tenure. Also, in the Budget of that year, the Business Expansion Scheme (BES), which provided for tax breaks for investors, was extended to investment in private rented housing. This was in effect the first ever fiscal subsidy in Britain specifically to private landlords.

While the BES has had some effect (see Crook and Kemp 1991), the introduction of a modest temporary supply-side subsidy together with deregulation of rents were not enough to reverse the long-standing weak position of private landlordism in Britain, which stems from a variety of demand- and supply-side reasons (see Whitehead and Kleinman 1986; Whitehead et al. 1994). While the decline of the sector did slow down and even reverse somewhat around the turn of the decade, the reasons for this were associated more with the slump in the owner-occupied sector, creating both unsold properties for letting, and households (particularly younger households) wary of entering the owner-occupied market, rather than flowing from changes in the legislative framework.

It remains to be seen whether there are longer-term changes in attitudes and behaviour, in regard to tenure preferences in particular, as a result of the continuing slump in the owner-occupied market, the reduced fiscal support for home ownership, and the continuing residualization of the social rented sector. If preferences, expectations and behaviour change in the light of these experiences, then there may be both demand- and supply-side pressures for an expansion of the sector, catering primarily for a wider group of younger, employed and mobile households. But a major role for private renting can be ruled out.

2.4 OUTCOMES

What sorts of outcomes have these policies led to? In examining this question, one has to acknowledge the inherent difficulties in separating the effects on housing outcomes of, on the one hand, policy factors and, on the other, exogenous economic and demographic trends. With these caveats in mind, I first set out the demand and supply positions in the British housing system, before going on to look at housing needs, and then at polarization and segregation in housing outcomes.

2.4.1 Housing Demand and Supply

The level of housing demand and of housing needs is a function of both demographic and economic factors. I look first at demographic and social changes, before going on to consider the influence of economic variables such as income growth and distribution.

Population growth in the 1980s was considerably slower than in the 1960s: in the UK the rate was 2.5 per thousand in 1988 compared with 8.1 in 1960. But the number of households grew much faster than the population. The UK population increased by 3.12 million between 1961 and 1971, but by only 0.42 million between 1971 and 1981. Between 1981 and 1991, population increased by 1.46 million. However, the number of households rose steadily over the same period, from 18.2 million in 1971 to 19.5 million in 1981 and to 21.9 million in 1991. This has meant a fall in average household size from 2.9 in 1971 to 2.7 in 1981 to 2.5 in 1991 (Central Statistical Office 1995).

The number of households in England grew by 191,000 p.a. between 1981 and 1991, and is projected to fall slightly to 183,000 p.a. between 1991 and 2001 and to 172,000 p.a. in the decade 2001-11 (Department of the Environment 1995).

In terms of household structure there has been a shift away from 'traditional' married couple headed and/or nuclear family households towards a greater proportion of single-person, single-parent and elderly households. In the UK, marriages fell from 459,000 in 1971 to 350,000 in 1991 and to 299,000 in 1993 (*Financial Times*, 23 August 1995), with the number of first marriages falling from 369,000 in 1991 to 222,000 in 1991 (Central Statistical Office 1995). The marriage rate fell from 7.1 per 1,000 eligible in 1981 to 5.4 per 1,000 eligible in 1992.

The divorce rate in England and Wales rose from 11.9 per 1,000 marriages in 1981 to 13.9 in 1993 (*Financial Times*, 23 August 1995). The United Kingdom has the highest divorce rate in the European Union, with the exception of Denmark. The number of decrees absolute granted in the UK rose from 79,000 in 1971 to 171,000 in 1991. In the UK, single-parent families, as a proportion of all families with dependent children increased from 9 per cent in 1971 to 20 per cent in 1991 (Central Statistical Office 1995). The number of lone-parent households is projected to increase in

England from 981,000 households in 1991 to 1.202 million in 2001. Cohabiting couples are projected to increase from 1.222 million to 1.447 million over the same period, while married couple households will *fall* from 10.547 million to 10.217 million (Department of the Environment 1995).

There has been also an increase in the numbers of single-person households. This has several causes: earlier exit from the parental home, higher divorce rates, greater numbers of single elderly living independently, and so on. Single persons comprise about 26 per cent of all households in England. This proportion is projected to rise to 31 per cent in England (Department of the Environment 1991).

The level of housing demand and, in particular, the extent to which housing needs can be expressed as effective demand in the marketplace, is a function not just of demographic and social variables, but also of economic variables, particularly income growth and its distribution, unemployment and inflation. Over the last two decades, despite two recessions, there has been a steady increase in real GDP and in real household incomes, not just in the UK, but throughout the European Union. Between 1971 and 1993, household disposable income in the UK rose by 80 per cent in real terms. But this economic growth has not been evenly distributed; unemployment rose from 5.6 per cent to 10.3 per cent between 1976 and 1993 (Central Statistical Office 1995) and income inequality has worsened (see Chapter 6).

To summarize, then, the number of households has continued to rise, particularly 'non-traditional' household types such as single-parent and single-person households. Incomes have also continued to increase but economic restructuring and the growth and persistence of unemployment have led to a widening in the distribution of that income, and to greater economic inequality. Unemployment fell in the second half of the 1980s during the consumer-led boom of the Lawson years, before rising sharply again from 1989 to 1992, in part as a consequence of Britain's finally abandoning the Thatcherite attempt at an independent anti-inflation policy and joining the exchange rate mechanism. Subsequently, the competing claims of monetary discipline inside the ERM and domestic political and economic considerations proved impossible to reconcile and Britain was forced out of the ERM in September 1992. Despite lower interest rates and a growing budget deficit, unemployment continued to rise sharply in late 1992 before falling slowly through 1993 and 1994. Even this recent fall in unemployment must be seen in the context of a continuing shift from full-time to part-time jobs, and the rise of temporary and less secure employment contracts.

A key factor in 1980s Britain was that real incomes for those in work rose considerably. Coupled with liberalization and deregulation of the housing finance market, this led to a prolonged and ultimately unsustainable boom in the British owner-occupied market. Throughout this period, moderate inflation reduced the real user cost of housing, although not to the extent experienced in the 1970s. By the end of the decade, the British housing market was characterized by high real interest rates, and, for the first time in the post-war period, falls in *nominal* as well as in real house prices, leading to the problems of mortgage arrears, repossessions and negative equity discussed in section 2.3.1 above.

How did the supply of housing respond to this pattern of demand? Total housing starts peaked at 221,000 p.a. in the early 1980s and 250,000 p.a. in the later 1980s (Table 2.2). Currently (1994) starts are about 200,000 p.a. Within this total, private sector output more than doubled from just under 100,000 p.a. in 1980 to 220,000 p.a. in 1988 before falling back in the early 1990s. Starts by local authorities have declined almost to zero over this period. Housing association starts remained in the range 10,000 to 20,000 for most of this period, with rapid expansion after 1991, partly through the one-off housing market package (see 2.3.2 above).

Changes in the stock are a function not just of new supply, but also of losses to, and changes within, the existing stock. In the UK, slum clearance fell from an average of 55,000 p.a. in the 1970s to 30,000 in 1981 and to less than 10,000 p.a. in the late 1980s (Central Statistical Office 1991, Table 8.2). 'Other changes' - i.e. net gains from conversions and other causes, and losses other than from slum clearance - have fluctuated in the range of minus 2,000 to plus 3,000 in the 1980s.

2.4.2 Housing Needs

As shown in 2.4.1 above, there have been both increases in the level of housing demand and changes in its composition. To some extent these increases in demand have been met through market mechanisms, leading to equivalent changes in the level and composition of supply. But there has also been market failure, together with the existence of additional housing needs which cannot be expressed as effective demand in the market.

Table 2.2 Housing starts, Britain, 1980-1993 (thousands, per annum)

	LA	HA	Private	Total
1980	42	15	99	155
1981	26	12	117	155
1982	35	18	141	194
1983	35	14	172	221
1984	27	13	158	198
1985	22	12	166	200
1986	20	13	181	214
1987	20	12	194	227
1988	17	14	220	250
1989	15	15	170	201
1990	9	19	135	162
1991	4	22	135	161
1992	3	34	120	157
1993	2	41	143	187
1994	2	41	159	202

Notes
LA = local authorities (including new towns and government departments.
HA = housing associations.

Source: Department of the Environment, Housing and Construction Statistics.

In the mid-1970s as part of the Housing Finance (later Housing Policy) Review the Department of the Environment undertook a medium-term forecast of housing output covering the period to the end of the 1980s. This produced a projection of output over the following fifteen years based around the two ideas of market-driven demand in the owner-occupied sector plus enough public investment to ensure the same rate of progress in eliminating unmet need over the survey period as over the immediate past.

This type of detailed forecasting exercise was not to be repeated. The Conservative government elected in 1979 explicitly rejected the notion of quantitative national targets for housing output. The ideology of the Thatcher and post-Thatcher governments has stressed individual freedom, consumer choice and rolling back the state. Put most simply, there was and is a belief that free markets are more efficient than central planning, and that the operation of the price mechanism in bringing together demand and supply in the housing market will lead to greater total social benefits than the administrative allocation of housing (Monk and Kleinman 1989).

In fact, over the 1980s the stock of dwellings did not increase fast enough to cope with the increase in the number of households. The number of households in England increased by 1.711 million between 1981 and 1991, while the number of dwellings increased by only 1.644 million (Housing and Construction Statistics). The government's main policy aim was to increase the level of owner-occupation, which it did, from 56 per cent in 1981 to 66 per cent in 1992 (UK figures).

The rented sector, on the other hand, declined in absolute as well as relative terms; the number of rented dwellings fell by nearly 1.4 million between 1981 and 1993 (Table 2.1). Despite the collapse of local authority housebuilding and the impact of the right to buy, local authorities still owned three in five of the rented stock in 1993. In terms of the flow of social rental units available to meet housing needs, I have elsewhere estimated that the total supply from both local authorities and housing associations in England, and including new construction, relets and gains from conversions, fell by about 13 per cent, from 304,000 in 1979-80 to 264,000 in 1989-90 (Kleinman 1991).

The overall tightening of the housing system has shown up in lower vacancy rates and in the increased levels of homelessness. Households accepted as homeless and rehoused by local authorities in Great Britain increased from 70,000 in 1979 to 180,000 in 1992 while the number of statutorily homeless households placed in temporary accommodation by local authorities rose from under 5,000 in 1979 to 63,000 in 1992, before falling slightly to 54,000 in 1993 (Wilcox 1994). The implicit vacancy rate for the housing stock as a whole fell from 3.8 per cent to 3.2 per cent between 1981 and 1991, implying increased stock utilization and hence greater pressure.

In the absence of official estimates of the level of output necessary to meet housing needs, a number of studies have been undertaken by academics, professionals and lobbying organizations. In general these utilize one of three types of methodology (Whitehead and Kleinman 1992). *Net stock* approaches attempt to measure different types of need arising from inadequate provision within the existing stock - such as substandard units and concealed households - plus forecast household growth, and thereby estimate the number of units required to meet those needs now and in the future (Audit Commission 1992; National Housing Forum 1989). *Affordability* studies examine the number of households unable to gain entry into owner-occupation given specified affordability criteria who can therefore be expected to require social provision of one kind or another (Bramley 1989, 1990, 1991). *Gross flows* approaches derive from the last official attempt at a medium-term forecast in the Housing Policy Review of the mid-1970s. The gross flows of both households and dwellings through the system, including inter-tenure moves, are modelled explicitly (Whitehead and Kleinman 1992; Kleinman et al. 1994). From this are derived both market-driven private sector output and the level of unmet housing need, taking into account projected social housing output and including the backlog in terms of unfit occupied units and some concealed households.

Despite the very different methodologies and assumptions used, all these recent studies show a substantial level of unmet housing need both currently and over the next decade. The central estimate is that about 100,000 social rented units are needed p.a., about four times current output (Whitehead and Kleinman 1992). More recently, the Department of the Environment in its official projections of household growth to 2001 estimated the demand for additional units of social housing to be in the range of 60,000 to 100,000 per annum (Department of the Environment 1995). While precise quantification of housing need is impossible, all the evidence suggests that unmet housing needs have increased considerably in recent years.

2.4.3 Polarization and Segregation in Housing Outcomes

In the early 1980s, there was considerable debate about whether, and to what degree, the council sector was becoming residualized; or, to put it another way, whether the housing system was becoming polarized between affluent home owners and poor council tenants. (See for example: English

1982; Clapham and MacLennan 1983; Malpass 1983; Forrest and Murie 1983; Robinson and O'Sullivan 1983; Hamnett 1984; Robinson et al. 1985; Bentham 1986; for a discussion see Kleinman 1988.) Surprisingly, by the mid-1990s such discussion had almost entirely disappeared. This was not, of course, because the issue had disappeared. Rather, the working assumption was that residualization, or polarization certainly had taken place, was continuing, and was irreversible. In the popular imagination - as displayed for example, in films or TV series - the image of the council estate immediately connotated poverty and exclusion, in much the same way as a terrace of decaying private rented houses had done two decades earlier.

Information on the concentration of poverty and disadvantage in the social housing sector over the 1980s and 1990s can be obtained from large sample surveys such as the General Household Survey and the Labour Force Survey. Several relevant indicators are brought together by Wilcox (1994). Labour Force Survey data show that between 1981 and 1991, the proportion of all household heads in full-time work fell from 58 per cent to 54 per cent. However, among council tenants it fell from 43 per cent to 25 per cent, and among housing association tenants it fell from 42 per cent to 29 per cent. By contrast, among mortgagors the rate fell only from 92 per cent to 86 per cent. Lone parents, as a proportion of all household types rose from 7 per cent in 1981 to 9 per cent in 1991, but from 12 per cent to 18 per cent in the council sector, and from 9 per cent to 13 per cent in the housing association sector.

Data from the General Household Survey show that economically inactive households increased from 33 per cent to 39 per cent as a proportion of all households between 1980 and 1992; however, as a proportion of all households in the council sector economically inactive households rose from 42 per cent to 62 per cent, and in the housing association sector, from 52 per cent to 59 per cent. The proportion of council tenant households headed by someone in a non-manual or skilled manual occupation fell from 38 per cent to 23 per cent over the same period.

Data on average incomes of heads of households by tenure are given in Table 2.3.

Table 2.3 Average income of head of household by tenure, Britain (£ per week)

Tenure	1972	1980	1992
Owners:			
Outright Owner	25	81	194
with mortgage	39	142	320
Tenants:			
Local Authority	22	68	110
Housing Association	-	66	120
Private unfurnished	19	60	149
Private furnished	21	87	170

Source: General Household Surveys, collated in Wilcox 1994, Table 28.

As the table shows, in 1972 the average income of council tenants was 56 per cent that of mortgagors. By 1980, this had fallen to 48 per cent and by 1992, to only 34 per cent. That is, while in 1972 mortgagors had incomes on average less than twice those of council tenants, twenty years later, their average incomes were three times higher. Incomes in the housing association sector were similar to the council sector.

Family Expenditure Survey data show that in 1992 31 per cent of households had an income below £160 per week. In the council sector, however, the figure was twice as high - 63 per cent of households, with 58 per cent the figure for housing associations. At the other end of the income scale, fewer than 10 per cent of council tenant households had an income above £320 per week, compared with more than one-third of households in total, and nearly two-thirds of mortgagors (Wilcox 1994, Table 29b).

What has caused this polarization? This concentration of poverty and disadvantage in the social sectors could have occurred through one or more of three main mechanisms. First, there may have been changes in the characteristics and attributes of social sector tenants compared with owners over time - for example, the ageing of households in the sector, and any increased likelihood (compared with owners) of council tenants to become unemployed. Second, there has been the process by which a section of the council tenant population has transferred tenure *without* moving, via the right to buy. Third, through the effects of transfers of moving households between tenures and differential entry and exit into the two main tenures.

The reasons for the changing employment circumstances of council tenants between 1978 and 1991 have been carefully analysed by Alan Holmans (1993). He argues that the increase in the proportion of council tenants with no earning member has been going on for at least a quarter of a century, but has been much more rapid since 1978. There are, in Holmans's view, three main reasons for this: transfers to owner-occupation through sales to sitting tenants; the general increase in unemployment; and ageing, 'in particular many of the post-war generation of tenants reaching retirement age' (Holmans 1993, p. 79).

As far as unemployment is concerned, Holmans finds that

The economic recession brought about a disproportionately large increase in unemployment among council tenants between 1977-78 and 1984, including other household members of working age as well as household heads. Less than one-third of the national increase in unemployment had been reversed by the time of the 1988 survey. When however unemployment increased again from 1990 onwards owner-occupiers were proportionately worse affected than council tenants. (Holmans 1993, p. 79)

Hence, Holmans concludes that there is no evidence, at either a national or regional level to support the proposition that council tenure *per se* has an independent effect on unemployment, acting either through physical location or through the generation of a 'culture of dependency'. (Holmans concedes that either or both of these factors may nevertheless operate at the level of the individual estate.) 'Between 1988 and 1990, unemployment fell among council tenants at a faster rate than among owner-occupiers, and between 1990 and 1991, unemployment rose less among council tenants than among owner-occupiers' (Holmans 1993, p. 80). Nevertheless, council tenants as a group were particularly vulnerable to the rise in unemployment between 1977-78 and 1984, and this, together with the fact of higher unemployment rates through the cycle in both the 1980s and 1990s, compared with the 1960s and 1970s, is one part of the explanation for the pauperization of the sector.

The right to buy had a huge effect on the employment circumstances of council tenants, not only because the number of transfers was so high (1.3 million) but also because a far higher proportion of purchasers than of all tenants were in employment. Nearly two-thirds of purchasers in 1981-83 were in full-time employment at the time of the 1991 survey, while of those households who were still tenants in 1991, only a quarter were headed by someone in full-time employment: 'That so high a proportion of sitting tenant purchasers were in employment means that transfers to owner-occupation on the scale experienced from 1978 to 1991, over a quarter of the 1977-78 stock, had a powerful effect on the employment circumstances of tenant.' (Holmans 1993, p. 83).

The ageing aspect is very much a cohort effect, as the very large post-war generation of tenants reached retirement age during the 1978-88 decade. Holmans estimates that about half of the reduction in the number of employed council tenant household heads was due to the effects of the right to buy, and apportions the total reduction as follows:

Right to buy and other sales	80,000
Increase in unemployment	230,000
Other	540,000
Total	1,570,000

As Holmans estimates the ageing effect to comprise between 200,000 and 250,000 households, this implies that between 390,000 and 340,000 of the reduction was through turnover effects, that is differential patterns of entry and exit from the main tenures.

My own analysis of Labour Force Survey data sheds more light on these turnover effects.[2] Table 2.4 gives data for 1981 and 1991 comparing characteristics of those moving from social housing to owner-occupation with those moving in the other direction. Note that all households are *moving* households, that is sitting tenant purchasers are excluded.

Already in 1981 there were clear differences between the sorts of households travelling in each direction: three times as many household heads moving from owner-occupation to social housing as moving in the other direction were divorced, while the proportion in employment was ten percentage points lower in that direction. But by 1991, the differences were far more marked. Over a quarter of those moving to social housing from owner-occupation were divorced, almost ten times the proportion moving in the opposite direction. Only a third were married, compared with nearly three-quarters of those moving from social housing to owner-occupation. Only 40 per cent of movers from owner-occupation to social housing were employed, half the figure moving in the opposite direction, while the proportion who were retired was nearly six times as high. Comparison of sitting tenant purchasers in the social sector with households moving from social tenure to owner-occupation through purchase of a different dwelling, shows that the moving group were even more likely to be in employment than the sitting tenant purchasers.

Table 2.4 Characteristics of movers between social housing and owner-occupation (percentages)

	1981		1991	
	Social housing to owner-occupiers	Owner-occupiers to social housing	Social housing to owner-occupiers	Owner-occupier to social housing
Marital status				
Married	82.2	71.6	72.2	34.2
Cohabiting	N/A	N/A	13.9	8.2
Single	13.8	12.6	11.1	9.6
Divorced/				
separated	3.1	9.5	2.8	27.8
Widowed	0.9	6.3	0	20.5
Total	100.0	100.0	100.0	100.0
Econ activity				
Employed	94.7	83.2	77.8	39.7
Unemployed	3.1	4.2	5.6	13.7
Retired	1.8	9.5	5.6	30.1
Student	0	0	2.8	0
Other	0.4	3.1	8.2	16.5
Total	100.0	100.0	100.0	100.0
Sample	225	95	36	73

Source: Evans and Kleinman, own calculations.

More broadly, we can compare the characteristics of those entering the social sector with those entering owner-occupation. In 1981, about two-thirds of social entrants were married, with 9 per cent divorced or separated. Over 70 per cent of entrants to owner-occupation were married, with 4 per cent divorced or separated. In 1991, a new category of cohabiting was introduced. The proportion of new owner-occupiers who were married fell to just over 40 per cent, while for new social tenants married households fell to 25 per cent. Divorced and separated entrants rose to 18 per cent for social housing, compared with 8 per cent for owner-occupation. In terms of employment, entrants to owner-occupation changed little: 88 per cent were employed in 1981, and 90 per cent in 1991. But among new social tenants, the employment rate fell sharply from 54 per cent in 1981 to 35 per cent in 1991.

One final significant point: according to the LFS data, only 71,000 of the 1.77 million moves in 1984 involved movement in either direction between social housing and owner-occupation (4.0 per cent of all moves). In 1991, this had fallen still further to 57,000 out of 1.75 million (3.3 per cent of all moves). These very low figures are consistent with a bifurcated or polarized housing system in which movement within tenures is the norm, and movement between tenures a rare exception.

2.5 ASSESSMENT

The evidence presented in this chapter bears out the hypothesis that both housing policy and housing outcomes in Britain have undergone a process of bifurcation. The concerns of policy have become steadily more divergent over time between the two main sectors and this policy divergence is reflected in the polarization of housing outcomes.

The concerns of social sector policy have related to its role as a residualized or welfare tenure. More than anything else, the concepts both of council housing and more generally of social housing have increasingly been seen as problematic in themselves. The drive has been if not to privatize the sector entirely, then at least to make it more market-like, mimicking, even if only at the level of rhetoric, how real markets work. So tenants are referred to as 'customers', even where they have no real choices, and where the level of effective demand is minimal in the absence of massive income transfers organized through the state in the form of housing benefit.

Private sector policy has been geared around deregulation, access to owner-occupation, and the price and availability of mortgage finance. More recently this has been extended somewhat to concerns about falling capital values, arrears and repossessions. Within this, there have been contradictions in government policy, a conflict which was largely hidden in the 1980s but became more overt in the 1990s. Broadly, what does an 'enterprise culture' mean? Does it imply that the state should encourage *and support* the expansion of owner-occupation, or does it mean that the state should withdraw its support from all housing sectors? For a long time in the 1980s it was assumed to mean the former although behind the scenes, the second view was steadily gaining ground, especially in the Treasury.

In the 1990s, government concerns grew about the cost of continuing support for owner-occupiers, about the principles on which it rested, and increasingly about the macroeconomic effects of house-price inflation and equity withdrawal. In particular, there were concerns about the excess consumer demand fuelled by house-price inflation, about the speculative and inflationary psychology it encouraged, and about the destabilizing effects of pronounced house-price swings on expectations and preference formation. To some extent this reflected a growing 'Europeanization' of economic policy, and a desire to match the post-war German record of low inflation and the more recent French espousal of a strong currency and competitive disinflation. By the mid-1990s, this view was ascendant, as evidenced by the falling real and indeed nominal value of MIRAS, by the absence of measures to support house prices, activity or confidence, and by the restrictions in social security support to home owners.

Concerns in social sector policy, although centred around nominally similar concepts of deregulation, privatization and a greater role for markets, in practice occupied a separate universe, one in which demand is almost entirely dependent on income transfers, and where the operation of the housing system even at the most local level is very largely determined by central government rules and criteria. As the sector became more and more residualized and separated from the mainstream, the rhetoric of empowerment, localism and bootstraps activity became ever more strident: a sure sign that main programme resources were being reduced. The policy isolation was reflected also in the political weakness of the sector in response to policy change and financial cutbacks. The lack of national protest, and even national debate in the face of, in effect, the abolition of council housing after 75 years can be contrasted with the prolonged, fundamental and highly publicized debates over the introduction of the internal market into the 40-year-old National Health Service. Of course, the reasons for this are not difficult to find: the National Health Service, like state education, caters for the vast majority of the population, and not just for the poorest quarter. Social housing is no longer a national arena for debate, but more like an isolated laboratory in which policy experiments can be carried out, protested only by those who can be dismissed by government ministers as the 'professional housing lobby'.

What can we conclude about housing policy and social exclusion in Britain then? If we define social exclusion narrowly, as referring literally to exclusion from society, then it remains the case that British housing policy is a force for social *inclusion*. The social sector, despite the pressures on it, remains geared to housing need: in particular, there is a legally defined right to housing, enforceable through the courts, for a defined category of households. Social housing provides a route to affordable permanent housing for a range of households that would be unable to secure accommodation in a purely private system. Similarly, home ownership, despite its casualties, meets the choices as well as the needs of millions of British households. Access to owner-occupation has widened considerably over the last two decades to include households for whom home ownership would not have been possible in earlier periods.

Nevertheless, housing policy in the last 20 years can scarcely be described as helping to create a more equal society. Poverty has become increasingly concentrated in the social sector, and policy has not only reinforced and supported this process, but has undermined the very notion of social provision as an alternative to the market, rather than as a safety net, grudgingly supplied by the state from limited resources.

On one reading, housing policy in Britain might therefore be seen as the paradigm of an 'Anglo-Saxon' social policy - that is, one that stresses market forces, economic individualism, a residual view of collective provision, and a rejection of social corporatism, with the promotion of owner-occupation as the key ingredient. But this is to over-simplify. First, as we have seen there are genuine contradictions in a policy of owner-occupier support: economic liberalism in fact implies reduced rather than increased support for home-owners. But second, if we describe British policy as the quintessential example of an 'Anglo-Saxon' policy regime, we are left with the problem of explaining how very similar developments have taken place in other, corporatist countries. It is to these issues that I now turn.

NOTES

1. At present (1995) only tenants of *non-charitable* housing associations have the right to buy.
2. Work carried out jointly with Martin Evans.

3. France: 'Qui Dit Marché, Dit Exclusion'

3.1 INTRODUCTION

The general direction of housing policy in France, as in Great Britain, changed radically in the 1980s and 1990s. Sustained economic growth during what Anglo-Saxons call the 'long boom', and the French refer to as '*les trentes glorieuses*' meant that housing conditions in France as in Britain steadily improved for the majority of households, and that output and expenditure grew in both public and private sectors. From the mid-1950s in France, governments assumed responsibility for ensuring that housing conditions improved, and that a separate dwelling was available for each family. The period was characterized by continually rising housing expectations, together with a major role for the state in ensuring the fulfilment of these expectations.

This golden age came to an end with the stagflation of the late 1960s and 1970s, and in particular the oil price rise and subsequent world recession. Continually rising real expenditure on social policies could no longer be painlessly afforded out of an expanding GNP. More difficult decisions now had to be made involving trade-offs between social expenditures on the one hand, and the need to maintain capitalist profitability and investment - the basic motor of the system - on the other. At the same time, in France as in Britain, the role of the state in housing policy came increasingly under attack. Housing subsidies were seen as profligate, difficult to bring under budgetary control, and insufficiently directed towards the achievement of specific policy aims. In physical terms, social housing - particularly that built in the mass housing era - rather than being seen as one aspect of progress and the advance of the welfare state, was increasingly seen as problematic and alienating. In social terms, planners and architects were accused of breaking up traditional communities and social networks in pursuit of unrealizable utopian fantasies about urban living.

There were thus two related crises: first, and more generally, the fiscal crisis of the welfare state, linked to the more uncertain economic environment; second and specifically, a crisis of confidence in mass housing brought about by the loss of faith in technocratic solutions. These came together to produce a decisive switch in state housing policy in both countries away from planning and towards the market.

In many ways, then, housing policy in France underwent similar changes to policy in Britain; indeed it is possible to point to a specific piece of legislation, the 1977 Housing Act, as the watershed, marking a new stage in the evolution of policy (Blanc 1993). But this similar shift in the broad direction of policy takes place in a different institutional, historical and political context to Britain - in a corporatist rather than an Anglo-Saxon welfare-state regime. By examining housing policy in France over the last 20 years we can begin to look at the question of what difference the type of welfare-state regime has made to policy formation and to housing outcomes.

In France as well as in Britain, there was a shift towards more market-orientated policies from the mid-1970s onwards. But this policy shift should be seen as a contingent rather than a necessary event. Moreover, the political and institutional context in the two countries differs significantly: for example, a socialist government was in power throughout most of the 1980s in France, in contrast to the Conservative dominance in Britain. We would therefore expect to find both similarities and differences in comparing the consequences of this policy shift in the two countries.

3.2 HOUSING POLICY 1975-1995

Lefebvre et al. (1991) usefully divide post-war French housing policy into three phases. During the period 1945-60, the Treasury played a predominant role. The economy during this period was characterized by capital shortages and relatively disorganized financial circuits. In this context, the state played the role of channelling savings, and distributing them as long-term loans under favourable conditions. In the 1960s and 1970s, the banking system predominated. The overriding national policy priority was the need to provide cheap finance for industry. Loans were made available at reduced rates for particular economic sectors - a system of specialized loans, whose distribution was monopolized by particular institutions. Hence the financial system was characterized by a segmentation of credit markets, quantitative credit controls and an absence of competition.

Finally, in the 1980s and 1990s, financial markets become dominant. Counter-inflation policy led to an ever more severe credit squeeze; state intervention lost its legitimacy, and economic liberalism became the dominant creed, both among policy makers and the general public. Housing in France is, in the view of these authors, now treated essentially as a private investment good, financed by private resources, largely as it was prior to the Second World War. Subsidy is concentrated on the poorest (Lefebvre et al. 1991). They conclude that, except for a few years in the immediate post-war period, state intervention in the housing market has been driven by circumstances, rather than being actively desired by political leaders (p. 88). In drawing this conclusion they come close to the position of Harloe (1995) who concluded that 'major growth [of mass social housing] ... has only occurred under historically specific circumstances which involved periods of generalized societal crisis and/or restructuring for capitalist regimes' (Harloe, 1995 p. 523).

Calcoen (1992) divides the post-war period slightly differently: a first stage between 1950 and 1965 of quantitative and qualitative scarcity, leading to an emphasis on a policy of construction. New construction (including social rented housing) benefited the middle categories of the population most, not the poorest. By the beginning of the 1960s, the state began to consider building at lower standards for the poorest groups. The period 1965-75 saw the progressive disengagement of the state, with greater recourse to savings and bank credit. Finally, the major reform of 1977 ushers in the third stage, characterized by: the encouragement of owner-occupation; a simplification of supply subsidies linked to the increase in personal support; and more emphasis on renovation as against new building. However, what was not foreseen was the transformation in the economic context, with rises in unemployment and in real interest rates. This rapidly thwarted the hopes and ambitions of the authors of the 1977 reform, who had envisaged that the extension of personal support and the vacancies created in the social rented sector by moves to owner-occupation would ease problems of homelessness and access to housing by opening the sector to poorer groups (Calcoen 1992).

The 1977 Housing Act followed the two major reports by Nora and by Barre. The Nora Report dealt with rehabilitation and recommended that the state should do more to encourage the improvement of existing dwellings. Public intervention should be concentrated on the less well off - in other cases, outcomes could be left to market forces. The Barre Report argued that the then current system was confusing and difficult to administer; that decision making was overcentralized, inflexible and insensitive; that public funds tended to benefit the better off, and that the effect on increased levels of public expenditure was inflationary (Pearsall 1984).

The French government accepted the broad principles of the two reports - markets should be given greater prominence, with the state playing a secondary role (Pearsall 1984). The resulting 1977 Housing Act had the following objectives:

* to allow market forces to express themselves;
* to increase the contribution made by households themselves by raising rents and interest rates to market levels;
* to reduce the overall level of state aid, through targeting help on households, according to income, and not on dwellings;
* to increase the level of owner-occupation and choice;
* to promote improvement of the older stock;
* to simplify the finance system and improve administration.

In social housing, the complex system of grants, loans and supplementary finance was replaced by *prêts locatifs aidés* (PLAs), subsidized loans for new construction, and loans for the improvement of older rented housing (PALULOS). New and improved social rented stock would henceforward be let at higher rents than in the past, but tenants in properties built or improved with a PLA or PALULOS loan would be entitled to apply for a new means-tested housing allowance, APL (*allocations personalisées au logement*). Previous systems of housing allowance were partial, applying to specific categories of tenants only, while APL is a more general benefit, available to any tenant in a PLA or PALULOS financed dwelling who qualifies. APL is also available to owner-occupiers. The effect of this reform, as intended, was to target financial help on the poorest households, enabling them to gain access to the *habitations à loyers modérés* (HLMs).

In analysing the development of housing policy in the 1980s and 1990s, we also need to examine the economic policy context. In 1981, the new socialist government initially reversed the policy of the previous government. It saw the housing sector as playing an important role in a general Keynesian economic stimulus, and sought to increase the state's involvement with housing (Lefebvre et al. 1991, p. 254). Hence there was an increase in the number of subsidized loans to owner-occupiers, and of new building and renovations by HLMs. The resources ceiling for qualification for PAP loans was raised by 25 per cent, and there were increases both in APL and in the older housing allowance schemes. The objective was 405,000 new units and 150,000 rehabilitations in 1982. After 1983, however, economic policy changed considerably. 'Keynesianism in one country' was deemed to have failed - a conclusion with profound consequences for the definition of the range of feasible economic policies, not just in France, but throughout the European Community. The priority was no longer demand management and expansion, but the control of inflation, and defence of a strong currency, linked closely to the German mark (the *franc fort* policy). This led to a double squeeze on housing spending: first, from the fall in general government expenditure in order to reduce the budget deficit, and second from the specific nature of the expenditures undertaken on housing. The actions taken by government in the early 1980s had led to an increase in housing spending by the state. Now, one of the effects of disinflation and income stagnation was that APL recipients did not leave the system as quickly as expected (Lefebvre et al. 1991, p. 258).

In order to contain expenditure, government began reducing the number of PAP loans allocated, and did not revise APL scales upward. Income ceilings for applicants to social housing were either not revised at all, or only revised weakly. This effectively limited entry to the HLM sector to the lower-income groups. In Flamand's (1989) view, three facts dominate post-1977: insufficient new construction; the growing involvement of public authorities in housing; but, despite this second point, a growing number of persons who are excluded from access to normal housing. Lefebvre et al. (1991) see this last point as an unavoidable consequence of the greater influence of market forces: 'Qui dit marché, dit exclusion' (Lefebvre et al. 1991, p. 269).

The account by Lefebvre et al. (1991) provides the most comprehensive analysis of recent housing policy development in France. They give primacy to the effect of budgetary rigour and monetary orthodoxy in producing a profound change in housing policy and housing finance, carried through 'with neither debate nor law' (p. 221). The 1980s saw a change from an economy of housing construction to one of housing exchange. Budgetary rigour and economic policy within the EMS led to a 'modernization' of the French housing market, involving less segmentation of the circuits of housing finance and subsidy, and more intensive use of the existing stock. There was a progressive abandonment of policy reference to housing needs in order to justify falls in output. Britain became the reference point for

French housing policy, particularly in terms of the liberalization and deregulation of housing finance. In the owner-occupied sector, specialized loans at below-market rates (see 3.3.1 below) gradually disappeared, to be replaced by free-market loans. This is making the French housing market more like that of Britain, and hence more cyclical in character. Meanwhile, in the social rented sector, the availability of new financial products has led to problems in funding social housing, as disintermediation hits the Livret A accounts, the traditional source of loans for HLMs (see 3.3.2 below).

These authors conclude that the general direction of French housing policy is unlikely to change, as the goal of European economic and monetary union - the cornerstone of French economic policy - is still far from being achieved, and it would anyway need a real sustained increase in economic growth for more resources to be allocated to housing. Reducing the budget deficit requires either expenditure to fall or taxes to increase, and the latter is unlikely. In their view the origin of the difficulties faced by the housing sector lies in the high nominal and real interest rates required to maintain the external value of the franc, and in the continuing policy of wage restraint in order to contain French production costs (competitive disinflation).

3.3 THE FRENCH HOUSING SYSTEM

3.3.1 The Owner-Occupied Sector

In France, as in Britain, housing policy over the last 15-20 years has sought to increase the level of owner-occupation. However, the mechanisms utilized to do so have been very different. The mortgage finance market in France has, until recently, been a very segmented market, with several different channels by which the flow of savings can be tapped in order to finance house purchase, and hence different types of loans with different interest rates attached. Over the 1980s, however, the system has become progressively marketized, or to use the French term *banalisé* - that is, the complex, differentiated system is giving way to a more market-orientated system, in which all borrowers will pay the same rate of interest.

Traditionally, French home owners have used a package of loans to purchase the property. Contractual-savings schemes (*plans et contrats d'épargne-logement* or PELs) play a part in the French system, as do their equivalents, the *Bausparkassen*, in the German system. Individuals agree to save at least a minimum amount for a period of at least five years. They receive interest at below-market rates plus a government bonus. At the end of the contractual period they qualify for a below-market rate loan of 2.5 times the sum saved (the contractual sum saved is of course now available as a deposit). Such schemes have played a major role in the French owner-occupation system, with perhaps 40 per cent of purchasers making use of them. Typically, these schemes might provide about 40 per cent of the purchase price of the dwelling, so they need to be supplemented with other loans. They are mainly used by the higher occupational groups and the self-employed. Reforms introduced at the beginning of the 1980s meant that PELs became more general savings products rather than specifically housing-related savings schemes. But falls in the interest rate offered on PELs in the mid-1980s tended to shift their status back towards being a specialist instrument (Lefebvre et al. 1991, p. 207). In the 1980s, the size of *épargne-logement* deposits grew, as they offered a better return than alternatives. However, since 1988 they have been losing market share to other types of investment.

Mortgage finance is provided mainly by ordinary banks rather than by specialist lenders like the building societies in Britain. More importantly, there are several different types of loans. PAP loans (*prêts aidés à l'accession à la propriété*) are loans at below-market rates of interest which are available to households whose income is below a certain ceiling (Ghékiere 1991, p. 139). They can be used for new property, subject to price ceiling, or for existing property requiring improvement. Repayments are staggered, so that they are kept low in the first few years. In 1982, more than a third of lending on new houses was helped via PAP loans. The number of loans made has been steadily falling, and PAP finance is rapidly disappearing from the system (see below).

Prêts conventionnés (PC loans) are loans at higher rates than PAP loans, but still at rates which are subject to an 'agreement' (convention) rather than set by market forces. They are made available by banks, the rates being agreed between the banks and the Crédit Foncier de France, a typically French hybrid public/private organization with responsibilities for organizing the mortgage finance market. PC loans are also available for new or for existing properties requiring improvement. As with PAP loans, borrowers are eligible for APL (means-tested personal support with housing costs).

Finally, there are free-sector loans, where interest rates are set by market forces.

As Table 3.1 shows, there has been a sharp decline over the 1980s in the numbers of PAP loans made, from 127,000 in 1982 to 53,000 in 1994. Conversely, the number of free-sector loans has increased from 33,000 in 1985 to over 130,000 in 1994.

Table 3.1 Housing starts, France 1980-1991 (thousands, per annum)

	PLA	PAP	PC	Free	Total
1980	60	120	100	117	397
1981	56	126	82	136	400
1982	64	127	81	72	344
1983	58	115	90	70	333
1984	55	113	92	35	295
1985	65	93	105	33	296
1986	60	86	99	51	296
1987	54	78	114	64	310
1988	54	60	108	105	327
1989	50	51	105	133	339
1990	47	37	105	121	310
1991	60	33	85	125	303
1992	63	29	70	115	277
1993	72	31	50	104	257
1994	75	53	40	134	302

Source: Ministry of Housing.

Thus, over the 1980s the French owner-occupied market has moved fairly rapidly from one dominated by state allocation of finance at sub-market rates to one dominated by market allocation of finance at rates set by demand and supply. At the same time there has been another important and related shift away from a system dominated by purchases of new property, towards one in which there is a much greater proportion of purchases of existing dwellings. Sales of second-hand property as a proportion of all transactions rose from 50 per cent in 1984 to 74 per cent in 1990 (Benit 1994, p. 168). According to Lefebvre et al. (1991) this restructuring of housing markets accelerated in the second half of the 1980s, so that the second-hand market is now the most active part of the system, and more and more resembles the British owner-occupied market (Lefebvre et al. 1991, 272-3). These authors argue that housing markets will thus become even more responsive to changes in the macro economic climate and, in particular, to the financial environment. They expect the virtual disappearance of PAP loans to be followed by the disappearance of PC loans, so that eventually there will be complete '*banalisation*', that is a system in which essentially the same loan can be granted by any banking or financial institution, for any property transaction, and the granting of loans is thus separated from any specific form of support (ibid., p. 274).

In France, as in Britain, the owner-occupied sector in the 1990s encountered some difficulties. In France, these are often seen in terms of stagnation or '*blocage.*' The policy of competitive disinflation has meant, via high real interest rates and slow income growth, that owner-occupier households are carrying a higher burden of debt than they might have expected to. When combined with the rise in unemployment and in divorce and separation, this creates problems in particular for younger and poorer owner-occupiers (Flamand 1989; Durance 1992). In fact the *taux d'effort* (gross relation between annual loan payments and annual household income) fell for PAP mortgagors between 1980 and 1988 from 18.9 per cent to 12.4 per cent, and for PC mortgagors from 31.3 per cent to 25.4 per cent. However, for those with free-sector loans it rose from 26.6 per cent to 34.6 per cent, over the same period, peaking at 42.0 per cent in 1986. The number of transactions increased between 1980 and 1988 from 483,000 to 573,000 (CREP, quoted in *L'Observateur de l'immobilier* 22). But since then there has been first, a fall in transactions (*Le Monde*, 23 April 1992) and more recently a fall in prices. These effects are most pronounced in areas such as Paris where prices had risen most in the previous period - they doubled between 1986 and 1990 and tripled overall between 1983 and 1990 (Massot 1990; Taffin 1992). At the top end of the market in Paris, prices may have fallen by as much as 20-25 per cent, while elsewhere the fall has been much less.

Essentially, the system of PAP or PC loans with APL performed the same role in the French housing system as did the right to buy in the British system, that is, it improved access to owner-occupation for skilled manual households (Benit 1994). Indeed, Benit argues that access to owner-occupation for modest-income households is easier in France than in either Germany or Britain, because a greater proportion of mortgagors benefit from personal support, either through APL or through the older *allocations logement* (AL): in 1988 more than one in five mortgagors benefited in this way (Benit 1994, p. 140).

Over the 1980s, however, owner-occupiers have been damaged by two major aspects of the stringency of French economic policy. Real wages have stagnated on the one hand, while low inflation has increased the real burden of the mortgage debt taken on. Benit (1994) argues that there are important cohort effects: the fall in inflation has hurt in particular those who bought in the early 1980s. They took out loans (at fixed interest rates) at a time when nominal rates were particularly high, expecting inflation to erode the real value of the repayments; however, subsequently the direction of economic policy changed to the prioritization of sustained low inflation. Those borrowing from the mid-1980s on have had lower nominal (and hence lower real) interest rates to contend with and hence fewer problems. Flamand (1989) makes similar points about the fact that some young households did not foresee the salary stagnation and fall in inflation in the 1980s. The rise in unemployment and the impact of other events such as divorce, illness or birth of another child, can then easily upset household budgets.

The fall in house prices has been particularly concentrated among buyers of cheaper, PAP-linked individual houses in peri-urban developments. The effect of the relatively unpopular location is accentuated by the fact that while the original purchasers benefited from the low-interest PAP loans, subsequent buyers do not qualify, thus depressing the resale price (Benit 1994).

The fall in inflation created widespread problems for owner-occupiers. Between 1984 and 1988, nearly one-third of mortgagors renegotiated their loans, including 45 per cent of holders of PC loans. This led to supplements to the APL and a reorganization of PAP in October 1988 (Benit 1994). Problems can arise when family size changes, and households can lose entitlement to APL, a problem which applies equally to tenant households. In 1989, there were 200,000 households whose outgoings were above 60 per cent of disposable monthly income. In 1984, it was estimated that 13 per cent of households were 'overindebted'; of these 65 per cent had PAP loans, and a further 28 per cent had PC loans. As a consequence, lenders are now more prudent in terms of lending policies, requiring a deposit of at least 10 per cent from the household's own resources (that is, not from another loan), and being more cautious generally about loans and loan-to-income ratios.

What has been the impact of these changes? Lefebvre (1993) argues that they have increased exclusion from the housing market. Poorer households cannot gain access to owner-occupation. Modest-income households now access the second-hand rather than the new market, but lack the resources to improve the property, potentially giving rise to problems of stock deterioration. Those unable to move to owner-occupation stay as tenants but, with the decline of the private rented sector, landlords can be more selective about whom they will house. Households thereby excluded from the private rented sector add to the demand for social housing. Meanwhile, the non-revision of the income ceilings on access to social housing contribute to ghetto formation and management problems in social housing. Hence, Lefebvre links the changes in housing finance and the impact of marketization with the growth in polarization and social exclusion, a point to which I return in section 3.5.

3.3.2 Social Housing

Most social housing in France (89 per cent) is owned by the HLM (*habitations à loyer modéré*) organizations. These comprise two main types: public organizations, closely linked to the local authorities (*Offices Publics* and OPACs), and *sociétés anonymes,* which are linked to a variety of private and voluntary organizations (Ghékiere 1991, p. 140). In 1988 there were about 3.5 million social rented dwellings, representing 17.1 per cent of the stock. There is an income ceiling for applicants for social housing.

Since 1977, new social rented housing has been financed by the granting of a reduced interest rate loan to the HLM organization, the *prêt locatif aidé* (PLA). These loans are distributed by the Caisse des Dépôts et Consignations. A similar loan, PALULOS, is available for the improvement of older social rented housing. In addition to the PLA subsidized loan, new social construction benefits from a capital grant averaging 12 per cent for new build and acquisition-improvement and 20 per cent for rehabilitation. The source of the funds used for social housing are the popular Livret A savings accounts.

These financing mechanisms reduce the rent on a social unit below what would be charged if costs had to be fully covered. However, rents are higher than those which prevailed before 1977. This increase in average rents is offset by the eligibility of households living in a PLA or PALULOS financed social unit to apply for APL, the means-tested housing allowance, which is paid directly to the landlord. Hence the 1977 reform represents a conscious and deliberate attempt to shift the financing of social housing from a property-based to a household-based approach: average rents increase, but the poorest are protected through the housing allowance system. This change has enabled larger numbers of poor people to gain access to the social sector, but also has provided incentives for the better-off households to leave, as they have to pay higher rents, but with no entitlement to APL. Not surprisingly, this has consequences for social polarization, discussed in 3.5 below.

An additional source of funding is the so-called '1 per cent', a tax on all employers over a certain size, of 1 per cent of their salary bill. This tax is collected by local committees and distributed to social housing organizations to enable the provision of both rented and owner-occupied housing.

Throughout the 1980s, a series of programmes and initiatives have been launched with the aim of improving conditions on large HLM estates. *'Habitat et vie sociale'* was launched in 1977, followed by *'développement sociale des quartiers'* in 1982. These programmes have increasingly concentrated on more than just physical improvements to the housing stock and changes to management and administration, but including also community development, training and education, job creation, leisure facilities and so on (Emms 1990; Power 1993).

As in the owner-occupied sector, economic liberalization has had profound impacts on the financing of social housing. The French system of social housing has been highly dependent on access to low-cost funds via the Livret A accounts. In recent years, this source of funds has been hit by disintermediation as French households have increasingly switched their savings away from this traditional home for small savings towards newer types of savings vehicles offering higher returns. In 1989, there were net withdrawals of FF35 billion from Livret A accounts, rising to withdrawals of FF51 billion in 1992. In particular, the Livret A accounts are suffering from competition from PEPs (*plans d'épargne populaires*) and other newer financial products (Durance 1992).

Government has tried to slow this *'décollecte'* via a number of measures, including modernizing the Livret A product and requiring HLMs to put all their treasury surpluses into Livret A accounts. In addition, government has secured partial access to the Livret Bleu accounts of the Crédit Mutuel (Durance 1992). But the problem of *'décollecte'* remains. One result is greater use of alternative sources of funds - both internally generated by the HLM organizations and those provided externally through the 1 per cent housing tax on employers. In fact only 0.45 per cent of this tax is now available for financing social housing, the remainder going to the *Fond National d'Aide au Logement* (FNAL) which distributes *allocation-logement sociale*. The 1 per cent housing tax has become more and more important in the financing of social rented housing, especially in high-cost areas like the Paris region (Taisne 1990; Fribourg 1992; Durance 1992). More generally HLM organizations are under increasing financial pressure, caught between high financing costs on the one hand and, on the other, the fact that their tenants are increasingly drawn from the poorer and more disadvantaged strata, meaning that their rent-paying capacity is limited. Consequently the risks of arrears and bad debts, and the costs of management have increased.

3.3.3 Private Rented Sector

In France, as in Britain, there has been concern about the decline in the size of the private rented sector, although the sector remains much larger in France than in Britain. The number of privately rented units fell from 4.8 million in 1961 to 4.1 million in 1988, a reduction from 33 per cent of the stock to 20 per cent (Ghékiere 1991, p. 129).

The Quillot Law of 1982, passed by a socialist government, strengthened tenants' rights and was opposed by property and industrial interests. But by 1986, under a 'cohabitation' government of the Right, the Mehaighnerie Law freed up the rents of new and vacated units, and allowed rents to be revised annually in line with the construction cost index. Rents on current contracts were to be freed in 1991 (1995 for lettings in large cities) (Flamand 1989), but this was cancelled by the Mermaz-Malandain Law of 1989. Further reforms to encourage private renting were announced in May 1993.

Between 1984 and 1988 the private rented sector in France declined by 441,000 units; altogether there was a loss of 700,000 in the 10 years to 1988 (Louvot 1992). However, the tax incentives brought in under the Quiles (September 1984) and Mehaighnerie (June 1986) plans have had some effect - private rented sector construction has risen from only 5,000 in 1985 to over 20,000 in 1990.

The reduction in the private rented sector has also meant a reduction in what is called the *de facto* social rented sector (*logements sociaux de fait*). This refers to a reduction in the supply of poor quality but cheap rented accommodation, accessible and affordable by poor and marginal households. The private rented sector in France has undergone a process of *normalisation* in which marginal housing - such as maids' rooms (*chambres de bonne*) and furnished hotels - as well as the wholly rented building are disappearing (Massot 1990). In the big cities, in particular, recent decades have seen the disappearance of much of this marginal housing, also known as *faux logements*. In the Paris area, the numbers of such *faux logements* fell from 254,000 in 1968 to 105,000 in 1982 (Lacoste 1990) and to only 78,000 in 1990 (Census data).

Demarginalization of the sector is also caused by improvement of former unfit units (perhaps 200,000 per annum) and the dropping out of older units from the 1948 Law rent control and protection (50,000 per annum). New private construction is mainly for co-ownership, while older rented blocks are broken up through sales of individual apartments. One-third of landlords do not wish to be landlords, and current profitability is weak. *Normalisation* is leading to greater homogeneity in terms of the physical characteristics of the stock, but greater heterogeneity in terms of capital values, based mainly on location. Massot (1990) concludes that it would be a pity if private renting were squeezed out in France in the way which it has been in Britain; a balanced market requires a private rented sector: home ownership cannot be a universal tenure, and social sector expansion is limited by the cost of land and the decline in the Livret A source of finance.

3.4 OUTCOMES

3.4.1 Housing Demand and Supply

As with Britain, I shall look first at demographic and social changes, before going on to consider the influence of economic variables such as income growth and distribution.

In France as in Britain, population growth in the 1980s was considerably slower than in the 1960s: in France the population grew by 4.8 per thousand in 1988 compared with 9.6 in 1960. But the number of households grew much faster than the population: by 17 per cent between 1962 and 1982, while the number of households increased twice as fast. As a result, the average size of household fell from 3.10 in 1962 to 2.70 in 1982 and further to 2.57 in 1990 (INSEE Census data). In the Paris region, average household size fell from 2.73 to 2.48 between 1962 and 1982, and is projected to fall to 2.15 in 2015 (Lacoste 1990).

Trends in household structure have been similar to Britain, with a shift away from traditional married-couple-headed and/or nuclear family households towards a greater proportion of single-person, single-parent and elderly households. In France the number of marriages fell from 417,000 in 1972 to 285,000 in 1984 (Flamand 1989), and to 276,000 in 1992 (Taffin

1992). The marriage rate in France fell from 5.8 to 5.0 per thousand eligible between 1981 and 1989, while the divorce rate per thousand marriages rose from 6.8 to 8.4. The number of lone parent households is projected to increase in France from 897,000 in 1982 to 1.139 million in 1990 (Taffin 1992).

In both countries there has also been an increase in the number of single-person households. This has several causes, such as earlier exit from the parental home, higher divorce rates and greater numbers of single elderly living independently. Single persons comprised about 26 per cent of all households in both England and France in 1989. This proportion is projected to rise to 28 per cent in France in 2000 (Louvot 1989).

As in Britain, over the last two decades there has been a steady increase in real GDP and in real household incomes in France. Taking the whole period 1970-89, real GDP per head has increased by about 50 per cent in both France and the UK, while real earnings have increased rather more in France than in the UK. But a different picture emerges if we concentrate on the last decade. GDP growth in Britain was 26 per cent between 1980 and 1989, compared with only 15 per cent in France, while UK real earnings rose by 21 per cent compared with 8 per cent in France over the same period. OECD figures show that real net take-home pay stagnated in France during the 1980s, while rising an average of 0.5 per cent per year in the rest of the OECD (OECD 1992,1994). Unemployment has risen substantially in France from the low levels of the 1970s, reaching 12.0 per cent of the labour force in October 1993; unemployment among young people is particularly acute.

The overall demographic and economic pattern underpinning housing demand is thus broadly similar in France to that described in the previous chapter for Britain: the number of households has continued to rise, particularly non-traditional household types such as single-parent and single-person households. Real incomes have grown more slowly than in Britain, and there has been considerable growth in unemployment.

While the broad demographic and economic trends in France are similar to those in Britain, there are also important differences in terms of economic policies and economic performance. In both countries, there has been a slowdown in growth compared with the 30 years after the war, and in particular, the rise and persistence of unemployment, with a growing component of long-term unemployed. But in France, unlike in Britain, there has been a consistent and (in its own terms) successful anti-inflation policy since the early 1980s, based around membership of the ERM and the *franc fort*. This has brought benefits in terms of France's inflation rate falling below that of Germany in June 1991 (OECD 1992). The inevitable consequence of this deflationary policy stance has been prolonged high unemployment in France, the political consequences of which eventually played a large part in the virtual collapse of the ERM in August 1993.

These differences in economic policy and in economic performance have had important consequences for the housing markets of the two countries. In France, the operation of the housing system has been slowed considerably by the combination of stagnant real earnings, high real interest rates and the impact that low inflation has on the user cost of capital to mortgagors. That is, owner-occupiers who borrowed in the early 1980s on the expectation that high or at least moderate inflation would speedily reduce the real debt burden have been sadly disappointed. In France, there was something of a housing boom between 1986 and 1990, but it was not so pronounced as in Britain.

In both countries, unemployment and the numbers in poverty have increased, meaning that in each case, the burden of economic difficulty is falling disproportionately on a relatively small section of the population. On the other hand, there is a clear difference in that while French social housing output has been maintained at a consistent level of about 50,000-60,000 new dwellings per annum, in Britain, social housing construction virtually collapsed in the 1980s. This leads on to the central question of the extent to which housing needs are being met both currently and in the future, discussed in 3.4.2 below.

In France, after the initial post-war reconstruction period in which priority was given to industrial development, a relatively high proportion of resources, by European standards, was devoted to housing investment. This policy was partly a consequence of the lower quality of the existing stock in France and the later timing of rural to urban migration by comparison with other countries, hence the need for new construction. In the 1950s and 1960s it also reflected the dominant role of the state. Housing investment as a proportion of GDP remained far higher than in Britain, for example, in the 1970s and 1980s - in 1975 the figures were 8.4 per cent for France and 4.4 per cent in Britain, falling to 5.5 per cent and 3.4per cent in 1985, respectively.

As in other European countries, there was a move away from new construction and towards rehabilitation from the 1970s on, as the crude shortage of dwellings was overcome. Nevertheless, in France, output was still at a relatively high level in the early 1980s, with starts of 400,000 or more in 1979, 1980 and 1981. This fell by about 25 per cent in the early 1980s, so that since 1984, starts have fluctuated around 300,000 (see Table 3.1 above). The figure of 300,000 units remains a psychological barrier in French housing policy. When, in late 1991, it appeared that output for 1992 might fall below this level, a variety of measures were introduced to give a boost to the housing market (Mouillart 1992). Nevertheless, output did fall to a low of 277,000 in 1992 (*Le Figaro*, 10 May 1993). The Balladur government announced in May 1993 a package of assistance to the housing sector, with the objective of raising output to above 300,000 again (*Le Monde*, 11 May 1993).

Within this total, subsidized rental starts, mainly by HLM organizations, have in fact remained fairly constant, only once being outside the range 50-60 thousand p.a. On the other hand, subsidized owner-occupation via low-interest PAP loans has fallen from 135,000 in 1979 to only 33,000 in 1991. Starts using regulated loans (*prêts conventionnés*) have fluctuated in the region 80,000 to 115,000, but have declined steadily since 1987. Starts financed by free-market loans fell from 136,000 in 1981 to only 33,000 in 1985 but then rose to 125,000 in 1991.

Hence, output in the early 1990s has fallen by comparison with output earlier in the 1980s, and has fallen considerably by comparison with peak output in the 1960s and 1970s. In France there were over 500,000 starts in 1975, including 115,000 in the subsidized rented sector (Froger 1992). Stock changes in France are characterized by greater volatility than in Britain, with larger numbers of losses and changes of use as well as higher new construction. Over the period 1982-87, about 34,000 units p.a. were demolished, and another 77,000 were lost through fusion of two or more small units into one larger one (Louvot 1989, pp. 31-7). Offsetting this was an estimated additional 53,000 units p.a. through conversion gain. Finally, 66,000 houses were converted into business premises, and a similar number (62,000) moved the other way. In total, the annual net loss from the stock was estimated by Louvot to be 62,000 p.a. Louvot breaks down these changes by the three categories of principal residence, secondary residence, and vacant property. Principal residences actually show a net gain over the period from the balance of demolitions, conversions and changes of use, of 8,000, second homes a loss of 7,000, while vacant units decline by 63,000. Louvot's work shows that properties generally pass through a stage of long-term vacancy, before dropping out of the stock altogether.

Hence, annual losses from the stock are much higher in France than in Britain. In the UK, net losses ran at about 15,000 in 1983, falling to 10,000 in 1987, while in France they were between four and six times higher over the same period. This in part helps to explain the higher level of output in France, as a greater amount of new provision is needed in order to replace units leaving the stock.

These differences in the operation of the housing system also come out if we compare vacancy rates. According to Census data, vacancy rates in France were 7.8 per cent in 1982 and 7.2 per cent in 1990.[1] Vacancy rates in Paris increased from 1.6 per cent in 1962 to 9.8 per cent in 1982 and 9.1 per cent in 1990 (Taffin 1992). Vacancy rates in Britain were much lower. Official figures for the number of households and dwellings in the 1980s imply a vacancy rate of about 4 per cent at the beginning of the decade, falling to about 3 per cent by the end of the decade (see Chapter 2 above).

The higher vacancy rates and greater volatility experienced in France relate to particular characteristics of the stock. More recent urbanization in France compared with Britain means that there is a higher level of dereliction and abandonment of the stock in parts of rural France, as well as changes of use from principal residence to second home. In addition, the French private housing stock has undergone a process of *normalisation*, as described above in section 3.3.3. Differences in the structures of the two housing systems may mean that different vacancy rates are required in order to keep each system functioning, that is that the equilibrium vacancy rates of each country are different.

We can see, then, that the policy shift towards the market has had different effects on output in France as compared with Britain. In France, new social rental housing has remained more or less constant - the change has come mainly *within* the owner-occupied sector, with a shift away from owner-occupied social housing, and towards that financed by free-sector loans.[2]

Although policies in both countries have favoured owner-occupation, the tenure patterns remain different (Table 3.2).

Between 1970 and 1988, owner-occupation increased by 15 percentage points in Britain, compared with 9 percentage points in France. Private renting declined by 9 percentage points in each country, but this means that the private rented sector is still twice as large in percentage terms in France as in Britain. In 1988, more than half of all rented dwellings in France were owned by private landlords, compared with just over a quarter in Britain. The relative sizes of the social rented sectors have become more similar over the last two decades - in France because of the growth of the sector, in Britain because of its decline.

Table 3.2 Housing tenure, Britain and France (percentages)

	1970	1970	1988	1988	1992	1992
	GB	Fr	GB	Fr	GB	Fr
Owner-occupiers	50	45	65	54	67	54
Private tenants	19	29	10	20	9	21
Social tenants	31	11	25	17	24	17
Other	-	4	-	9	-	8

Note: Figures for France 1970 do not sum to 100 per cent; no explanation given.

Sources: Ghékiere 1991; OPCS *General Household Survey* 1992; INSEE, *Enquête Logement* 1992.

3.4.2 The Demand/Supply Balance and Housing Needs

According to Mouillart (1992) construction over the period 1954-75 was roughly in line with needs. But since the end of the sixth plan in 1975, there has been growth in the level of unsatisfied demand. Quantitative estimates of housing needs are a combination of estimated new household formation, a vacancy reserve to ensure adequate mobility within the stock, and replacement of the more dilapidated parts of the stock (Louvot 1989; Mouillart 1992). New household formation can be further subdivided into the pure demographic increase, resulting from changes in marriage and divorce rates, and that resulting from decohabitation, that is increases in the number of single parents and the earlier departure of children from the parental home.

Since 1975, the fall in construction has been much greater than the slowdown in the growth of the number of new households, so that the adaptation of demand to supply works via a fall in the rate of replacement of the stock. As a result, units stay in service longer, and improvement and maintenance are reduced. In addition, there is a reduction in mobility, and less decohabitation because of economic pressure from unemployment, high real interest rates and a tighter housing market. Mouillart estimates that unmet needs have been running at about 44,000 p.a. since 1976. Hence by the 1990s in Mouillart's view, more than 500,000 units had been lost, a figure which one can relate to the estimate of 400,000 homeless cited by

Housing Minister Besson (Mouillart 1992, p. 34). This shortage not surprisingly affects the poorest and most vulnerable households most. In addition, mobility becomes more and more difficult and there is an increased fall in stock quality.

Official INSEE projections suggest a need for about 362,000 new units per annum on average over the period 1990-95. This comprises 246,000 needed for household growth, over 60,000 replacement demand, a vacancy reserve of 22,000 and 47,000 in the second homes sector (Taffin 1992). The level of demand is projected to fall in the second half of the 1990s. For 1995-2000, the INSEE estimate is 314,000, of which 207,000 is from net household increase. Louvot estimates that demand for principal residences might be only half as great in 2000-2005 as in 1975-82 (Louvot 1989). As far as types of housing are concerned, the demographic trends perhaps suggest a greater demand for smaller units and for flats rather than houses. But this is likely to be more than offset by the strong recent trends which show clear household preferences for more space and for *la maison individuelle* (single-family house) (Merlin 1988). Finally, Mouillart (1992) makes the point that the sum of local needs will always be greater than the national aggregate total, because the system does not fully adjust across submarkets.[3] These spatial aspects are important - but data relating to local submarkets are often not available.

The existence of unmet housing needs has prompted the French government into action. At the end of the 1980s there was an estimated 200,000-400,000 homeless households, plus 2 million badly housed (Froger 1992). At the same time, there were 2 million vacant dwellings, of which about 300,000-400,000 are in urban areas, and some of which could be brought into use. According to the French housing ministry, the right to housing is a national priority. This concept of a right to housing is closely tied to the notion of social inclusion and the reinsertion of marginal groups. The concept is first employed in the Quillot Law of 1982, and incorporated in rather more detail in the Besson Law of 1990.

The Besson Law introduced a number of specific measures. Each departement must have a plan for housing for the poorest households, established under the joint authority of the prefect and the president of the general council of the departement, after consultation with a wide range of parties (Froger 1992). Each departement must also set up a solidarity fund to be used for paying rent deposits, rent payments, support and training (Bayley 1994). Recognizing that several thousand households could be housed in the cheaper parts of the existing stock, the government introduced a new low-interest loan - the PLA *d'insertion* - available to HLMs and other organizations to purchase private sector property for letting to poorer households, with a target of 10,000 units p.a. in 1992 and 13,000 in 1993 (Froger 1992). The role of the prefect in nominating homeless or badly housed persons to the social stock has been greatly strengthened (Bayley 1994; Froger 1992)

Out-turn has been below target however, at about 7,000 units p.a. Problems include the small-scale nature of the PLA-I programme, which does not generate economies of scale and the fact that landlords only get 80 per cent of the normal social rent on these lettings (although the capital grant towards construction costs is higher, at 20 per cent rather than the usual 12.75 per cent). There are also problems of nimbyism from the local authority: communes have to give planning permission and in most cases guarantee the loan. In many cases, communes take the view that they do not want any more poor people in the area (Bayley 1994).

The Besson Law also extended means-tested housing allowances, including to young people living in hostels (*foyers*), and increased the budget for the *fonds de solidarité départementale*, used to avoid evictions of families in arrears (Froger 1992).

Second, the 'Loi d'orientation pour la ville' (LOV) was passed in 1991. This aims at favouring social mix at the local level and countering ghettoization. The decentralization of the early 1980s devolved most planning powers to the level of the commune. A major part of the LOV is to encourage the provision of social rental housing in those communes which form part of large conurbations but currently have only a low proportion of social housing (Comby 1992). Communes which are part of a conurbation of 200,000+ persons, but have less than 20 per cent social housing and less than 18 per cent of households in receipt of housing benefit, are required to provide more plots for social housing construction (Guibert 1992).

These measures are not insignificant, but represent more aspirations and goals rather than a directly attainable set of policy outcomes. As one commentator puts it, the right to housing is more than just symbolic, but it does not imply the *realization* of that right - unlike, for example, the introduction of the *revenu minimum d'insertion* (RMI), the guaranteed income (Calcoen 1992). In May 1993, the incoming centre-right Balladur government announced a more substantive programme of financial help to the housing and construction sectors including reforms to help the private rented sector, another 20,000 PAP low-interest mortgage loans to lower-income home buyers, and 11,000 more PLA loans for social rental construction in the HLM sector. However, at the same time, the government announced a freeze on housing benefit spending and a slowing down of the previous government's proposal to reduce the level of transfer taxes (*droits de mutation*) on property sales (*Le Monde*, 14 June 1993). The policies of the new government hence show both continuities with the previous administration, as well as perhaps a somewhat greater emphasis on stimulating private enterprise.

Overall, in France just as in Britain, the efficacy of housing policies in meeting housing needs has been profoundly affected by changes in housing finance, and the greater market orientation of the system. In both countries, deregulation has meant that most home owners must now pay the market cost of mortgage finance, and not a rate that is kept below market levels by either a government-supported cartel (Britain) or directly subsidized state loans (France). As a result, home owners have greater choice, and easier access to loans and hence to owner-occupied housing during the boom period. Conversely, the sector is now more vulnerable to general economic shocks, and perhaps also to systemic failure.

In the social housing sector, greater market orientation is producing major tensions. In Britain, this takes the form of housing associations having to take difficult and often unwanted decisions about the trade-offs between output, quality and rent levels. This reflects a radical and important change in the nature of housing associations, from being managers of a physical stock of housing to being managers of a financial asset, secured against the physical value of the stock (Pryke and Whitehead 1991). In France this takes the form of an emerging crisis of social housing finance resulting from the disintermediation of the Livret A accounts, a crisis which is masked rather than resolved by greater reliance on the 1 per cent *logement* and internal sources of funds. In both countries, the underlying tension is between the social goals which housing associations and HLM organizations are expected to perform, and the market means by which they are expected to carry it out.

3.5 POLARIZATION AND SEGREGATION IN HOUSING OUTCOMES

It is widely perceived that social polarization and tenure segregation have increased in French housing. French social housing, until comparatively recently, was not seen as housing for the poor, but rather as housing for a mix of skilled manual and white-collar workers. But a combination of factors have worked together to change this. First, the expansion of owner-occupation has meant that some of this latter group have moved out of social housing and into owner-occupation. As we saw earlier, the policy of PAP or PC plus APL can be seen as broadly equivalent to the right to buy in Britain.

Second, the private rented sector has been both declining in size, and improving in quality, leading to the loss of large numbers of smaller, cheaper, sometimes furnished, units which previously had acted as a pool of *de facto* social housing. This diminution in the *de facto* social sector has increased the demand from poor and marginal households for social housing.

Third, the social sector itself has been changing. Social landlords are now under greater pressure to house the homeless and other disadvantaged groups, APL means that social housing is affordable by the poor, while the rise in average rents means that better-off households have an incentive to leave, particularly as those whose incomes rise above the income ceiling (*plafond des ressources*) can be charged an additional rent (*sur-loyer*).

Taken together, these changes are producing a pattern where middle and high-income groups are in private housing, households with low but regular income are in acceptable social housing, and those on precarious incomes are in poor quality social housing (Blanc 1993). Blanc comments

> The crisis of HLM rented housing is primarily related to changes among its clients. Traditionally, HLMs housed a population with a low-middle and regular income. The poor were in the private sector, in slums and in dilapidated housing. The present housing policies have two main consequences:
> * the former HLM tenants tend to become owner occupiers and they move out;
> * slums and substandard housing are regressing. Then the poor have no other choice left and they tend to apply for HLM housing. (Blanc 1993, p. 212)

Similarly, Taffin has argued that the policy to move the better off into owner occupation, leaving vacancies behind which can be used by the poorest, has worked only too well (quoted in Flamand 1989, p. 329). So tenants become poorer while mortgagors, strongly indebted and with slow salary growth, get larger subsidies for longer. There is thus a concentration of poorer and more vulnerable households in the HLM sector, with the *taux d'effort* weighing more heavily on household budgets. Problems are created, too, for the landlord organizations, as arrears rise. This limits both their investment capacity and their management capacity, and pushes them in the direction of selecting their tenants more narrowly (Flamand 1989).

Evidence on social polarization by tenure in France is available from INSEE's *Enquête Logement* (Housing Survey), carried out every four years. Table 3.3 gives data on tenure by socio economic group for 1978 and 1988.

Table 3.3 Tenure by socio economic group, France, 1978 and 1988 (percentages)

Tenure	Professional managerial intermediate	Manual etc.	Retired/ non-active	Total
1978				
Outright owners	27.3	15.4	57.3	100
Mortgagors	53.9	38.2	7.8	100
Social tenants	25.6	53.6	20.6	100
Private tenants	36.6	34.9	28.3	100
All households	35.6	32.1	32.3	100
1988				
Outright owners	26.4	9.2	64.3	100
Mortgagors	60.7	28.9	10.4	100
Social tenants	35.4	35.4	29.3	100
Private tenants	49.8	23.7	26.6	100
All households	42.7	22.2	35.0	100

Source: INSEE, *Enquête Logement* 1978, 1988.

In 1978, more than a half of mortgagors were in the non-manual socio economic categories, compared with about a quarter of social sector tenants, and just over a third of all households. By 1988 (there were some changes in categorization) more than 40 per cent of all households were in the non-manual category. In the social sector, the proportion had risen to 35 per cent, but among mortgagors it had risen still further, to over 60 per cent. There is some evidence that the social sector is becoming bipolar: while the proportion in the non-manual categories rose from about 25 per cent to about 35 per cent, the proportion who are retired or otherwise economically inactive rose from 20.6 per cent to 29.3 per cent.

Table 3.4 Tenure by socioeconomic group (detail) France, 1988

	Owner	Mort-gagors	Social Tenants	Private Tenants	Other	All
Farmers	5.2	3.0	0.1	0.2	0.6	3.0
Profess-ional senior manage-ment	6.9	9.7	2.1	6.2	7.7	6.7
Higher exec.	4.4	14.5	3.8	7.4	12.4	8.5
Intermed clerks	5.4	22.9	11.8	11.2	17.0	13.7
Skilled manual	6.8	23.7	23.0	11.8	16.7	16.1
Unskilled manual	2.4	5.2	12.4	7.0	7.7	6.1
Retired former non-wage earner	14.9	1.3	1.4	4.4	2.7	6.4
Retired former wage earner	41.8	7.9	20.2	36.7	13.6	22.1
Other non-active	7.6	1.2	7.7	5.4	7.5	6.5
All	100	100	100	100	100	100

Source: INSEE, *Enquête Logement* 1988.

Further detail on the social composition of tenures in 1988 is given in Table 3.4 from where it can be seen that the higher socioeconomic groups are over-represented among mortgagors and under-represented among the ranks of social tenants. Conversely, unskilled manual households, and other non-active are over-represented in the social sector. The crucial break comes between skilled and unskilled manual households. Skilled manual households make up 23.7 per cent of mortgagors and 23.0 per cent of the social sector, compared with 16.1 per cent of the population as a whole. But unskilled manual households (6.1 per cent of all households) make up only 5.2 per cent of mortgagors, but more than double that proportion (12.4 per cent) of the social sector. The private rented sector, as in Britain, is heterogeneous: the 1948 law sub-sector, not surprisingly is dominated by retired households (more than 40 per cent) while the rest of the sector caters for a range of groups, with over-representation particularly among higher executives, intermediary positions and clerks.

Table 3.5 Tenure by income octiles, France, 1988 (percentages)

	Outright owners	Mortgag -or	Social tenants	Private tenants	All
Lowest income	15.0	1.0	5.3	9.4	9.8
Second	17.6	2.7	8.3	11.2	11.6
Third	14.1	6.3	14.9	15.0	13.0
Fourth	13.3	10.6	17.2	15.3	13.8
Fifth	13.4	19.4	24.1	17.2	17.1
Sixth	12.3	23.8	19.5	16.3	16.6
Seventh	7.7	20.1	8.3	8.9	10.6
Highest income	6.5	16.0	2.3	6.4	7.5
All	100	100	100	100	100

Source: INSEE, *Enquête Logement* 1978.

Data on tenure by income are given in Tables 3.5 and 3.6. Tenure by income (in eight categories) in 1978 is shown in Table 3.5. In 1978, higher-income groups were over-represented among mortgagors, with about 60 per cent of mortgagors being in the top three categories, compared with about 35 per cent of the population as a whole. Lower-income groups were over-represented among outright owners. Social housing was an interesting case: both the lowest two octiles and the highest two were under-represented - there was a concentration of households in the middle of the income distribution. The private rented sector, by contrast is shown to have been extremely representative of the population as a whole, at least in income terms.

Table 3.6 shows tenure by income (ten categories rather than eight) in 1988. Outright owners once again show an over-representation of lower-income deciles, and an under-representation at the top end. Being a mortgagor is clearly very related to income, with an under-representation of the bottom five deciles and over-representation of the top five. The private rented sector is again very representative of the overall distribution of income. But there has been a marked change in the social rented sector: now all five lower deciles are over-represented, while all five higher ones are under-represented. Lower-income groups are clearly more concentrated in the social sector in 1988 compared with 1978.

This finding is confirmed by Table 3.7, taken from Lefebvre et al. 1991. While in 1973, there were twice as many HLM households in the highest income quartile (24 per cent) as in the lowest quartile (12 per cent), by 1988 this pattern had been more than reversed, with only 12 per cent in the highest quartile but 30 per cent in the lowest quartile.

Finally, while there is clearly income segregation by tenure in France, the scale of it is not so great as in Britain. Benit (1994) provides diagrams showing the cumulative distribution of households by income in each of the main tenures for France, Britain and Germany. The separation between the curves is not so great in France as in Britain; also the curves for private and social tenants are much closer in France than they are in Britain.

Table 3.6 Tenure by income deciles, France, 1988 (percentages)

	Outright owners	Mortgagors	Social Tenants	Private tenants	All
Lowest decile	12.2	1.3	10.1	10.5	9.6
Second decile	12.8	2.5	12.3	10.9	9.8
Third decile	11.5	4.6	13.3	12.5	10.3
Fourth decile	11.6	6.2	14.0	11.1	10.3
Fifth decile	9.6	8.9	12.0	10.4	10.0
Sixth decile	9.1	10.7	6.6	10.1	10.0
Seventh	8.5	13.6	9.8	9.3	10.0
decile	7.3	15.6	8.6	8.8	10.0
Eighth decile	8.4	17.9	5.7	7.5	10.0
Ninth decile	8.9	18.5	2.9	9.0	10.0
Highest					
decile	100	100	100	100	100
All					

Source: INSEE, *Enquête Logement* 1988.

Table 3.7 HLM sector households by income bands, France, 1973-1988

	Lowest quartile	Second quartile	Third quartile	Highest quartile
1973	12	29	35	24
1978	18	30	33	19
1984	26	33	28	13
1988	30	33	25	12

Source: Mission économique de l'Union Nationale des Fédérations d'Organismes d'HLM, quoted in Lefebvre et al. 1991.

3.6 ASSESSMENT

Lefebvre et al. (1991) in their major study of housing policy and finance in France draw several important conclusions. First, the French housing market has been *modernized*, in the sense of displaying less segmentation, a restructuring of assistance, the disengagement of the state, and deregulation and *banalisation* of the housing finance system. In this process, the authors argue that Britain in particular and Anglo-Saxon economic liberalism has been the key reference point, although policy in France has not progressed (or regressed) as far along this axis as in Britain. One consequence of this is likely to be a more cyclical French housing market.

Second, the emphasis of policy has switched to the existing stock. There has been a move from a production-orientated to an exchange-orientated housing economy. The traditional French link between housing subsidy and new construction has been broken, or at least weakened.

Third, housing markets are now more responsive to, and affected by, changes in macroeconomic conditions. In particular, the restrictive budgetary, monetary and wage policies of the post-1983 French governments, based around the anchor of the *franc fort* have had major impacts on housing. This has tended to swamp the real political will behind the right to housing strategy. This macroeconomic stance is closely linked to the economic and political commitment to the European monetary system and the goal of economic and monetary union.

Fourth, the change in economic and financial policy in the 1980s amounts in effect to a major reform, yet this reform was not expressed in legislation, nor indeed in any political debate. This is confirmed by Durance, who argues that there was no great legislative reform, but rather an evolution of economic and financial arrangements which, together with small modifications has led to substantial changes in housing finance (Durance 1992, p. 81).

Fifth, there is now less reference to housing needs. The better off do have a right to housing, while the poor have at best a right to shelter, with no choice in the process. This parallels the bifurcated development of housing policy in Britain, described in Chapter 2 above.

Hence, in France as in Britain, housing policy took an explicit turn towards the market in the late 1970s and 1980s. This had two types of effect. First, there were direct effects in terms of the switch from renting to owner-occupation, the rise in social rents, the greater reliance on means-tested personal subsidies, and other policy changes. But of greater long-run importance were more fundamental changes which have made the housing system as a whole more closely influenced by conditions in financial markets and the state of the national economy. Different aspects of this greater sensitivity - and vulnerability of the housing systems towards changes in market conditions - have been discussed above.

In both countries, the turn towards the market has been presented as a necessary, indeed almost inevitable, development, reflecting the view that markets are the most effective way of allocating resources. But in both countries, the state continues to play a vital role in supporting market relationships - for example, through housing allowance systems, through the planning machinery, by underpinning the housing finance system, and so on. In both countries, also, the state has been forced to some degree to confront some of the consequences of the failure of market-orientated policies. In Britain, the movement towards a fully liberalized financial system has been more pronounced. Social output has virtually collapsed compared with previous decades, and government has successfully managed to distance itself from direct responsibility for 'headline' issues such as housing shortage and homelessness. However, at the same time, the strong ideological attachment to, and encouragement of owner-occupation has recently rebounded on the British government to some extent, with the collapse of the housing market in the early 1990s, sharp falls in house prices, and the emergence of negative equity.

In France, the story has been less dramatic, but essentially similar. Social output has been maintained, but at a much lower level than in the 1970s. Deregulation has not proceeded so far or so fast, and access to owner-occupation via state-allocated low-interest loans remained an important, if declining, aspect of the system in the 1980s. But the direction of policy is very much the same, and the combination of monetarist austerity at the macro level, with disintermediation in the circuit of social housing finance and a greater proportion of free-market loans in the owner-occupied sector, has led to *blocage* and reduced expectations in the housing sphere. Indeed, ironically the path of monetarist orthodoxy was adhered to more closely in nominally socialist France than in outwardly Thatcherite Britain in the 1980s (see 6.4 below).

Differences do, of course, remain. Comparing France with Great Britain one finds a greater role for the state in the allocation of housing finance, a relatively unsophisticated and less competitive mortgage market, and, despite the decentralization programme, a greater recognition by government that housing is a national, and not entirely a local responsibility. This recognition is a major aspect of the Besson Law, for example. While low compared with earlier decades, housing output in France in the 1990s remains at a far higher level than in Britain. However, despite the rhetoric, in France there is nothing like the legally enforceable right to housing which is enjoyed by at least some groups in Britain (that is homeless households in priority need).

In neither country has the shift towards the market produced a situation where needs are being fully met. In Britain, a growing body of evidence predicts increased homelessness and housing shortage throughout the 1990s. In France, the policy response to shortage may appear stronger on the surface, but the underlying reality is not so different.

In both countries housing policies and housing outcomes now depend more on factors external to the housing system. That is, the marketization of policy has meant that the achievement of housing policy objectives is subordinated to the performance of the national economy, and the perceived needs of economic policy - in particular, monetary policy of a particularly conservative kind. In addition, more recently, systemic weaknesses have come to the fore, as a result of a combination of internal housing policy failures together with the more general effects of economic recession. This might lead to a radical reappraisal of the relationship between state and market in the housing sphere. At the moment, however, it seems more likely that in both countries the general thrust of current policies will continue - modified perhaps by some short-term reflationary measures in response to the economic and political cycles.

French housing policy in the mid-1990s is thus perhaps best characterized as a *hybrid*. Examined as *social* policy, it displays many of the features of the solidaristic or corporatist model: a non-residual approach to social provision; clear and continuing responsibilities for all levels of government; corporatist and consensual arrangements; the continuing (if reduced) existence of special circuits and specialist institutions. But examined as an aspect of *economic* policy, we get a different picture, one in which 'Anglo-Saxon' features are more apparent: deregulation, liberalization, market forces, targeting of help, the ending of specialist arrangements.

In conclusion, then, we can see clear evidence of polarization in housing outcomes and bifurcation in housing policy in France, as we have done in Britain. But the processes are not so advanced in France as their equivalents are in Britain. However, the differences do not seem to be assimilable easily to a simple dichotomy between neo-liberal/Anglo-Saxon and corporatist/solidaristic. It is in solidaristic France that economic monetarism has been most consistently applied, with important consequences both for housing policy and for housing outcomes.

NOTES

1. According to the Enquête Emploi (Employment Survey) they grew from 9 per cent in 1982 to 9.4 per cent in 1988 (Louvot and Renaudat 1990).
2. Note that some *secteur libre* construction is for private rental rather than owner-occupation.
3. This point has also been made in the British context by Bramley (1989, 1990).

4. Germany: From Social Market to Free Market

4.1 INTRODUCTION

In Germany, housing policy since 1945 has to be seen within the context of the commitment to a social market economy. While housing policies in all countries reflect a mixture of state intervention and market forces, the particular form taken in Germany reflects this wider vision. By this I mean the consistent emphasis on market provision within a framework of laws, and the reliance on market forces, supplemented by regulation and limited state support. Housing is not provided as a social service, but government retains important responsibilities both for ensuring the housing standards of the mass of the population, and of meeting the needs of the most disadvantaged.

Any study of German housing policy in a comparative context will bring out both similarities and differences with policies in France and Britain in particular, and in other EU countries more generally. Many of the main trends in German housing policy in recent years, such as the switch from 'bricks-and-mortar' production subsidies to means-tested personal housing subsidies, or the reduction in new social housebuilding, or the encouragement of owner-occupation, are common to most EU countries. But the exact form of these policy developments reflects the specific German context.

In a comparative context, a number of aspects of the German housing system immediately stand out. First, there is the importance given to market conditions. Policy is sensitive to the current stage in the economic cycle, and policy makers try to work with the cycle rather than cut across it. What would in other countries be described as changes in policy are sometimes defended in Germany as changes in emphasis, because of different economic conditions, rather than shifts in direction. This was certainly the case following the limited re-introduction of federal housing subsidies in the late 1980s.

Second, social housing takes a very specific form in Germany. The term 'social housing' therefore describes a method of *financing* housing together with a set of *regulations* and *responsibilities* about allocation of tenancies, rent levels and standards, rather than refers to a physically identifiable stock of dwellings. Flats which were at one time let as social housing can, once the subsidized loans with which they were built have been paid off, be let as non-social private rented housing. One result of this is that there is in general less segregation of social and private housing. Social housing is more evenly spread throughout the stock:

> Compared to Britain, the spatial distribution of the different segments of the housing stock throughout the cities of West Germany is relatively homogeneous. Old, and therefore cheap, social housing can be found in central locations with high accessibility and in attractive environmental settings with tall trees, having been built during reconstruction on the site of buildings demolished during the war. (Kreibich 1991, p. 78)

However, while this is the general pattern, there are also large estates of social housing built on the peripheries of the major cities during the 1960s and early 1970s. According to Power, fourteen 'giant' estates, each with over 5,000 dwellings in blocks of thirteen storeys or more, were built in this period (Power 1993, p. 129).

Third, while in Britain the private rented sector has declined continuously over the last fifty years and now plays only a very minor role in the housing system, and in France there is considerable concern about the more recent decline of the sector, in Germany private renting remains a large, diverse sector, housing more than two out of five households. Its diversity means that it plays a major role in providing accommodation for all income levels. Investors in the sector include individuals as well as companies.

Fourth, and as a corollary to the last point, fewer households are owner-occupiers, by comparison not only with Britain, but also with other EU countries. Although policy has supported the encouragement of owner-occupation, and the level of home ownership has risen in recent years, it remains the lowest in the EU. The reasons for this are complex. The greater size and diversity of private renting means that there is an alternative to owner-occupation for middle- and higher-income households. House prices are much higher in Germany, even taking into account relative incomes. High house prices and the way that housing finance is organized mean that owner-occupation is not an option for lower-income households as it is in Britain, and that first-time buyers need to spend a number of years saving for a deposit and to qualify for a *Bausparkasse* low-interest loan (see below).

Depreciation allowances for home owners can only be obtained once in a lifetime, which discourages early entry and trading up on the British model: 'A young first-time buyer buying a small house with a low income gets little subsidy but loses the chance of obtaining a higher subsidy later in life' (Hubert 1994, p. 10). Entry to owner-occupation usually occurs in the middle of the life-cycle, and there is relatively little trading up and down within the stock. The average first-time buyer in Germany is aged 36 and stays in the property for 28 years. This contrasts strongly with the British pattern of early entry to owner-occupation and frequent movement, often of a speculative nature, within the sector.

Fifth, although means-tested housing benefit (*Wohngeld*) has been available in West Germany since 1965, a much smaller proportion of tenants is dependent on benefit to pay their rent. In 1992, only 10 per cent of tenant households and 1.2 per cent of owner-occupier households[1] in the western part of Germany were in receipt of benefit. The number of recipients in the former GDR was much higher: 31 per cent of tenant households and 20 per cent of owner-occupier households. But this is still far below British levels, with more than 60 per cent of social tenants in receipt of housing benefit.[2]

Finally, the development of housing policy and the housing system in Germany has been crucially affected by the economic situation. For most of the post-war period, until very recently, West Germany has been characterized by low inflation, low and stable interest rates and, compared with other EU countries, low unemployment. This has had profound effects on the housing market. Low inflation and unemployment has contributed to a 'savings culture'. Fixed interest rates on housing loans (to both owner-occupiers and investors) has until recently been the norm. Germany has not had the 'Anglo-Saxon' experience of high inflation, negative real interest rates, house-price booms, and windfall gains for mortgagors. Home ownership in Germany is both expensive and a long-term commitment; and it is perceived to be so by the mass of housing consumers. Conversely, the environment for investment in rented housing has been more attractive than in other countries not only because of the specific legislative and taxation arrangements, but also because of the relatively stable economic conditions underpinning loan repayments, rent levels and costs.

Since unification in 1990, much of the economic and social stability which has underpinned, and in part explains, the nature of the post-war West German housing system has come under threat. Inflation is rising, as is unemployment, and in the early 1990s, real take-home income began to stagnate. In addition, the relatively balanced urban and regional system which obtained in the old Federal Republic, and which contrasted greatly with both Britain and France, each of which is dominated by its capital city region, came to an end. In its place came a very unbalanced distribution between west and east together with the possibility of a much more skewed urban hierarchy developing as Berlin sought to become a 'global city' to rival London and Paris (Dangschat 1993). Alongside this, in the wake of the great changes of 1989 and subsequently, came the large migrations of *Aussiedler*, *Übersiedler* and non-German refugees which put additional pressures on the housing system.

German housing policy is, therefore, a story of a relatively stable system in the forty years or so after 1950, based around the core West German idea of the social market economy, which in the last few years has been faced with a very different economic and social situation.

4.2 HOUSING POLICY IN THE POST-WAR PERIOD

The federal nature of the political system in Germany makes for a relatively complex policy-making and implementing environment, with roles for the Federal government, the *Länder* and the local authorities. The Federal government determines its own overall level of support to housing, while the *Länder* have considerable power to determine their own housing policy within these constraints. In particular, the *Länder* decide on the form of support to social housing, and its allocation between home ownership and rental programmes. The *Länder* are required at least to match federal funds, and in practice they contribute more (Boelhouwer and van der Heijden 1992). The allocation of federal resources between states is formula based, mainly reflecting population size. Local municipal authorities can and do contribute their own resources to housing programmes. These local authorities have both direct control over local social housing companies that they own, as well as indirect control via a system of nomination rights (see below).

There is, therefore, considerable scope for differences in housing policy at the level of both states and cities. Moreover, as outlined below, national housing policy has gone through different phases, reflecting both economic developments and changes in political power at the federal level. However, as a general comparative point, the formulation and implementation of housing policy in Germany rests on a considerable degree of consensus-building and agreement between different levels of government, and between government at all levels and other agencies. This is, of course, not specific to the housing sphere, but reflects institutional aspects of the Federal Republic in the post-war period, such as coalition politics and the broad commitment to the social-market economy. However, it is important to emphasize that this does not mean that housing policy has somehow been 'de-politicized', but rather that the form that the politics of housing takes differs in Germany from that in Britain. The constitutionally defined relationships between the different levels of government in Germany protect state and local governments from the centralization of power at the national level which has been the dominant characteristic in Britain over the last fifteen years. But there are nevertheless conflicts between federal and other levels of government in Germany over questions of housing policy.

Very broadly, we can divide housing policy in the post-war period into five decade-long categories (Tomann 1990; Boelhouwer and van der Heijden 1992). The immediate post-war period was characterized by an acute crude shortage of dwellings, caused by a combination of war damage and an influx of refugees. In 1950 the shortage was estimated at between 5.5 and 6 million dwellings. The first phase, the 1950s, was hence a period of reconstruction. The First Housing Act in 1950 introduced rent controls and subsidies to new housing. Loans covering 40 per cent to 50 per cent of the costs of construction were provided by the state interest free to both private investors and non-profit associations. In exchange, landlords had to accept government controls over allocation of the dwellings, protection for tenants and minimum standards with regard to size and quality. These conditions were to apply during the period the loan was in force only; at the end of this period, unless the landlord is a municipally-controlled association, the dwelling ceases to be part of the social sector and becomes part of the private sector. This principle has continued in German housing policy with important consequences in the 1980s and 1990s, as much of the stock built with subsidies comes out of the social sector, as we shall see below.

The 1950 Act was followed by the Second Housing Act in 1956, which, subsequently modified and extended, remains in large part the framework for social housing. Instead of direct government loans, investors obtain loans on the private capital market. The government however, provides interest subsidies for a certain period of time to enable the dwelling to be let at a below-market rent. This social rent is determined by the government, and size and quality of the dwelling are also regulated. Apartments built under these provisions can only be let to households whose income is below a certain level. A second category of social housing, which has received public funds since 1967, can be let to middle-income tenants whose incomes are up to 40 per cent above the ceiling for the first category of social housing (Duvigneau and Schonefeldt 1989).

In the 1960s, the second phase, full employment and the effect of additional supply in creating a more balanced housing market, led to a reduction in the role of the state. Rent controls were gradually phased out, so that by 1968 they remained only in Hamburg, Munich and Berlin. Housing benefit was introduced in 1965, and supply subsidies were extended to owner-occupation as well as social rented housing (Tomann 1990).

The third phase of policy in the 1970s saw a return to greater government involvement under SPD-FDP coalition governments. Chancellor Willy Brandt declared that the government's aims were to increase owner-occupation among broad strata of the population, develop a long-term programme of social housing construction and improve housing benefit (Boelhouwer and van der Heijden 1992, p. 122). This led to a housing boom, with output peaking at 714,000 in 1973, before falling rapidly to under 400,000 in 1976. After 1976, under Chancellor Helmut Schmidt, there was a change in policy towards improvement rather than new building, and a greater emphasis on owner-occupation rather than renting. This change in policy was justified in part by the overall balance between the number of households and dwellings. Urban renewal was encouraged by the 1971 Urban Renewal Act and subsequent legislation, which provided for the costs of renewal to be shared between the three levels of government. Under the last SPD-FDP coalition government of 1980-82, there were sharp rises in interest rates and a reduction in the resources available to government. A more market-orientated policy was gradually introduced, a move which continued and accelerated under the CDU-FDP coalition which took power after 1982. In 1982, the government introduced the 'additional rent tax' (*Fehlbelegungsabgabe*). This allowed (but did not compel) the states to levy an additional charge on social tenants whose incomes exceeded by 20 per cent or more the income ceiling for social housing, the money raised being required to be used to provide more social housing by local authorities

(Boelhouwer and van der Heijden 1992, pp. 125-6). This was an attempt to correct for poor targeting of subsidies which meant that some tenants in subsidized dwellings were on average or above-average incomes.

✓ The fourth period of housing policy, between 1983 and 1989 is marked by the greater influence of neoliberal economic ideas and consequent policies of deregulation and liberalization. While in Tomann's (1990) view it would be wrong to speak of a fundamental change of policy, there has certainly been a shift from supply subsidies to housing allowances and to deregulating social housing. The new government's policy aimed to relax rent controls further, provide more assistance to owner-occupation, remove tax exemptions for social housing companies and further cut the level of subsidies.

In 1986 the government abolished federal subsidies for social rented housing. Even more radically, in June 1988, the government decided to abolish the special tax status of non-profit housing companies, effectively turning them into private landlords. Changes were made to the rent legislation to permit rises above the rate of inflation, and the tax framework for owner-occupation was reformed in 1987. Owner-occupation was treated as a consumption rather than an investment good and hence both mortgage interest tax relief and tax on the imputed rental value of the property were abolished (Boelhouwer and van der Heijden 1992, p. 129). New tax allowances for owner-occupiers related to family size were, however, introduced and subsequently increased.

The fifth and current period of housing policy is one characterized by extreme pressures in the housing market, and policy responses by government to this increasing pressure. By the end of the 1980s, 'balanced' housing markets had clearly given way to excess demand and acute shortages of accommodation, particularly but not exclusively in the big cities. From an assumed surplus of dwellings of 100,000, the 1987 Census showed a shortage of one million units. One poll in a major urban area in the early 1990s found that 46 per cent of people saw housing need as the most important problem, ahead of environmental pollution (44 per cent), traffic (34 per cent) and crime (17 per cent) (Wilderer 1993). The causes of this are complex. The number of households continued to increase, as household size fell; in addition, real disposable income rose throughout the 1980s. Living space per person rose considerably, from 24 square metres per person in 1968 to 35.5 square metres per person in 1987. Urban renewal and redevelopment and conversion of inner-city apartments to larger units or to commercial uses had reduced the supply of poorer quality, cheaper accommodation. At the same time, the increase in demand was coming from young people, students, small households and immigrants, who required precisely this type of accommodation.

Hence the new shortage or new crisis in the West German housing system arose initially for essentially domestic reasons. But these pressures were compounded by the flow of migrants. Government responded to these pressures with a variety of policy measures. Private investment was encouraged through improvement in the tax treatment of housing investment. Federal subsidies to social housing were re-introduced, albeit mainly under a new 'third subsidy system', which was less generous than previous federal subsidies and operated for a shorter period. This new subsidy system was more flexible, and involved greater negotiation and agreement with states and local authorities. Altogether, about DM40 billion was allocated for social housing for the four years 1990-93, representing about 500,000 new social units (Boelhouwer and van der Heijden 1992, p. 133). By relaxing certain building regulations the government aimed to promote additional supply through the conversion of commercial premises, attics, and so on.

Overall, the federal housing minister in 1989 set a target of one million new dwellings over the following three years - a target that was in fact very nearly achieved (see below). Housing policy in the 1990s shows the degree of sensitivity of the Federal government to the new housing shortage. At the same time, the policy response maintains the underlying philosophy of looking to the market to meet most housing needs, and using state activity to support and supplement, not to replace the market. One of the major issues for housing policy in the 1990s is of course the condition and ownership of the former state-owned stock in the new eastern *Länder*. This is discussed in 4.6 below.

4.3 THE GERMAN HOUSING SYSTEM

4.3.1 The Owner-Occupied Sector

Despite a long-term policy orientation towards increasing the level of owner-occupation, home ownership among Germans remains low by Western European standards. Nevertheless it has increased over the last twenty years from 36 per cent in 1970 to 42 per cent today (Haffner 1991). House prices are high in Germany, with a ratio of 6 to 7 of house prices to average earnings. This is about twice as high as the ratio in Britain for, example.

There are no direct equivalents to building societies in Germany. Mortgage loans are provided by savings banks, mortgage banks and commercial banks. These first mortgages are restricted by law to a maximum of 60 per cent of the purchase price of the property. Home owners must therefore top up their first mortgage with second and third loans and/or a cash deposit. Second loans are often obtained from *Bausparkassen* - specialist housing contract-savings institutions whose operations are described below.

Traditionally, the German mortgage market has been dominated by *Sparkassen* (savings banks) and *Hypothekenbanken* (mortgage banks), which still provide half of total lending (Tomann 1993). In the 1980s there were numerous takeovers of mortgage banks and *Bausparkassen* by commercial banks, creating financial conglomerates providing a range of financial services. Loans have traditionally been at fixed interest rates, but in recent years greater volatility in inflation and interest rates has led to greater use of variable rate mortgages and renewable interest rate loans (where the rate is fixed for 5-10 years at a time). Mortgage banks are legally restricted to providing only mortgages to residential properties and loans to public corporations. They can grant second mortgages up to 15 per cent of their total outstanding loans. During the 1980s, their market share declined from a quarter to about one-fifth (Tomann 1993). Savings banks are almost all owned by local or regional government. By law they can only operate in the relevant local or regional area. They provide a range of retail banking services. Savings banks have the biggest share of the mortgage market - about 30 per cent (Tomann 1993). Like British building societies, they fund mortgages via short-term deposits. This makes them vulnerable to movements in inflation and hence short-term interest rates. Again, like British building societies, they cope with this by offering variable rate mortgages and by relative rigidity of interest rates to depositors (that is savers' rates do not change as frequently as money market rates) (Tomann 1993).

Bausparkassen are specialist housing savings institutions. There is no direct equivalent in Britain, but they are, for example, similar to the *plans d'épargne-logement* (housing-savings plans) used in France. They work as follows. The saver contracts for a given amount and agrees to deposit a certain sum per annum, usually 5 per cent of the total amount of the contract. The saver can then choose to receive interest on this sum at a rate of either 2.5 per cent or 4.5 per cent p.a. In addition, the saver receives a bonus of 10 per cent p.a. of the sum saved, plus an additional 2 per cent for every child under 18, up to a maximum of DM800. The bonus is tax-free, but there is a qualifying income ceiling.[3] The scheme used to be even more generous: until 1975 the bonus was 25 per cent, and 14 per cent up till 1988.

When the amount saved reaches 40 per cent or 50 per cent of the contracted sum (depending on which version of the scheme was selected), the saver receives the total contracted sum, depending on the availability of funds. The remaining portion is given as a loan, at an interest rate of either 4.5 per cent or 5.75 per cent, usually over a 12-year period.

The *Bausparkasse* system is hence a separate financial circuit. Imbalances between the supply of and demand for funds are met by changes in the length of waiting time for the loan rather than by changes in interest rates. The system expanded until the late 1970s, promoted by the special tax treatment and premia. This preferential treatment was reduced during the 1980s, reducing the attractiveness of the system, a development which was compounded by the consequent longer waiting times. Recently, the system has received a boost from unification, with a boom in contract saving in the new *Länder* (Tomann 1993).

Hence the typical home buyer makes use of a package of loans. This might include a first mortgage from a mortgage or savings bank, a *Bausparkasse* loan, and a third loan from a commercial bank. In practice, this is much less complicated than it sounds. As many mortgage banks and *Bausparkassen* are owned by commercial banks, the borrower will often be making a single monthly payment to cover all three loans, and indeed may not even be aware of the details of how the payment is made up. However, the complexity of loans and local operation of many financial institutions may be a significant factor in the low mobility found in the owner-occupied sector.

Owner-occupiers are not taxed on the imputed rental value of their home, nor do they, in almost all cases, have to pay capital gains tax. On the other hand they do not receive tax relief for mortgage interest payments. Losses during the construction period and depreciation (for 8 years) are tax deductible. Moreover home owners (but not tenants) receive a tax credit for each child in the family (*Baukindergeld.*) This was introduced at DM600 but was subsequently raised, first to DM750 in January 1990 and then to DM1,000.

Muellbauer's (1994) comparison of owner-occupation in Germany and Britain brings out several important differences. He concludes that German housing markets function in a 'radically different' environment to that of Britain. While the owner-occupied market in Britain is influenced strongly by speculation, in Germany, it is determined more by 'fundamentals' - that is demography, population change and income growth. The housing supply side in Germany 'has been more hostile to house price booms ... the German tax system is less biased towards owner occupation. A large private rental sector offers continuous alternatives to owner occupation' (Muellbauer 1994, p. 246).

While in Britain in the 1970s real mortgage rates for borrowers were often negative, in Germany bank mortgage loans were always at positive real rates of interest, and even *Bausparkassen* loans were only below inflation for short periods in 1973-75 and 1978. Coupled with the lower gearing (loan-to-value ratio) in Germany, this has meant that the rate of return on owner-occupation in Germany has sometimes been negative and has never been spectacular, unlike the experience in Britain. Muellbauer argues that the econometric evidence suggests that housing supply in Germany is better matched with rising income and a rising population. 'This is consistent with the view that Germans buy houses primarily as places to live while for the British, the portfolio investment motive is a very important consideration' (Muellbauer 1994, pp. 244-5).

4.3.2 Social Housing

Social housing is provided both by private landlords and non-profit housing enterprises (*Gemeinnütziges Wohnungsunternehmen*). There are more than 1,800 non-profit housing enterprises which belong to the Gesamtverband Gemeinnütziger Wohnungsunternehmen (GGW) based in Cologne. The total is made up of more than 1,200 co-operatives, who together own about one million units; 540 private limited-dividend companies; and 60 public limited companies. These 600 limited-dividend companies own an average stock of 5,000 units each. The fifty largest companies have an average of 20,000 units, and together own one-third of all social housing (Power 1993). The largest social housing company, Neue Heimat, at its peak owned a gargantuan 400,000 rental units. Neue Heimat crashed spectacularly in the 1980s in a major financial corruption scandal. Much of its stock has now been dispersed to other social housing enterprises.

Altogether the non-profit sector owns 3.4 million dwellings (1985) of which some 2.3 million units are still receiving subsidies. Social housing enterprises are sponsored by employers, trade unions, churches and by local authorities. Social landlords claim to compete with each other in terms of the quality of service they offer and value for money, especially on large estates where several enterprises are involved (Emms 1990). In practice they will also be competing for some tenants with the private rented sector.

The Federal government provides subsidies to social housing, but the form of those subsidies is controlled by the states. Both states and local authorities can add their own subsidies. The basic structure of support is that part of the building cost is covered by loans at below-market rates. Subsidy is calculated as investor's costs minus a predetermined social rent, below market rent. So the investor (social housing enterprise or private landlord) will break even, provided actual costs remain at or below calculated costs, and provided the levels of arrears and voids are controlled. The subsidies are degressive: the interest rate tapers up over time to the market level, and hence the social rents will also rise over time. In addition to these 'built-in' increases, rents can rise if the level of interest rates generally rises, or if there are increases in operating costs such as management and maintenance expenditure (Hubert 1992).

Typically a market rent for a new unit might be about DM20 monthly per m^2 while a social rent might be about DM8-9. Rents are set on a scheme-by-scheme basis - there is no rent pooling across the stock, as in Britain. Consequently, rents of social units can differ markedly depending on their time of construction. It can often be the case that older, centrally located and therefore more attractive flats have lower rents than newer flats much further away from the centre of town. The additional rent tax (*Fehlbelegungsabgabe*) is one attempt to deal with this problem, as is the use of degressive subsidies. While the subsidized loan remains in force, the dwelling must be let as social housing. When the loan expires, the local authority no longer has nomination rights to the dwelling.

Applicants for social housing (both tenants and owners) must have incomes below a certain ceiling. This income ceiling has been, however, relatively generous. The local housing office (*Wohnungsamt*) checks a household's income, and if it is satisfied that the household income is below the ceiling, issues a certificate of entitlement (*Wohnberechtigungsschein*). The applicant can then present this certificate to any of the private or non-profit landlords providing social housing in the area.

Local authorities have nomination rights to local non-profit social landlords whom they sponsor, that is, they can allocate tenants to vacancies that arise. Other landlords providing social housing are free to choose from among applicants in possession of an entitlement certificate. Hence in some cases, the local authority-sponsored housing associations can become a 'reception pool' for special needs and so-called problem groups (Heinz 1991, p. 92).

Large cities where access problems are particularly severe can be declared 'areas with increased housing need' under section 5a of the Housing Assignment Act (*Wohnungsbindungsgesetz*). In these cities, local authorities also have nomination rights into the stock of other social landlords operating in the area. These organizations can choose from a list of three applicants supplied by the city (Heinz 1991, pp. 92-3).

In common with Britain, France and other countries, there has been a change in the type of households gaining access to social housing over the last two decades. Social housing in Germany, as elsewhere, was not originally intended for the poorest groups in society but rather for skilled and white-collar workers. More recently this has changed, with a more diverse pattern of households found in the sector. The reasons for this are complex. The expansion of owner-occupation has led to the exit of some better-off households from the sector. Social housing subsidies are now more targeted, as production subsidies have been reduced, while greater reliance is placed on means-tested housing allowances (Hills et al. 1990). This has the dual effect both of making newer and more expensive social housing affordable by poorer households, while also making it less attractive for better-off groups. This latter effect is in principle compounded in those areas where an additional rent tax is levied on households whose incomes rise above the income ceiling, although the rent tax does not appear in practice to have any effect on tenants' mobility. At the same time, the more balanced housing market of the 1970s led to vacancies in the social housing stock, and less pressure generally, encouraging a more flexible approach to allocations. Finally, although the private rented sector in Germany remains large, much of the poor quality, cheap segment of the sector, particularly in central city areas, has been lost through urban renewal, improvement/enlargement, and conversion to business use (Kreibich 1991). As a result, the types of household that rely on the social sector for their housing are relatively poor and fairly diverse. As Kreibich puts it:

> The typical client is no longer the worker's family with several children, but the old couple or the widow living on a pension and, as new tenants, the young couple with only one child and one, or even one-and-a-half, regular and average incomes, or the single parent household. (Kreibich 1991, p. 66)

As an example of this, Table 4.1 gives details of applicants and allocations for social housing in Cologne.

Table 4.1 Social housing: applicants and allocations, Cologne 1987

Groups	New applicants		Allocations	
Young families	3,144	(21.5%)	1,579	(24.3%)
Elderly	2,309	(15.8%)	1,402	(21.6%)
Students, etc.	3,789	(25.9%	893	(13.7%)
Single parents (1/2 children)	1,938	(13.3%)	1,200	(18.4%)
Single parents (3+ children)	212	(1.5%)	173	(2.7%)
Families (3+ children)	1,227	(8.4%)	398	(6.1%)
Handicapped	1,986	(13.6%)	860	(13.2%)
Totals	14,605	(100%)	6,505	(100%)

Source: Amt für Wohnungswesen der Stadt Köln, quoted in Kreibich 1991.

From the 1970s on, there was increasing concern about both social and physical problems on large outer city social housing estates. Although the scale of these problems, and the degree of social segregation by housing tenure and location is considerably less than in Britain and France (Emms 1990) nevertheless there were increasing concentrations of households on social security, the poor, the old, the unemployed and foreigners (Power 1993).

From 1983 onwards, Federal government money under the urban programme (*Städtebauförderung*) began to become available both for research on experimental projects and physical renewal schemes in social housing (Emms 1990; Power 1993). These funds were supplemented by state and local authority expenditures, as well as contributions from the social housing enterprises themselves. Renewal schemes combined physical renewal measures with changes in management style and a greater role for tenant participation. In some cases efforts were made to change the social mix - for example in Hamburg and Bremen, the rent tax was abolished to encourage better-off households to stay in the sector (Power 1993).

The change to the taxation status of non-profit housing enterprises, coupled with other changes in the 1980s which made the early repayment of subsidized loans more attractive means that the size of the social housing sector is rapidly shrinking, despite the recent increase in output under the 'third subsidy system' (see below). Kreibich (1991) calculates that in Cologne half of the social housing stock in 1987 will have changed status by 1997, and another estimate suggests that half the stock of 4 million dwellings nationally will have left the sector by 1995 (van Vliet 1990). This development will increase trends towards polarization in the German housing system. In the past, polarization (or residualization of the social sector) has not been as severe as in Britain because of the nature of the social sector and the existence of a large diverse private rented sector. But with the upgrading of much of the private rented stock, and the disappearance of a large proportion of the social sector, the poorest and most disadvantaged will more and more have to rely on the part of the social sector which remains under the control of the city authorities. These households 'will be increasingly concentrated in problem estates with unfavourable design (e.g. high-rise, high-density), peripheral location and rising rents' (Kreibich 1991, p. 77).

Hence by the early 1990s, there were four separate groupings in the social rented sector: those owned by traditional private landlords, rapidly moving out of the socially controlled sphere and becoming part of the private rented sector; co-operatively owned social housing; non-profit housing owned by local authorities; and the rest of the former non-profit sector, most of which is destined to join the first group. Harloe (1995) estimated that of the 4 million social rented dwellings in 1984, 1.5 million are in the first category, and will hence join the private rented sector; 0.8 million are co-ops (but in practice rarely allocated to the most needy); 0.7 million are owned or managed by local authority-owned social rented companies; and perhaps one million other non-profit rented units set to become private rented units. He comments that

> The radical steps taken in the 1980s to reduce the scale of the social rented housing sector resulted in a more rapid and extensive privatization than that achieved by the other main proponent of this approach, the British Conservative governments. (Harloe 1995, p. 467)

Furthermore, Harloe identifies as a crucial factor the political vulnerability of the sector, particularly after the Neue Heimat scandal, but more generally because of a widespread view that the non-profits had lost their earlier social mission. He concludes:

> The changes in the 1980s resulted in the reduction of social rented housing to two distinct forms of provision: cooperative housing, serving sections of the better-off working and lower middle class, and a relatively small, residual stock under the control of the local authorities which continued to house a high proportion of low-income groups. (Harloe 1995, p. 503)

4.3.3 Private Rented Housing

Investment in housing has been relatively favoured in the German taxation system (Tomann 1990) and there is a particularly favourable tax treatment for new investment in private rented housing (Hubert 1993). As a result, Germany continues to have a large private rented sector, the largest in the EU, in which higher-income private individuals as well as large commercial companies are investors (Oxley and Smith 1993). Until 1990, investors were not required to pay the (relatively low) annual land tax for the first ten years after construction (this advantage has now been abolished as part of a more general tax reform). As with other investments, relevant costs - interest, depreciation, management and maintenance - can be deducted from revenue for income tax purposes. Losses from rented housing can be offset against income from other sources. The depreciation allowances are an important source of subsidies to private rented housing (Hubert 1993).

About half of the sector was built before the Second World War. Although there has been, and continues to be, high levels of new construction for private renting in Germany (unlike in Britain where there has been virtually no new private rental construction for more than fifty years), the level of output has fallen recently: in 1989 it has been estimated that only about 30,000 new units for private letting were completed, 14 per cent of total output (Oxley and Smith 1993, p. 12).

Rent levels for new tenancies are unregulated, and hence set at market levels. Tenants have security of tenure, with landlords only able to secure possession on certain specified grounds. For existing tenants, the key concept is that of *Vergleichsmiete* (rent of a comparable dwelling). Landlords can increase the rent by reference to the rent of other contracts that have been agreed locally during the last three years, subject to an upper limit that existing rents cannot be increased by more than 30 per cent within a three-year period (currently reduced 'temporarily' to 20 per cent within three years). The aim is to prevent rents for existing tenants lagging too far behind those of new contracts. Recent evidence, however, suggests that rents on new lettings are in fact considerably higher than rents of longer-standing tenancies, reflecting both current shortages and the effects of the rent review legislation (Hubert 1993).

Private renting in Germany, unlike in Britain, is a large, diverse tenure providing for a wide range of mainstream needs. In a number of important ways it is still seen as the 'normal' tenure. It provides a realistic alternative to either owner-occupation or social renting for millions of households. The majority of households who become owner-occupiers will spend many years as private tenants first. The operation of the sector provides a good example of the philosophy of a social market economy: a reasonably strong regulatory framework which emphasizes quality within which entrepreneurial activity provides for needs. The price to consumers is moderated by a combination of state controls and competitive market pressures.

However, in the last few years, housing shortages have led to a breakdown in the broad political consensus on housing policy. In particular, the government appears divided between those who favour further legislation to limit rent increases for sitting tenants, and those who fear this will mean the re-imposition of rent controls and hence disincentives to investment (Hubert 1993).

4.4 HOUSING OUTCOMES

4.4.1 Housing Demand and Supply

The demand for housing is a function of demographic, social and economic trends. In terms of demography, the number of households in Germany has continued to grow, accompanied by a decline in average household size, trends which are broadly in line with experience in other European countries. As for economic factors, GDP per head at constant prices and constant purchasing power parities rose by about 50 per cent between 1970 and 1989, about the same as in France, Britain and the EU as a whole. Earnings, however, have not risen as fast in Germany over this period as elsewhere (Kleinman 1992, p. 6). In 1993, all-German GDP fell by just over 1 per cent and for the first time in 11 years, private household consumption did not increase, but remained flat. Falling real income was resisted by lowering savings (OECD 1994).

Unemployment in the 1970s was relatively low in Germany, reaching only 3.8 per cent, for example, in 1979. However, after 1982, it rose to 8-9 per cent for the rest of the decade, before falling to 6.3 per cent in the 'unification boom' in West Germany in 1991. Recent trends in unemployment are shown in Table 4.2. Unemployment remains twice as high in east as in west Germany; in addition there are many who are working short time. In the OECD's words 'Germany has not been immune from the OECD-wide trend towards slower growth and higher unemployment. Over the past 20 years, growth rates have declined with each new business cycle.' (OECD 1994, p. 69). Furthermore, unemployment is now the 'number one policy problem and concern' (OECD 1994, p. 74).

Table 4.2 Unemployment, 1991-1993

Unemployment rate	West Germany %	East Germany %
1991	5.5	10.8
1992	5.8	14.8
1993	7.3	15.1

Source: OECD 1993.

Table 4.3 gives details of the supply of new housing in the former West Germany since 1970. From an annual total of nearly 500,000 in 1970 (and over 700,000 in 1973) output fell sharply to only just over 200,000 p.a. in the mid-1980s. From then on, as the private sector responded to higher rents and unmet demand, and government responded to housing need and public pressure, completions have steadily increased, almost doubling by 1992. The target set by the housing minister of one million new homes in the period 1990-92 was almost achieved - Hamm (1993a) argues that it was only the delay in the execution of some contracts that prevented the target being reached. Output in 1993 and 1994 exceeded 400,000, and a total of over 500,000 was forecast by the Deutsche Institut für Wirtschaftsforschung (DIW) early in 1995.

Table 4.3 Housing supply, West Germany (thousands, per annum)

Year	1-2 family buildings	Multi-family buildings	Total*
1970	196	249	478
1975	195	210	437
1980	249	114	389
1985	152	133	312
1986	141	86	252
1987	125	71	217
1988	123	63	209
1989	141	74	239
1990	127	97	256
1991	134	135	315
1992	137	185	375
1993	151	223	432
1994	170	250	400
1995 (forecast)	175	275	520

Note: *Includes units in existing buildings.

Sources: Duvigneau and Schonefeldt 1989; Hamm 1993a; DIW 1995.

Further details on the supply of social housing are given in Table 4.4. Output of social housing fell from over 100,000 at the beginning of the decade to under 40,000 at the trough in 1988. It then expanded rapidly to about 100,000 in each of the years 1990-92. In 1992 there were in addition another 18,000 social units completed in the new *Länder*. In 1993, it is expected that 150,000 new social units will be built in east and west Germany together (Hamm 1993b).

Table 4.4 Social housing output, West Germany, 1980-1992 (thousands)

Year	Rented	Owner -occupied	Total
1980	40	57	97
1981	46	47	93
1982	59	40	100
1983	59	45	104
1984	40	40	80
1985	30	39	69
1986	17	35	52
1987	13	28	41
1988	13	26	39
1989	39	26	65
1990	62	29	91
1991	64	32	96
1992	64	35	100

Source: Hamm 1993b.

Looking at the allocation of the programme between rental and owner-occupied housing we find that the proportions have changed markedly at different times. In 1986 and 1987, two-thirds of the programme was for owner-occupation, while in the last few years almost two-thirds has been for rental. In recent years a growing proportion of social output has been financed through the more flexible, but less generous and less permanent 'third subsidy system'. Introduced in 1989 (although not accepted by all *Länder*) this now accounts for about one-third of total social output (Hamm 1993b, Table 1).

With the exception of Denmark, West Germany had the highest proportion of dwellings per 1,000 inhabitants in the EU (Ghékiere 1991, p. 41). Between 1978 and 1987, the stock of dwellings grew by almost 4 million - 16 per cent of the 1978 stock (Table 4.5). There were 2.5 million more owner-occupied homes at the latter date, while the social rented sector had fallen by some 700,000.

Table 4.5   Change in housing stock, West Germany, 1978-87   (millions, percentages)

	1978	%	1982	%	1987	%
Owner occupiers	8.5	37.5	9.3	40.1	11.0	42.0
Rented	14.1	62.5	13.9	59.9	15.3	58.0
- private	10.1	44.8	10.4	45.0	11.9	45.4
- social	4.0	17.7	3.5	14.9	3.3	12.6
Total	22.6	100	23.2	100	26.3	100

Source: Ghékiere 1991, p. 284.

House prices in Germany are relatively high in relation to incomes. Calculations by the Nationwide Building Society show that the price of an average-value house in West Germany in 1984 was equivalent to about 20,000 hours of work by the average worker, compared with about 9,000 hours in Britain and about 10,000 in France (quoted in Whitehead et al. 1992). Putting it another way, the ratio of average house price to GDP per head in 1988 was 8.6 for West Germany, 6.3 for the UK and 5.1 in the Netherlands (Holmans 1991 quoted in Whitehead et al. 1992). These inter-country comparisons cannot be exact - for example, there will be differences between countries in the quality of the 'average' house - but the data give a broad indication.

Rents in Germany have risen faster than inflation for most of the last decade, and in 1992 rents rose faster than incomes too. This trend has continued: in May 1993 the annual rent rise was calculated to be 5.7 per cent with a particularly strong rise of 7.7 per cent noted in the social rented sector (Hamm 1993a).

Urban renewal policies in the last twenty years have been relatively successful in renewing the physical fabric of central city areas, and improving urban environments. The very success of such policies has, however, worsened the position of the economically weaker groups in society. This has come about both through the physical displacement of poorer households as an area gentrifies, and through the loss of cheaper inner-city private rental housing through modernization and conversion.

Conflict between local residents and public authorities in Berlin over urban renewal is fairly well known (see Hass-Klau 1986, for example). But gentrification and social change associated with housing and urban renewal have also affected other cities. Dangschat points out that the economic revitalization of Hamburg was accompanied by a rise in the numbers on social assistance from 151,000 in 1987 to 167,000 the following year, and an increase in homelessness from 8,000 to 26,000 between 1988 and 1989 (Dangschat 1990).

4.4.2 Housing Needs

From the mid-1980s on, the 'balanced housing markets' of earlier in the decade gave way to a new housing shortage. While this new shortage was most severe in the big cities, it was by no means confined to them. The crisis of the 1980s hence differed from the so-called 'new housing shortage' of the 1970s which was more geographically specific. The origins of the shortage were mainly internal: increased household formation and rising expectations combining with reduced construction activity. In addition urban renewal, the modernization and rehabilitation of the private rented sector, the shrinkage of the social housing stock through transfer to private renting, and the encouragement of owner-occupation had led to a reduction in cheaper rented properties, particularly in the inner areas of the larger cities. The 1987 housing survey revealed that the existing stock of dwellings was smaller than the estimate accepted by the Federal government when it decided to stop assistance to new social housing (Harloe 1995, p. 469).

This 'internal' shortage was swiftly compounded by large-scale migration from Eastern Europe and elsewhere. The number of *Aussiedler* migrating to the Federal Republic increased from 80,000 in 1987 to 200,000 in 1988, 40 per cent of whom went to North Rhein-Westphalia (Kreibich 1991, p. 75). Altogether some 4 million persons are estimated to have migrated into the western part of Germany between 1988 and 1993. (Bundesministerium für Arbeit und Sozialordnung 1993, p. 102.)

The results of this renewed housing pressure were rapidly rising rents, longer queues for social housing and increased homelessness. Increased housing demand has not translated into increases in owner-occupation. Most of the new households - students, young people, foreigners - do not have the economic ability to become home owners. Pressure was therefore put on the social sector at the same time as the size of the sector was diminishing. From 1988 the problem reached crisis proportions, with many cities resorting to bed-and-breakfast accommodation, and the use of gymnasia, for example, for emergency accommodation. The director of housing of the city of Cologne said in 1988: 'We are fully booked up. There is absolutely no available flat in social housing' (quoted in Kreibich 1991, p. 75).

This new housing shortage and consequent high rents affected not just the poorest, but a wide range of households, including younger households with middle incomes entering the housing market for the first time, especially in the bigger cities and the more prosperous regions. Indeed, it was the fact that the housing shortage was affecting a relatively wide group, which pushed the government into action - the Federal government responded with measures that were mainly directed to those groups with political clout, especially younger white-collar and skilled manual workers (Harloe 1995, p. 470). The government's aim was to increase the level of private housebuilding, mainly for middle-income groups. The new third subsidy system was both more limited and of shorter duration than previous social housing subsidies, and in some cases the income limits for access to social housing could be set aside:

> So it was clear that this programme was targeted at the more politically important middle-income demand rather than the poorest households. (Harloe 1995, p. 471)

Despite the success of the housebuilding programme announced by the Federal government in response to the crisis, the problems continue. The gap between demand and supply remains and the Deutsche Institut für Wirtschaftsforschung (DIW) estimates that at least 500,000 flats need to be built each year to fight homelessness effectively by the year 2000 (Wilderer 1993). The shortage, according to Wilderer (1993) continues to affect middle-class as well as less well-off households. But the brunt of the problem is, of course, borne by the poorest. Estimating the number of homeless in Germany is difficult because there is no legal definition which adequately covers all groups (Osenberg 1993). However, the number of homeless people who were directed into casual wards by law in North Rhine-Westphalia rose from 43,000 in 1989 to nearly 60,000 in 1992. In 1990, a federal working group on homelessness estimated 130,000 single homeless, 300,000 persons in casual wards, 100,000 persons in hotel rooms, 100,000 persons in asylums and psychiatric hospitals, and 200,000 immigrants in transitory lodgings (Osenberg 1993). In 1993 a new federal programme was announced focusing on homelessness and the housing situation of single parents.

4.5 POLARIZATION AND SEGREGATION IN HOUSING OUTCOMES

Until recently, social polarization by housing tenure has been much less prevalent in Germany than in either Britain or France. As Harloe writes, in West Germany there were

> relatively few areas of concentrated low-income settlement in social rented housing. In fact, the largest low-income concentrations occurred not in social housing but in areas of older inner-city accommodation, which had, for example, housed many of the migrant workers that had come to Germany in the 1960s and 1970s. (Harloe 1995, p. 467)

The reasons for this are several: the existence of a large and diversified private rented sector; the dispersed nature of the social housing stock; and the allocation policies of those managing social housing.

Alongside this relative lack of socio-spatial segregation (at least until recently) there has been considerable income polarization between owner-occupation on the one hand and renting on the other. The average income of owner-occupiers in West Germany in 1988 was 67 per cent higher than that of tenants. This compares with a gap in France of 29 per cent, while the average income of British owner-occupiers is 61 per cent higher than private tenants and 128 per cent higher than social tenants (Benit 1994, p. 149). Income and tenure in Germany are thus highly correlated, as Table 4.6 shows. In the poorest group nearly three-quarters are tenants, with less than a quarter owners, while in the richest group these proportions are reversed.

Table 4.6 Income group by tenure

Net income	All households	Tenants	Owner-occupiers
DM per month	%	%	%
Below 1,200	94.9	72.6	22.3
1,200-1,800	98.0	68.7	29.3
1,800-2,500	99.3	58.9	40.4
2,500-3,000	99.7	52.7	47.0
3,000-4,000	99.8	44.4	55.4
4,000-5,000	99.8	34.4	65.4
5,000-25,000	99.7	24.1	75.6
All households	98.5	55.7	42.8

Source: Hubert 1994, p. 12.

Furthermore, such tenure segregation appears to be increasing. Between 1978 and 1987, the proportion of owners in the bottom quintile in the income distribution fell from 32.3 per cent to 29.9 per cent; in the top quintile it rose from 43.8 per cent to 51.5 per cent (Ulbrich 1993).

From the mid-1970s on, however, there was increasing concern about social segregation and polarization. In 1985 a study identified 233 high-rise high-density peripheral social housing estates that had been built in the 1960s and 1970s. Together these amounted to 500,000-600,000 dwellings, the vast majority of which were social rented housing. These estates were unpopular, especially with families (Harloe 1995, p. 468). While by the 1980s there was evidence both of physical problems and concentration of social problems, 'unlike France or Britain ... there was no significantly funded national programme to deal with the problems of these areas, only scattered experiments and local initiatives' (Harloe 1995, p. 469).

This growing concentration of social problems in the social rented sector has come about partly through housing market change - the loss of cheaper inner-city private rented units and the shrinkage of the social sector - and partly because of the rise of unemployment. While in 1981 pensioners made up 62 per cent of those claiming housing benefit, and the unemployed only 5 per cent, in 1990 pensioners now comprised only 34 per cent of the claimant group, while the unemployed now amounted to 16 per cent (Bundesministerium für Arbeit und Sozialordnung 1993, p. 103). Hence, as Harloe concludes:

> There was a huge rise in the numbers in urgent housing need after 1989, with the breakup of the GDR and the other socialist countries. This situation was one aspect of the development of what the Germans call the 'two-thirds' society. On the one hand, a majority continued to benefit from rising incomes and improving living conditions. On the other hand, there were the 'new poor' - the unemployed (swelled by rapidly rising numbers in the Eastern Länder as their economy collapsed), single-parent households, low income young workers and large families. (Harloe 1995, p. 470).

Because of German citizenship law, based on the *ius sanguinis* (blood law), few members of ethnic minorities are German citizens. Since 1973, and the shift to permanent settlement and immigration control, the term foreigner (*Auslander*) has generally replaced 'guestworker', and has rapidly acquired pejorative connotations (Ginsburg 1992 Castles 1984). 'Foreigners' in 1990, comprised 8.2 per cent of the population; the largest single group are Turks, who comprise about 1.7 million, or one-third of the foreign population (Ginsburg 1992, p. 195).

Minorities in Germany often live in the very worst housing conditions. For example, 60 per cent of Turkish families in Berlin lack a bathroom and 25 per cent lack an inside toilet. Turkish households on average pay higher rents for the same size and type of accommodation compared with German households (Gude 1991). Foreigners have difficulty in gaining access to social housing and stay longer on waiting lists (Blanc 1991). Social housing organizations often discriminate against foreigners or adopt informal quotas to limit the number of families in a particular block. In general, the approach of public authorities to problems of discrimination and exclusion, in Germany as in France has been to advocate a 'colour-blind' approach rather than to pursue policies of ethnic monitoring and equal opportunities as in Britain.

Equal opportunities issues are much less visible in Germany than in Britain. Germany has not to date seen itself as a country of immigration, still less a multi-ethnic society. Minority households are in a relatively weak position legally and politically, and indeed continue to be referred to as 'foreigners' despite many years of residence or in some cases having been born in Germany. About 60 per cent of foreigners have been resident more than ten years and 70 per cent of 'foreign' children under 16 were born in Germany (Ginsburg 1992). As a consequence of these important legal, political and cultural differences, issues of race and housing are articulated in a very different way in Germany compared with Britain (Blanc 1991). Germany has no legislation explicitly addressing the question of racial discrimination comparable to the Civil Rights Act in the USA or the Race Relations Act in Britain (Ginsburg 1992).

4.6 HOUSING ISSUES IN THE NEW *LÄNDER*

The housing issues and policy choices faced by the Federal government and public authorities in the new *Länder* are similar to those faced by reform governments elsewhere in Central and Eastern Europe (see Turner et al. 1992, for example). The difference in the former East Germany is, of course, the timescale involved - the housing system of the former GDR has undergone not a gradual process of transformation but a sudden incorporation into a Western market system.

In the GDR, housing was supplied not as a commodity for which consumers paid a (subsidized) price, but as part of an alternative, non-market reward system. Rents were extremely low, and did not cover the costs of even basic management and maintenance, let alone the construction debts. A large part of the real costs of housing were thus carried by the state. Average living space in the GDR was about one-third below West German levels.

From the 1960s on, housing construction in the GDR was dominated by large-scale system-building using pre-fabricated materials. By such methods, giant estates such as Marzahn in Berlin were built. The proportion of state-owned stock rose to more than two in five dwellings by 1989 (Table 4.7).

In addition, there was little if any incentive to maintain and repair the housing stock adequately. New building proceeded on the basis that once built the dwellings would need little or no further work, while the extremely low controlled rents in the private sector discouraged any spending on the stock.

Table 4.7 Housing stock, GDR, 1971-1989

	1971	1981	1989	1971	1981	1989
	thousands			percentages		
State-owned	1,698	2,447	2,889	28	37	41
Co-op	596	974	1,230	10	15	18
Private	3,763	3,141	2,883	62	48	41
Total	6,057	6,562	7,003	100	100	100

Source: Kohli 1993.

The lack of expenditure on repair and maintenance, and the increasingly poor quality of new construction has bequeathed a major problem of stock quality. Over half the flats in the new *Länder* require some work, and more than one-quarter are classified as being in severe disrepair (Kohli 1993).

The policy response by the Federal government to the problems it has inherited involves privatization, modernization and improvement of the stock, increases in rents, the introduction of housing allowances and the goal of creating viable credit-worthy landlords and increasing investment in the sector. Under the unification contract, state-owned properties were transferred to local authorities, who are supposed to privatize the stock step by step, first creating communal housing companies, and then selling on to investors, and in particular, to tenants (Kohli 1993). Outstanding debts were transferred to the local authorities along with the stock. The one million or so co-operatively owned units remained with the co-ops. However, while the co-ops own the dwellings many did not own the land on which they stand, and had to negotiate with the local authority to purchase the land. As there was no price recommendation in the unification contract, these negotiations have proved to be protracted (Kohli 1993). In addition, there are estimated to be over a million ownership claims from those claiming to be former owners (or their successors) of houses and flats in the new *Länder*.

The continuing debt on the stock is a major problem. The 2.7 million units which passed into the ownership of the local authorities has an associated debt of at least DM22 billion. Not surprisingly there was considerable dispute between the *Länder* and the Federal government about who should shoulder the burden of this debt (Kohli 1993). Eventually, however, a solution was found in which companies owned by local authorities and co-ops will be relieved from any debt exceeding DM150 per m^2 provided that they sell 15 per cent of their stock, preferably to the present tenants, within the next 10 years. A proportion of the proceeds goes into a special fund, and there are incentives to sell quickly (Hubert, private communication). The Federal government has provided considerable funds so far for rehabilitation of the stock. Together with contributions from the *Länder*, Kohli (1993) estimates that this would be sufficient to modernize and repair a quarter of the stock.

The second main strand of policy is in regard to rents, with a goal of raising rents gradually to West German levels. The first stage was in October 1991, when basic rents were raised by DM1.0 per m^2 per month, and DM3.0 per m^2 per month in payment for utilities. From 1 January 1993, there were further rises of between DM1.20 and 2.40 per m^2 per month (Kohli 1993; Dick 1993). These rent rises were accompanied by an extension of the housing allowance system to the new *Länder*; indeed imposing these rent increases would have been politically impossible without this. Housing allowances are currently more generous in the new *Länder* than elsewhere (e.g. they cover heating and hot-water costs) but this difference is being phased out and will disappear from 1995. By June 1992, there were 3.2 million housing benefit claims, 80 per cent of which were made on 1 October 1991, when the first stage of the rent increase was implemented. Nearly 2 million households receive housing benefit, almost 30 per cent of households in the new *Länder*. This comprises 31 per cent of tenant households (10 per cent in the west) and 20 per cent of owner-occupiers (1.2 per cent in the west).

As far as sales to tenants are concerned, there are, not surprisingly, differing potentials within the stock. The pre-war stock is probably the most attractive, but subject to former-owner claims. Post-war, but low-rise, stock is probably the most viable for sales to sitting tenants, and Kohli (1993) estimates that perhaps one million of the 2.7 million stock could be sold to tenants. The Federal government has brought in special measures, including a 20 per cent subsidy of the purchase price to tenants, up to a maximum of DM7,000 for the first and DM1,000 for each subsequent family member. These subsidies are in addition to the normal help to owner-occupiers discussed above. However, tenants often have little equity and are affected by or worried about the rise in unemployment. Also, many of those who could buy do not want to buy their current flat - often poorly designed and too small for current family size. The Federal government is sponsoring a number of model schemes, involving some 6,500 units, as a form of demonstration project (Kohli 1993). Sales totalled 2,500 in 1991 and possibly 18,000 in 1992.

Output is increasing in the new *Länder*. Hamm (1993a) finds evidence of a strong growth rate in housebuilding activity in 1992, and argues not only that there is a good chance that housebuilding will get going on a large scale, but also speculates that it will act as the engine of recovery in the east. Social output was 18,000 units in 1992, and could rise to 30,000 in 1993 (Hamm 1993b). This has to be seen against the background of the poor starting position of housing conditions in the east, and the new needs that are thrown up by rapid economic change, and the associated rise in unemployment. According to Buskase (1992), there are about 500,000 households in East Berlin, Sachsen-Anhalt, Saxony and Thuringia looking for accommodation, of which more than 100,000 are classified as in urgent need. Homelessness did not previously exist in the GDR, a consequence partly of low rents and protection from eviction, and partly of the legal impossibility of such a state - people found homeless could be charged with being 'outcast' (*asozial*) and sent to jail (Osenberg 1993). With the changes, homelessness is rising and is a particular problem for the young, and for those previously living in company housing who lose their job and their home if made redundant (Osenberg 1993).

4.7 ASSESSMENT

Over the last twenty years, the stock of housing in West Germany has both expanded and been considerably improved. Most households are able to obtain adequate accommodation, and have seen their standards of housing consumption rise considerably. The German housing system is characterized generally by high quality and space standards. But a growing minority live in inadequate accommodation, unable to gain access to the mainstream stock. As in other areas of social policy, there is clear evidence of the emergence of a 'society of two-thirds'. At the same time although there is considerable tenure polarization by income, the level of socio-spatial segregation is probably less than in Britain and France. A much smaller proportion of households depends on housing benefit to secure adequate accommodation. Despite the existence of many large social housing estates with a familiar catalogue of physical and social problems, in general social housing is distributed more evenly through the stock.

Home ownership remains a goal of German housing policy, but has not been pursued as relentlessly as in Britain. Certainly, in Germany, owner-occupation is not regarded as a right. On the contrary, owning one's own home is seen as a major commitment, to be entered into only when one is already firmly established within both the labour and housing markets. Lending policies are more cautious, the system is more regulated, and speculative trading within the owner-occupied sector relatively rare.

The development of housing policy in Germany in recent years shares several similarities with policies adopted in Britain and elsewhere (Kleinman 1992 Ghékiere 1991). There has been a greater emphasis on targeting state aid, by moving from production-based subsidies to personal housing allowances. Owner-occupation has been expanded, although at a slower pace than elsewhere in Europe. Greater choice and quality for the majority has co-existed with unmet needs and worsening conditions - particularly in regard to access - for a minority. Central government support to housing has been reduced as a result both of a political commitment to shift provision from state to market, and because of pressures on public expenditure. A greater proportion of housing costs has been shifted on to consumers.

However, to argue that German housing policy is converging to the same kind of 'Anglo-Saxon' policy as in Britain would be to ignore important differences between housing policy in Germany and housing policy in Britain. The housing crisis of the mid-1980s led to a strong policy response by the Federal government, who clearly saw it as their responsibility to take measures to bring the housing market into balance. This contrasts strongly with British policy under the Conservatives which has been characterized by a piecemeal approach, and in particular a rejection of quantitative targets for housing output.

Second, housing policy is shared between the different levels of government in Germany. The continuing importance of, and, within defined limits, independent action by, regional and local authorities in Germany contrasts strongly with the centralization of power in Britain which has left local authorities with little autonomy, particularly in financial matters.

Third, despite the rhetoric about markets in Britain, there is a greater practical importance given to markets in Germany in terms of accomplishing housing policy goals. Policy measures are very much governed by the state of the housing market, and the current point in the economic cycle. Paradoxically, then, housing policy in Germany makes less of a totem of marketization, while in practice being more closely attuned to market conditions.

Fourth, there is less adulation of home ownership as a total solution. Renting is seen as a normal choice for millions of households, and policy initiatives deal at least equally with the private rented as well as the owner-occupied sector.

Currently, the housing system in Germany is undergoing a considerable amount of change. New pressures come from without - the impact of EU integration, and the waves of migration from the east; and also from within - the social and economic costs of unification, and the rise in both inflation and unemployment.

European economic integration will have important effects, both direct and indirect, on the national housing policies of the individual EU member states (for a discussion see Priemus et al. 1993 and 1994). There will be direct effects through increased capital mobility. Tomann (1993) sees two important consequences of the opening up of financial services in the single European market for German housing finance. First, that mortgage lenders from elsewhere will come into the domestic market, either by cross-border trading or through the establishment of branches; second, that the integration of the securities market will offer new opportunities for securitization, although he argues that a European market for mortgage-backed securities is still a long way off. In a more competitive market, current providers of second-lien mortgages, which are relatively expensive in Germany, could be vulnerable to British-style providers of 90+ per cent mortgages including mortgage insurance. *Bausparkassen* in particular might be thought to be under threat in this way, although Tomann concedes that they do have a specific niche in the market.

Freedom of movement in the single market will have rather less of an impact in Germany as the main migratory pressures are from outside the EU. The migration issue will continue to be important in the housing policy sphere. The impact is two-fold. First, there is the issue of responding to need and demand for housing, both quantitatively and qualitatively. Second, and more fundamentally in the long run, is the question of the adaptation of German housing policy and practice to the fact that Germany is now a country of immigration, and is becoming a multi-ethnic society. Issues such as equal treatment and equal access, and how to deal with racial harassment and xenophobia will become more important, although the extent to which policy will respond to this new agenda is not yet clear.

Third, there is the continuing imbalance between demand and supply in the market. Access difficulties, and homelessness will ensure that housing remains a politically salient issue in the 1990s. Allied to this is the fate of social housing. Despite the recent partial revival of federal subsidies to social housing, the sector will continue to decline as a proportion of the stock. Whether the private market will be able to cope with the new and different housing pressures of the 1990s remains to be seen.

Fourth, there is the privatization and modernization of the housing stock of the new *Länder*. There are many legal and administrative issues still to be solved, as well as the continuing question of how the costs of this process should be apportioned between the Federal government, the *Länder* and the tenants/owners. More fundamentally, what will be the long-term effects of privatization and higher rents, particularly in the context of rapid economic and social change? Will the housing system in the east come to resemble that in the west, or will there continue to be 'two Germanys' in housing terms, despite there formally being only one system?

Finally, will owner-occupation rise to 'Anglo-Saxon' levels, or will the traditional dominance of the rented sector continue? For some, the growth of owner-occupation is a natural and universal phenomenon, and hence it is Germany's laggardly behaviour which requires explanation. For others, the German experience shows that the Anglo-Saxon obsession with promoting owner-occupation and comprehensive deregulation, are not the only ways to run a modern capitalist housing system. In the 1990s the issue will be the degree to which the specificities of the German system survive in a more integrated Europe.

German housing policy over the last forty years has been characterized by a high degree of political consensus around the boundaries of state and market, and around the extent of the state's responsibilities for different types of need. In the future, many of these constants will be called into question: what types of need, from which types of household have a claim on the state and what sorts of policy mechanisms are appropriate to try to deal with them?

Hence, in Germany as in France and Britain, both policy and outcomes have been characterized by greater bifurcation and polarization. The extent of bifurcation is perhaps somewhat less in Germany than in the other two countries. However, this mainly reflects the greater economic and social homogeneity that prevailed in the old Federal Republic. This homogeneity is now being transformed through the absorption of the poorer East

Germany, through the impact of immigration, and through the realities of integration into a more diverse European Union.

As with the other two countries, ironies abound. Germany has proved relatively resistant to neoliberalism, with a regulated and protected housing finance system, yet has gone further even than Britain in privatizing its social rented housing. The rhetoric is much less stridently pro-market than in Britain, for example, yet in practice policy and instruments are much more closely attuned to market conditions. Increasingly, it is the underlying imperatives of economic integration, the single market and free trade that are the important drivers of housing policy rather than the traditional principles of solidarity and the social market.

NOTES

1. *Wohngeld* can be claimed by owner-occupiers as well as both private and social tenants.
2. The comparison with the former DDR does of course in part reflect the fact that rents in 1992 were considerably below levels in either Western Germany or in Britain.
3. The construction premium for savings contracts (*Bausparvertrage*) entered into after 1991 is now to be paid only after the loan has been allocated, or after a minimum of seven years, instead of yearly (Borkenstein 1993).

5. Europe: Bringing in the (Super) State?

5.1 THE EUROPEAN DIMENSION

The last 20 years have seen considerable progress towards a more integrated Europe, both economically and politically. This has had an important impact on national housing policies, notwithstanding the formal position that the European Union has no competence in the sphere of housing (see 5.2 below). This has been not only because of the *direct* effects of European social legislation and social activity on the housing systems of the member states, but also through the *indirect* effects of economic policies adopted at both member-state and Community level, in order to promote European Union. The completion of the internal market and the preparations for economic and monetary union have committed member state governments to a broad policy focus on financial deregulation, deflationary macro economic policies, reduced government expenditure, and the prioritization of anti-inflationary measures above all other policy goals, including full employment. A crucial aspect here is the asymmetry between the integrated European market, and the powerful economic forces thereby unleashed, and the fragmentary, politically fraught and weak progress towards any greater political integration, and in particular towards the kind of institutional and fiscal federalism which a single market/monetary union might be thought to imply.

There are five main ways in which the process of European integration might be connected with the development of housing policies in the member states.

1. The direct role that the European Union plays in housing (see 5.2 below).

2. Impacts from closer European union on national policy formulation. These would include both the direct impacts on housing from EU directives, as well as, more commonly, the indirect effects from greater co-operation and sharing of views between member-state governments; from greater direct contact between local government and housing providers in different countries; and from lobbying activities by housing producer and consumer groups.

3. European integration affects the underlying problems of poverty, unemployment, and social exclusion, with which public policy tries to deal. Because of the spatial aspects of this process - integration produces winners and losers - there are important consequences for housing. In northern and western Europe, for example, the losers, or the have-nots, are increasingly concentrated in social housing and in particular locations.

4. Housing policy can have effects on the process of integration itself. Much of the supposed economic gain from integration arises from the better employment of factors of production, which implies (at least in principle) labour mobility from regions and industrial sectors in decline to those in ascendancy. Such labour mobility implies well-functioning housing markets and administrative systems, which in practice do not obtain.

5. The commitment to economic integration. The completion of the Single Market Programme, the signing of the Maastricht Treaty, and the measures taken in advance of EMU have not imposed new policies on member states, but rather have reinforced and bolstered the existing commitments to deflationary policies, to market-led development, and to the reduction of public expenditure.

European integration in relation to housing is a two-fold process. First, there is a process driven by markets and by economic actors, a process which is world-wide and which is facilitated rather than driven by government action. When European governments agree to abolish exchange controls and deregulate financial markets, they do not by that action shape the economic and social consequences. But by doing so they put into play the forces that will shape that future. Second, there are the positive policies and actions governments take to further the cause of integration and union, either to advance the processes which market forces are anyway bringing about, or to protect existing populations from the full force of the consequences of this restructuring.

In principle, housing policy could be used, both by national governments and to some degree by the European Union, as part of a strategy for increasing solidarity and social cohesion by encouraging mobility, reducing spatial polarization and weakening class and status divisions based around tenure. More likely, however, it is a reflection of the bifurcation in housing policy which has taken place at national level, in which issues of access to owner-occupation, property values, residential quality and environmental preservation loom large for the comfortable majority, while more traditional housing policy concerns such as homelessness, housing need, the price and availability of social housing, crime and vandalism on housing estates, the quality of housing management, and so on are confined to a politically weak and economically marginal minority. The stress on so-called holistic or 'bootstraps' solutions by both national governments and supra national organizations reinforces this localism so that this second category of housing issues is seen as being essentially endogenous and self-generated, or even brought about principally by social pathologies and individual failures.

5.2   CURRENT ROLE OF THE EUROPEAN UNION IN HOUSING

Housing is not formally within the competence of the institutions of the European Union. Housing is mentioned neither in the Treaty of Rome nor in the Single European Act nor in the Maastricht Treaty. Moreover, the key principle of subsidiarity within the European Union means that policy making and implementation should occur at the most devolved level possible (Spicker 1991), and the trend in many European countries has been towards greater decentralization downwards, rather than centralization upwards. For these, as well as other reasons, housing policy will remain mainly within the competence of national, regional and local governments for the foreseeable future.

In practice, however, the European Union and its forebears have always been involved to some degree with housing (Ghékiere 1992; Matznetter 1993). First, since 1954 the European Coal and Steel Community has financed social housing for coalminers and steelworkers, based on a broad interpretation of Article 54 of the Paris Treaty. Over the last 40 years, more than 200,000 dwellings have been financed in this way via long-term cheap loans, both for owner-occupiers and for tenants. Just over half of these houses were built in West Germany.

Second, the European Community has played a role in the housing of migrant workers. Under a special programme set up in 1977, assistance has been given to organizations representing or working for migrants, to providing new and rehabilitated dwellings, to co-operatives and to establishing pilot projects. In addition, all national social housing programmes must be open to migrant workers.

Third, there has been since 1977 a small programme addressing the housing needs of the handicapped, directed mainly at cross-national exchanges of experience.

More recently, housing has received somewhat more attention within the EU because of the connections between housing on the one hand, and issues of social exclusion and poverty on the other. Housing has played a role in several Commission-funded social programmes. Hence in the 1980s there was an important shift in Community involvement from a sectoral concern with specific housing needs (key industrial workers, migrants, and so on) to a more integrated approach in which housing is incorporated within broader structural funds expenditures and objectives. The Poverty 3 programme in which 39 projects were funded to the level of 55 MECU over five years, contained housing components, as have other specialist programmes like HORIZON, LEDA and ERGO (Ghékiere 1992; Matznetter 1993; McCrone and Stephens 1995). Two housing/urban regeneration 'pilot projects' in London and Marseille were funded by the EC under Article 10 of the ERDF in the late 1980s. However, the scale of spending under both Poverty 3 and the urban pilot projects has been small in relation to the structural funds as a whole. The 'Quartiers en Crise' network focuses on the need to reintegrate neighbourhoods into the urban fabric, avoid polarization and promote urban social development. The main activity is promoting exchanges of experience, and the network now links some 25 cities across the EU.

In addition, the Commission has funded research projects on housing and social integration; housing and labour mobility; immigrants and housing in West Germany; young people's housing; and the effect of economic and monetary union on national housing policies (Matznetter 1993; Priemus et al. 1993, 1994).

At the political level, too, housing has become more visible. Resolutions on homelessness and on the right to housing have been passed by the European Parliament in 1987 and 1990. The resolution against social exclusion agreed at the meeting of European social affairs ministers in 1989 included a reference to access to housing (Ghékiere 1992). European housing organizations such as CECODHAS, the federation of European social housing providers, and FEANTSA, the European coalition for the homeless, lobby both the Commission and Parliament to take a more active role in housing issues. In 1991, several European networks came together to sign a European Charter Against Social Exclusion and For Housing Rights.[1]

The Commission has also been drawn into the housing field via the implications of the single market programme for the mortgage finance industry. In the 1980s a draft directive on mortgage credit was prepared, although this was later superseded by the general programme of banking liberalization within the SEM programme. Current EU arrangements for promoting a single market in mortgage credit, as in other financial services, are based on the principles of home country control and minimum harmonization (McCrone and Stephens 1995). That is, prudential supervision remains with the home member state of the organization, with the single licence granted by that state acting as a 'European passport' to be recognized throughout the EU. However, in practice, inter-country differences in regulatory regimes, institutions and traditions seriously inhibit the development of a true single market. McCrone and Stephens conclude:

> The lessons from those banks and lending institutions that have started operations in other countries is that the going is tough: there are no easy profits to be made and it is often necessary to conform to the institutional structures of the country concerned. A gradual increase in cross-border lending can be expected, but a single market in mortgage finance is clearly a very long way away. (McCrone and Stephens 1995, p. 220)

Taken together then, there are several elements in place which suggest at least some housing role for the EU. In the Euro-enthusiasm of the early 1980s, some commentators went further, and saw a *de facto* housing policy emerging: 'In effect, a "shadow" housing policy is developing incrementally, through the unexpected results of a disparate body of legislation' (Drake 1991, p. v). However, national housing ministers have made clear their opposition to any increase in the powers of the European Union over housing, and are clearly in favour of continuing the exclusive competence of the member states in the field of housing (Ghékiere 1992). European housing ministers do meet together, but technically these are informal meetings, and are specifically outside the formal structure of the Council of Ministers.

The current position (1995) is that while European institutions do not have a generic involvement with housing, in practice the Union does get involved in housing through two very different channels: first, because of the links between housing and poverty; and second because of the technical requirements of promoting a single market in financial services. But, as Matznetter puts it: 'Between the two poles, the shelters for the homeless and the housing projects of the multinationals, there lies the vast majority of European housing' (Matznetter 1993, p. 22).

5.3 MAASTRICHT, EMU AND NATIONAL HOUSING POLICIES

The signing of the Maastricht Treaty in December 1991 can be seen in retrospect as marking the high-water mark of the renewed impetus towards European integration which began with the re-launching of the integration process in the mid-1980s around the 'magic number of 1992' (Tsoukalis 1993, p. 47). Since then Euro-optimism has been broadly in retreat, particularly since the virtual collapse of the exchange rate mechanism in 1993.

Two points must be borne in mind. First, the European integration project has always slowed during recessions and gained momentum during periods of economic growth; the current mood may thus be cyclical. Second, despite the concentration on often technical economic and monetary variables, this is at heart a political issue. Depending on political predilection, different conclusions can be drawn from the same event. For example, commenting on the 1992 turmoil in the ERM, the *Financial Times* on 17 September 1992 argued that 'the prospect of EMU is [now] so remote as to be almost invisible'. Reacting to the same events, Mr Michel Camdessus, managing director of the International Monetary Fund, predicted that the European monetary system would emerge strengthened from the crisis, and indeed that events had illustrated the advantages of moving ahead towards greater economic and monetary integration (*Financial Times*, 18 September 1992). With economic and monetary union, the politics and economics are inextricably linked. Certainly, writing in 1995, the emergence of a 'two-speed Europe' now looks far more likely than it did in the late 1980s - that is, a situation in which a smaller group of countries move towards a monetary union, while Britain and other countries remain outside.

The Maastricht Treaty envisages the completion of the single market, a period of convergence defined by key indicators and then full monetary union. These have broad implications for housing systems and markets. The key point is that economic convergence and monetary union - or at least the attempt to attain them - will reinforce many of the trends in housing policies identified in this study.

The European Union is both a reflection of economic and social integration in Europe, as well as the main factor in the furthering of this integration. The integration process is both an effect of EU policy decisions and an 'autonomous' - or perhaps more accurately a market-led - development. Separating the effects of these two components is not easy.

This problem of separating the policy and market-led aspects is particularly complicated in regard to the housing sector. Housing policy is not recognized as a specific European Union responsibility nor is it an object for a common policy formulation. However, as demonstrated above, in practice EU activity in a number of related policy areas (competition policy, social inclusion, regional policy, and so on) has major impacts on housing issues. Policy-led developments within the EU as well as 'autonomous' market processes will therefore be relevant to the operation of national housing systems.

There are several different channels by which the process of economic and political integration in general, and EMU in particular, will impact on national housing policies. I discuss these under the following headings:[2] factor mobility; competition policy; economic growth; lower inflation; lower government spending; tax harmonization; and citizenship and social justice.

5.3.1 Factor Mobility

The significance of the Single European Act and the completion of the internal market lies in the fact that they provide for the free circulation not only of goods and services, but also (in principle at least) of factors of production also. As far as capital mobility is concerned, the issues are relatively straightforward. Although policy in most countries has moved in the direction of deregulation of housing finance markets and integration of the circuit of housing finance into capital markets in general, in many countries specialized housing finance circuits remain in which there is government allocation of funds, below-market cost of finance and rationing.

Free movement of capital would suggest greater integration of housing finance markets both with general circuits of capital and with housing finance markets in neighbouring countries. It also implies the possibility of greater cross-border activity by financial institutions and perhaps the eventual emergence of true European housing finance organizations, created through acquisition and merger. Such developments will of course depend crucially on the speed with which financial liberalization and deregulation is more generally applied throughout the EU. However, it is perhaps likely that integration of housing finance markets will proceed more slowly than some other financial services, given the importance of local knowledge in correctly assessing lending risks. Alternatively, the development of European secondary markets would allow the institutions to remain primarily national while debt could move across borders.

Labour mobility is a more complex issue. It is important to emphasize that the presumed gains in economic well-being which will result from greater economic integration in Europe rest on the assumption that there is perfect factor mobility - although the implications of this for labour are rarely spelled out. In the Commission's own estimate of the increase in European GDP which will result from closer economic integration, the bland and question-begging assumption was made that 'displaced factors are re-employed'.

In the abstract world of neoclassical economic theory, no government intervention would be needed: workers move in response to market signals given by differential unemployment and wage rates. In practice, a number of different factors will inhibit labour mobility, not the least of which is the lack of available affordable housing in those regions and urban areas where job opportunities are greatest. Closer economic integration in Europe is likely to widen the disparities in unemployment levels between declining and growing regions, creating at least the potential for increased labour mobility. At the same time it should not be automatically assumed that the removal of formal barriers to movement will necessarily lead to a large increase in labour mobility within the Community. Studies of the USA suggests that workers' mobility is not particularly sensitive to differences in either social benefits or after-tax income (Ermisch 1991). But whatever the desired level of labour mobility after 1993, evidence from individual countries suggests that inflexible housing markets can prove to be a serious handicap to labour-market adjustment.

The relationship between housing policies and labour mobility is important for reasons of social justice as well as economic efficiency. The Social Charter proclaims that freedom of movement is one of the 'fundamental social rights' of EU workers, although what this actually means in practice is not clear. But if the spatial patterns of job opportunities and of rates of economic development are going to be affected by the process of economic integration, then housing policies should be adapted in order to give all EU citizens a reasonable chance of obtaining the employment opportunities that do exist.

While the European Union is in principle committed to the idea of free movement of labour, in practice mobility in Europe has been declining, remains low, and is likely to continue to do so. The reasons for this are complex: higher living standards, the rapid reduction in fertility rates in the south of Europe, the increase in two-earner households, and perhaps the spread of owner-occupation. The completion of the internal market will increase some types of migration, for example, the young and the skilled; but overall there are unlikely to be any large-scale shifts of population (Simon 1990).

5.3.2 Competition Policy and Liberalization of Markets

The removal of frontier controls will of itself have little immediate impact on the construction sector, given the existence of different tendering procedures and practices, varying building regulations and administrative procedures (van Oostward in Bouw 1988). But a variety of EU directives are putting pressure on national construction industries to operate in a more competitive manner (Langeveld and de Vries 1990; Priemus 1991). These include directives on government tendering, on building products, on the recognition of qualifications, as well as the 'Eurocodes' category of European standards for use in building structures which came into effect in 1992 (Priemus 1991). But there is still a long way to go before real European tendering is established.

In the longer term, there may also be greater cross-border activity by social housing companies tendering perhaps for the management of existing stock as well as the construction of new units. For example, in Britain, the management of local authority housing (representing about 70 per cent of the entire rental stock) is now subject to compulsory competitive tendering.

5.3.2 Economic Growth

The promise of sustained non-inflationary economic growth is a key part of the argument for economic integration in Europe. If faster growth does eventually result from economic integration, this will have important consequences for housing. In principle, it could lead to simultaneous expansion on both the demand and supply sides, resulting relatively painlessly in higher levels of housing consumption. But in practice, we know that the supply of housing is relatively inelastic, while housing demand has an income elasticity close to unity - that is an increase in disposable income of 1 per cent leads to an increase in housing demand of about 1 per cent. We would therefore expect faster growth to feed through fairly quickly into increased housing demand. This would take the form of increased household formation, demand for higher space standards and higher amenity, and an increased concern with the overall environment of the dwelling as well as just basic shelter requirements. If past experience is a guide we would also expect increased demand for single-family individual houses rather than multi-family collective units and for owner-occupation as against renting. But the future may not be like the past: lower inflation and lower expectations about house-price growth may depress demand for owner-occupation versus renting (see 5.3.4 below).

Given the inelasticity of the supply side, it should not be assumed that this increase in demand would be met by adequate new investment. It is more likely to result in increased pressure in the housing market, showing up in price and rent levels and scarcity in particular areas. Access to housing for poorer households might well get worse. Increased preference for greater space and for individual units will also have important implications for land-use planning and for environmental policies. The environmental consequences, in particular, will have implications for the European Union as well as for local and national governments.

On the other hand, more pessimistic observers would argue that current moves towards further integration and monetary union in Europe will result not in faster growth, but in a permanent deflationary bias and stagnant real incomes. In this scenario, housing demand would remain fairly constant in real terms. New investment would remain low in the face of high real interest rates and weak demand. In this context, problems of disrepair, an inadequate rate of replacement of the stock, and of affordability and indebtedness would assume greater importance.

5.3.4 Lower Inflation

A commitment to stable prices is one of the guiding principles of the Maastricht Treaty. This principle finds concrete expression in the convergence criterion that the rate of inflation of each member state should not exceed by more than 0.5 percentage point the average of the three best performing member states. Whether this, or indeed any of the convergence criteria formulated in the Maastricht Treaty, should be taken to be realistic targets for member states is open to considerable doubt. What is not, however, in doubt is the commitment of member-state governments and the institutions of the EU to an anti-inflationary strategy as the key aspect of macroeconomic policy. This deflationary 'consolidation doctrine' (Katseli 1989) prevalent among policy makers at both national and supranational levels, reflects both the specific increased influence of finance ministers and central bankers, as well as the more general move away from Keynesian policies and interventionist solutions during the 1980s.

If EMU does succeed in bringing about permanently lower inflation throughout the EU, there will be a number of consequences for the operation of housing markets. Unanticipated inflation redistributes income and wealth from lenders to borrowers, and leads to windfall gains to asset holders such as home owners. This is a major reason why owner-occupation proved to be a good investment decision for households in many countries in the 1970s. Conversely, if the 1990s are to be a period of permanently low inflation, then the real costs of home ownership to households will probably rise. This will have important effects on tenure choice by households, and also on affordability.

France is an instructive example in this context. As we have seen, throughout most of the last decade it has pursued a tough anti-inflationary policy based around the *franc fort*. Households who bought property on credit on the assumption that inflation would quickly erode the real value of the debt have found the reality to be very different. Together with stagnant real incomes and persistently high real interest rates, this has led to *blocage* in the housing system as well as an increase in affordability problems. Commitment to ERM/EMU and a low inflation regime will clearly have most impact on previously high-inflation economies, reducing future growth in the asset price of owner-occupied property considerably below that experienced in the 1970s and 1980s.

A related question is that of interest rates. Convergence of long-term interest rates is another of the Maastricht EMU criteria. Lower and less volatile interest rates will, it is argued, provide a more stable environment for decision making by both producers and consumers. In terms of the housing market, this would imply a greater readiness to undertake new investment.

Lower inflation and lower interest rates will also impact on housing policies via the intermediary effects of house-price inflation rates and housing credit mechanisms. This raises a number of important research questions which require further analysis. For example, what effects will lower house-price inflation have on the attractiveness of housing *vis-à-vis* alternative investments, especially in those countries of traditionally high nominal house-price rises? At the same time, to what extent will lower house prices improve access to the owner-occupied sector for younger households, possibly increasing household formation rates? More generally, will a more stable environment in terms both of asset prices and of the cost of funds induce a greater orientation towards consumption rather than investment aspects of housing?

Methods of financing investment in housing, in both private and public sectors, might also be expected to change in a less inflationary environment, with a greater emphasis on fixed-rate borrowing, lower risk premia and perhaps longer repayment periods. However, the relationships between inflation rates, nominal interest rates and expectations of risk and return are extremely complex. They also depend crucially on the institutional response in each country and hence issues of greater capital mobility and of competition policy, discussed elsewhere, will also be relevant.

5.3.5 Lower Government Spending

A more direct impact on national housing policies will be experienced as a result of the mechanisms through which governments seek to achieve lower inflation. The Maastricht convergence criteria indicate that deflationary fiscal policies will need to be pursued for many years by the member states in order to attain and keep fiscal deficits at 3 per cent GDP or below and government debt at or below 60 per cent. Few people now believe that all member states will meet these targets in the proposed timescale.

But if we take these criteria at face value for the moment, it implies serious restrictions on government expenditure programmes. Reductions in spending will necessarily include housing expenditure, whether in the form of direct bricks-and-mortar subsidies, of housing allowances and personal support, or of indirect tax expenditures. There is no reason to believe housing would be exempt from the general austerity. Indeed, housing programmes are likely to be more vulnerable than demand-driven programmes such as social security. New pressures will emerge to improve the 'efficiency' of housing policies. Regulations and incentives to improve the efficiency of social housing management are also likely to continue, and there may be a gradual Europeanization of management and finance provision in social housing as the single market develops.

But pressure could equally be applied to tax expenditures (such as mortgage interest tax relief) which generally favour owner-occupiers rather than tenants. In numerous EU countries there is an array of evidence that tax breaks particularly aid high-income households and raise house prices. The tax expenditures on housing which expanded rapidly in the 1980s may therefore come under greater scrutiny in the future. For reasons of both equity and efficiency, member states may choose to direct at least part of the burden of greater fiscal austerity at the tax expenditure part of the equation. However, to do so runs the political risk of offending against the interests of owner-occupiers.

A serious attempt to try to adhere to the Maastricht conditions would therefore mean that the proportion of GDP going to public expenditure on housing (including tax expenditures) would fall. Even in the absence of the Maastricht convergence criteria, a continuing commitment to deflationary fiscal policies will mean pressure on housing budgets at all levels of government.

5.3.6 Tax Harmonization

At present there are considerable variations in the tax treatment of housing in the different member states. For example, while VAT is levied on new residential property transactions in most countries, it does not apply in either Britain or Germany (Haffner 1991). The tax treatment of owner-occupied housing varies widely. In some countries (Belgium, Denmark, Greece, Italy, Luxembourg, the Netherlands, Spain) owner-occupied housing is treated as an investment good, so that imputed rents are taxed while interest costs and perhaps some other costs are tax deductible. By contrast in France, Ireland, Portugal and the UK imputed rent is not taxed, but nevertheless there is some mortgage interest tax relief. In Germany there is a depreciation allowance, again with no tax on imputed rent (Haffner 1991).

If, as is expected by many, there is a gradual harmonization of fiscal policy, then there will be important effects on the financial position of both owner-occupiers and private landlords. This will in turn affect the prices of owner-occupied and rented units, perhaps the level of rents, affordability ratios, as well as influencing tenure choice. These impacts will, of course, differ across the member states, depending on the current fiscal treatment of housing.

5.3.7 Issues of Citizenship and Social Justice

Economic integration in the EU entails major structural change and social upheaval. The freer play of market forces in Europe will produce losers as well as winners, with whole industries, regions and urban areas in decline while others experience rapid growth with attendant problems of congestion. These massive structural adjustments will require a range of social policies if Europe is not to become more unequal, more divided and more conflict ridden. Included among these there will need to be an adequate housing policy response among the member states regarding both adequate housing for job migrants in the growth areas, and improving housing as well as social and economic conditions in the areas in decline.

The institutions of the European Union have continually emphasized the importance of social issues. Housing is a particularly important aspect of social policy in this regard as it determines to a large degree the life chances that individuals have. Issues of access to housing, of equal treatment and equal opportunities, not just for citizens of the member states but also for third-country migrants living within the EU borders will need to be addressed. Removing discrimination against ethnic and other minorities and against women thus becomes of crucial importance in the construction of an equal and democratic 'Social Europe'. The existence of large pockets of poor, disadvantaged and marginalized groups within an otherwise prosperous community is seen as being not only morally wrong, but potentially threatening. Given the polarizing trend within European housing markets, such groups are increasingly found in specific housing locations, mainly in the social housing sector. As a consequence, policies towards social housing have therefore become closely linked to issues of social exclusion and social integration. If the role of the EU in the 'fight against social exclusion' is expanded, this might imply some increase in the involvement of EU institutions in the housing sphere.

5.4 CONCLUSION

Examining the current and potential roles for European housing policy has brought out the tension between the relatively strong economic dimension of integration and its relatively weak social dimension. There is no European superstate, nor is there likely to be one in the foreseeable future, at least not one capable of making and implementing the type of federal social policy that would actually make an impact on the housing situation of the mass of European citizens.

It is clear that, even in its current indistinct, fragmentary and embryonic form, European housing policy, far from providing a distinctive solidaristic or social-democratic contrast to the policies of the three member states in this study, in fact displays similar symptoms of bifurcation. One strand of policy relates to issues of social exclusion, segregation and housing conditions for the dispossessed minority; the other strand deals with the framework for promoting stable market conditions for the majority.

The Maastricht convergence criteria amply demonstrate the rigidly orthodox, deflationary and anti-interventionist stance of the promoters of economic and monetary union. It is a profoundly conservative stance, mistrustful of state activity in principle (though not of increasing the powers of specific politicians and bureaucrats) and with an almost mystical belief in the healing properties of markets. However, as such it is not a product of 'Brussels' foisted on reluctant member states. Rather it is an accurate reflection of the received wisdom at member-state level, a world-view shared by elected representatives, senior civil servants and bankers. There are, of course, important tensions between the European Union, as a set of institutions, and the governments of the member states. But equally important are the shared assumptions which unite rather than divide these two levels of government - that is, a similar view on what is politically possible, on what the 'laws of economics' dictate, and on the need to control public expenditure and to prioritize the control of inflation over other macroeconomic targets. France is the paradigmatic case: the abandonment of 'Keynesianism in one country' after 1983 was a key turning point, not just for that country, but for the economics and politics of Europe as a whole.

The European dimension is inherently and inevitably contradictory. For many continental commentators, the 1980s in general, and economic integration in particular, represented the triumph of Anglo-Saxon ideas of free markets, deregulation and ultra liberal economic orthodoxy into previously state-managed domestic housing markets. This inevitably led to greater volatility, pronounced cyclical effects, social polarization and the erosion of a painfully constructed social consensus. For many British commentators on the other hand, 'Europe' promises (or threatens, depending on your political viewpoint) the imposition of large doses of continental corporatism, with its attendant intellectual baggage of social partners, social inclusion and consensus building. And so, while some equate 'Europe' with 'more market', others equally clearly equate it with 'more state'.

What might 'Europe' do for housing then? For optimists such as Drake and Ghékiere, it promises a new type of state intervention, a new source of funding, and perhaps even a broader, more 'holistic' approach than the narrow approaches of national and local governments. More likely, in my view, is that the project of European Union, through the completion of the single market and the pursuit of economic and monetary union, will effectively 'cement in' the narrow economic and fiscal orthodoxy which most governments anyway now espouse. This will make it even less likely for any radical measures to be taken, and will reinforce the existing tendencies to polarization.

NOTES

1. As well as CECODHAS and FEANTSA, these comprised OEIL, the European Organization of Unions for Integration and Housing of Young Workers; EUROPIL, the European Federation for Social Assistance and Integration through Housing; the European Network of Researchers; and AITEC, the International Association of Technicians.
2. This section draws extensively on the analysis in Priemus, Kleinman, Maclennan and Turner 1993, 1994.

6. The Wider Context: Welfare Division and Welfare Change

6.1 INTRODUCTION

The developments in housing policies over the last 20 years which I have described and analysed in the previous four chapters have taken place in a context in which there has been both major economic restructuring and important changes in the organization of the welfare state. Associated with this, there has been an increase in social polarization. These are very broad issues and a detailed examination of them is beyond the scope of this book. But in order to understand housing policy in its proper context, we do need to survey briefly the evidence on inequality and polarization; to examine the broad trends in welfare-state development in each of the three countries; and to look at the links between housing policies on the one hand, and urban change and economic restructuring on the other.

6.2 INEQUALITY AND POLARIZATION IN EUROPE

The official European Union poverty line defines as poor those households whose disposable income is less than half the average disposable income in the country in which they resided. On this basis O'Higgins and Jenkins (1989) estimated the number of poor people in the European Community as 38.6 million in 1975 (12.8 per cent of the population), rising to 39.5 million in 1980 and to 43.9 million in 1985 (13.9 per cent of the population). More recently these figures have been revised to give an estimate of 49 million for 1980 and 50 million for 1985 (15.4 per cent of the population), suggesting that the number of poor people stabilized in the first half of the 1980s (Schulte 1993, p. 41). Data presented by Cross (1993, Figure 2) shows that during the 1990s, the number of poor persons fell in Denmark, the Netherlands, France, Ireland, Spain, Greece and Portugal, while rising in Belgium and the UK.

As with all attempts to measure poverty, the particular definition used by the EU has both strengths and weaknesses. It employs a relative definition of poverty; indeed, some would argue it measures inequality rather than poverty. Second, although intended to generate a Europe-wide measure of poverty, the method used does not calculate the number of poor by reference to average income in the EU as a whole but instead sums the national totals of poor people, each calculated by reference to the average income in each member state. Atkinson (1991) showed that if a Community-wide poverty standard were used, the number in poverty would rise from 13.9 per cent to 17.4 per cent of the EU population. Moreover, Spain, Portugal, Ireland and Greece would together account for 55 per cent of all those in poverty, compared with 32 per cent at present (Atkinson 1991, p. 15).

The European Union estimates are intended to give a relatively straightforward 'snapshot' of poverty issues in the European Union. Other researchers have attempted to derive more robust cross-country estimates - a complex task given the conceptual and statistical difficulties. Gardiner (1993) provides a survey, bringing together evidence both on the rankings of 12 countries by level of income inequality, and on trends in income equality on a similar group of 13 countries. In terms of income inequality, Finland and Sweden have the least inequality, followed by Luxembourg, West Germany and the Netherlands. Canada and the UK are in the middle of the table, followed by France and New Zealand, Italy, Australia and the USA (Gardiner 1993, Table 3). Eight countries - Australia, Japan, the Netherlands, New Zealand, Sweden, United Kingdom, USA and West Germany - have followed a U-shaped trend, with movement towards greater equality giving way to greater inequality at some point in the 1970s or 1980s. Canada, France and Italy had stable distributions over the 1980s, while Finland and Norway experienced falling income inequality over the 1980s (Gardiner 1993, Table 4). Gardiner breaks down the overall changes in income inequality into a 'market income' effect, and a 'taxes and transfers' effect. In France, the latter was sufficiently large to offset the increase in market income inequality. In Germany taxes and transfers did offset the increase in inequality of market incomes, but not sufficiently to prevent a rise in inequality of disposable income. In the UK it appears that the effect of changes in taxes and transfers was to add to rather than offset the rising inequality of market incomes (Gardiner 1993, pp. 50-51).

Another way of measuring the growth of inequality and polarization in Europe is to examine evidence at national, regional and urban levels. At the national level, there is some evidence that divergence, in terms of both income disparities and unemployment rates between richer and poorer regions in the European Union has been growing, although the evidence is not conclusive, and there is some data pointing in the other direction. In the last decade, Ireland and Spain have gained on the EU average in terms of GDP per head, while for Portugal there has been no change, and Greece has actually lost ground (Begg and Mayes 1993, p. 150).

Begg and Mayes also point out that several of the least-favoured regions (Galicia, Asturias, northern England, Mezzogiorno, Wallonia) failed to keep pace with their respective member states. O'Donnell suggests that between 1960 and 1973, a period of relatively strong growth, there was some convergence of national and regional incomes, while between 1974 and 1986, with lower growth the trend was one of slight divergence (O'Donnell 1992).

Other writers come to similar conclusions. According to Nevin (1990), between 1958 and 1972, there was a narrowing of regional disparities in France, Germany and Italy, while disparities between member states were halved. Nevin ascribes this to a combination of higher growth rates in the poorer countries, and a fall in internal variance because of the movement of population from agricultural to industrial areas. Similarly, Cingolani (1993) finds that an index of per capita income disparity for the EU12 fell sharply in the 1950s and 1960s, but hardly changed between 1970 and 1990. However, the composition of the disparity changed: inter-country disparities fell, while the intra-country regional component remained almost the same. Collier (1994) argues that while there was convergence, at both country and regional level in GDP per head in the 1960s and up to the mid-1970s, since then there has been some convergence at country level, but inter-regional differences have widened. Collier also argues that regional disparities are greater for unemployment than for GDP per head, and that this gives a clearer indication of disadvantage and inequality: 'Per capita income measurements for a region can be close to the Community average but can hide large intraregional disparities; regional unemployment rates give a clearer indication of welfare differences within and between regions' (Collier 1994, p. 146).

Collier finds that regional unemployment disparities widened in the first half of the 1980s, although this trend was reversed in the second half of the decade. The European Commission's 'Employment in Europe' shows that the fall in unemployment between 1986 and 1991 was less in the Objective 1 (lagging) areas than in the unassisted areas: from 15 per cent to 14 per cent in Objective 1 areas against a fall from 9 per cent to 7.5 per cent in the unassisted areas. In the Objective 2 (industrial decline) areas, however, the fall in terms of percentage points was more than twice as great, from 13 per cent to 9.5 per cent (CEU 1993). At the urban level, Lever finds that the growth rate of cities in the 'core' was higher than that of cities in the periphery during the period 1975-85, but lower in 1985-89 and projected to remain lower in 1989-95 (Lever 1993, p. 947).

Some authors have argued that inequalities at regional and urban level will increase in the future, because of the impact of economic integration. In the past, EU integration had relatively low costs because it fostered intra-industry rather than inter-industry trade. But the current wave is likely to be very different, leading to greater specialization between regions, that is, to more divergent economic structures and hence to higher social and economic costs, the burden of which will not be equally distributed (Padoa-Schioppa (ed.) 1987, Appendix; Krugman 1991, pp. 81-2).

6.3 POLARIZATION AND THE WELFARE STATE

The wider context in which discussion and analysis of housing policies in each of the three countries should be placed includes both structural (economic and social) trends in the direction of greater inequality and polarization, and policy trends in regard to the welfare state in each country. A thorough analysis of each of these topics and the links between them would require an additional book. The treatment here is of necessity an outline only. Furthermore, although I have sought to keep the individual country discussions below broadly parallel, there are clearly differences in emphasis across the three accounts. Partly this reflects differences in the accessibility of relevant evidence, and my own knowledge of the broader material.

But there are other reasons, too. To some degree, the different emphasis and even tone in the discussions of polarization and welfare-state change in the three countries reflect characteristics of the welfare state and the wider society in each case. Hence in Britain, there is an extensive and detailed literature on inequality of income and on social inequalities generally, while concepts such as solidarity and social cohesion still appear unfamiliar, and indeed 'foreign'. By contrast, social cohesion and social integration appear prominently in debates about the welfare state and social change in France and Germany. In France, the growth of 'new poverty' and labour-market insecurity (*précarité*) provide a strong theme. In Germany, concerns about marginalization and about exclusion from the benefits and responsibilities of a social-market economy are prevalent.

6.3.1 Britain: Rising Inequality

There is considerable evidence that inequality has increased in Britain over the last 15 years, reversing the process of equalization that had been continuing for 70 years or more. The overall position can be summarized as follows. Between 1913 and 1938 there was a substantial narrowing of income differences, and by 1949 incomes were considerably more equal than in 1938. Between 1949 and 1964 income distribution remained fairly constant; the gap narrowed again between 1964 and 1974. But from the mid-1970s on, the trend towards greater equality comes to an end. The move towards greater inequality from 1977 to 1991 more than reversed all the 1949-77 movement in the direction of greater equalization. So incomes in the 1990s were more unequally distributed than at any time since 1949 (Hills 1995).

Atkinson (1993) and Gardiner (1993) provide useful surveys of the evidence. Using official 'Blue Book' data, Atkinson shows that there was a fall in income inequality between 1949 and 1976; most redistribution was from the top 10 per cent to the next 40 per cent, the share of the bottom 50 per cent changing little. In recent years, knowledge is more limited because of political influences on the collection of data. The Blue Book series was dropped in 1970 before being re-instated in 1975. Since 1981, estimates of personal disposable income are carried out every three years instead of annually. Between 1978-79 and 1984-85, the share of the top 10 per cent rose by 3.1 percentage points, wiping out two-thirds of the fall between 1949 and the mid-1970s (Atkinson 1993, p. 9).

Atkinson (1993) also presents Family Expenditure Survey evidence, which shows that the Gini coefficient - a measure of inequality which is zero if there is complete equality of incomes and 100 per cent if there is complete inequality, i.e. one person has all the income - increased from 29 per cent (1975) to 32 per cent (1985) to 38 per cent (1988). In addition, the government's own study of households with below-average income shows that the share of income, before housing costs, of the bottom fifth of the population fell from 10.0 per cent in 1979 to 7.4 per cent in 1991-92 (Hills 1995, Table 3).

More recent results for the UK, using Family Expenditure Survey data, are presented in Jenkins (forthcoming) and Coulter, Cowell and Jenkins (1993), and reported in Gardiner (1993). Jenkins (forthcoming) uses four different inequality measures which each show a pattern of falling inequality between 1971 and 1976, but considerable rises in inequality in the periods 1976-81 and 1981-86. On each measure, inequality was higher in 1986 than in 1981. Coulter et al. (1993) provide more detailed analysis of the same data sets. The income shares of the bottom five deciles rose between 1971 and 1976, but declined during 1976-81 and 1981-86. By 1986, each of these bottom five deciles had lower income shares than in 1971; conversely the shares of the top four deciles were higher. Inequality also seems to have increased rapidly in the second half of the 1980s. Quoting CSO data, Gardiner (1993) shows that there were 'big jumps' in the Gini coefficient from 1985 to 1987 and then again from 1989 and 1990.

How have these increases in inequality affected the real living standards of poor people? That is, is it the case that the living standards of all British households are increasing, but just that those of the poor are increasing less fast; or have poor people suffered a fall in absolute as well as relative income?

This issue is examined in detail in the summary of evidence to the Joseph Rowntree Foundation's Inquiry into Income and Wealth (Hills 1995). Between 1961 and 1979, the real incomes of the poorest tenth of the population rose faster than the average - before housing costs, the rise was 55 per cent for the poorest tenth compared with 35 per cent on average. But there was a sharp change after 1978: 'The incomes of the richest tenth accelerated away from the rest, while those of the poorest groups rose more slowly or stagnated right at the bottom' (Hills 1995, p. 29). Between 1979 and 1991-92 average real income rose by 36 per cent, and the real income of the top tenth grew by about 60 per cent. But the real incomes of the poorest tenth had not changed at all, if measured before housing costs, or had actually fallen 17 per cent lower than that of the equivalent group in 1979, if measured after housing costs.

What are the causes of this rise in inequality? Kuznets (1955) suggested that with economic development, economic inequality falls as per capita income increases. However, as Atkinson (1993) points out, Kuznets argued that this pattern came about because of the balance of conflicting forces, rather than as the consequence of some fundamental law, so we should not therefore be surprised about a change in the pattern.

Three factors in particular explain the rise in inequality: the shift from work in the composition of income; increases in earnings inequalities; and greater inequality in the non-work sector (Atkinson 1993). The shift in the size of the working population and the rise in inequality among those in work account arithmetically for almost all the change in inequality from 1975-85. From 1985-88, there is a different explanation. The size of the working sector did not change. Inequality in the work sector continued to increase, accounting for 60 per cent of the increase in income inequality in 1985-88. Also, inequality increased in the non-work sector, and there was a sizeable rise in the relative income of the work sector. These latter two developments account for the remaining 40 per cent of the rise in income inequality.

So the causes of increased inequality lie in a combination of labour-market developments, which affect income in the work sector, and government social security policy, which largely determines incomes in the non-work sector. There was a widening of inequality in gross individual earnings, with the decile ratio (the ratio of the earnings of the person 10 per cent from the top of the earnings distribution to the earnings of the person 10 per cent from the bottom) rising from 3.0 in 1975 to 3.2 in 1985 and 3.36 in 1988. After 1985, changes in social security led to a decline in the relative earnings of pensioners, and this was the major factor in the sharp fall in the real income of non-workers during 1985-88 (Atkinson 1993). At the same time, the reduced real value of social security benefits widens the gap between basic pensioners, and those in receipt of occupational pensions. Atkinson concludes that the 1980s saw a departure from the historical trend, with a definite rise in inequality, likely to be even more marked post-1985.

Similar conclusions are reached by Johnson and Webb (1993), who also identify changes in taxes and benefits; widening of the distribution of pre-tax earnings; and the shift from employment to both unemployment and self-employment. Using Lorenz curves, they show that each factor is relevant to the overall change in income inequality, and that, by reference to changes in the Gini and Atkinson coefficients, the tax/benefit changes appear to be the most important, followed by changes in economic activity.

Studies on the *spatial* aspects of inequality in Britain, and in particular relating to the question of whether polarization is increasing or not, are much less common. Green (1994) looks at the changing spatial distribution and segregation of poverty and wealth, including the question of whether spatial concentration and segregation of the rich and poor has become more or less pronounced over the 1980s. She uses 1981 and 1991 Census data, at ward, district and labour-market level. The study is thus based on areas rather than on households. In the absence of direct information on income and wealth, Green uses car ownership, unemployment and housing tenure, which have been shown to be reasonable proxies for poverty (Davies, Joshi and Clarke 1993).

Green uses three measures of distribution and segregation: *degree* - the proportion of households with characteristic X at district level; *extent* - the proportion of wards within a district in the top (bottom) 10 per cent of the national distribution of wards on that indicator; and *intensity* - the mean score of the three highest-ranked wards within each district. The focus of the study is hence geographical and ecological. Green finds that the degree of poverty is greater in the north than in the south, and greater in large cities compared with small and medium-sized towns; that the extent of poverty is most marked in the former coalmining and heavy manufacturing areas; and that the intensity of poverty is most marked in large northern metropolitan areas and in inner London. Green also constructs indices of dissimilarity and of isolation, quantitative measures of spatial distribution of variables. In absolute terms, increases in isolation were most apparent in large cities, with increased isolation (i.e. segregation) of the unemployed most marked in inner London.

Comparing 1991 with 1981 reveals a great degree of continuity in the spatial patterns of poverty and wealth. But there are also important changes, particularly, the degree, extent, intensity and segregation of poverty in inner London and other large metropolitan areas:

> In Inner London the 'core' of disadvantage expanded outwards during the decade, and in the most disadvantaged inner and east London boroughs 'poverty' became much more 'extensive': it is here that the increasing isolation of the 'poor' from the social and economic mainstream is particularly marked ... it would seem that important changes are occurring at the intra-urban scale - leading to a *polarization* of the social structure and increasing segregation of different population sub-groups in many large cities (with such processes being furthest advanced in London) (Green 1994, p. 13, original emphasis)

What role has the welfare state played in this increase in inequality? Britain, as both Esping-Andersen (1990) and Abrahamson (1992) allow, represents something of a hybrid or anomalous case in the typology of welfare states. The large range of non-means-tested benefits, the existence of redistributive services in kind such as the National Health Service, the education system and an almost unique system of publicly owned council housing which at its peak accommodated one in three of the population, and especially the universalist principles of the Beveridge model, clearly indicate that the British welfare state cannot be categorized simply as a minimalist, liberal safety-net. But at the same time, there is a strong element of what one might call 'latent dualism' within the system. Esping-Andersen (1990) explains this as follows

> the solidarity of flat-rate universalism presumes a historically peculiar class structure, one in which the vast majority of the population are the 'little people' for whom a modest, albeit egalitarian, benefit may be considered adequate. Where this no longer obtains, as occurs with growing working-class prosperity and the rise of the new middle classes, flat-rate universalism inadvertently promotes dualism because the better-off turn to private insurance and to fringe-benefit bargaining to supplement modest equality with what they have decided are accustomed standards of welfare. Where this process unfolds (as in Canada or Great Britain), the result is that the wonderfully egalitarian spirit of universalism turns into a dualism similar to that of the social-assistance state: the poor rely on the state, and the remainder on the market. (Esping-Andersen 1990, p. 25)

It is important to recognize that this latent dualism pre-dates, and cannot be reduced to 'Thatcherism'. Rather, the economic change after 1973, shifts in social and demographic patterns and the election of governments committed to an ideological shift towards the market combined to make these latent tendencies manifest. Nevertheless, since 1979, three main themes can be distinguished in regard to the welfare state.

First, there has been increasing concern by government about the supposed *negative economic effects of welfare-state spending*. This argument can take either a macroeconomic or a microeconomic form. In the early 1980s period of 'high monetarism', the argument was put in relatively technical terms. Increases in public expenditure were bad in that, if financed through borrowing, they 'crowded out' (through rises in interest rates) private expenditure, leading to lower economic growth in the long term. In addition, increased public deficits, as measured in the public sector borrowing requirement (PSBR) were inflationary. If the increased expenditure were financed through taxation, this would stifle economic activity and enterprise, both through the macroeconomic mechanism of reducing private demand,

and more importantly through the microeconomic mechanism of reducing incentives to work, savings and investment.

Later, as the pure doctrines of monetarism gave way to more pragmatic approaches to economic management, the grounds for concern shifted. Welfare-state expenditures would 'outstrip the nation's ability to pay' (Department of Social Security 1993b); economic progress was being threatened by a crisis of rising expectations and/or a 'demographic time bomb'. However, in practice, there does not appear to be a major problem of 'affordability' of the welfare state as a whole. Hills (1993) points out that over the medium term, welfare spending in Britain as a proportion of GDP has been stable, and official projections do not show a major shift in this:

> There are upward pressures, notably from the ageing of the population, from SERPS and from higher basic pension entitlements. But, even if benefit levels were to keep up with overall living standards (which is not current policy), the net effects of these three factors on the public finances over the next *fifty* years would add up to 5 per cent of GDP - no more than the recent increase related to recession over the past *three* years. (Hills 1993, p. 14, original emphasis)

The related microeconomic argument is that the taxation burden necessary to fund social spending reduces incentives to work, to save and to invest. Meanwhile, the existence of cradle-to-the-grave state provision inhibits the development of family, community and voluntary arrangements - in effect another form of crowding out. Among the New Right, the argument is not just that the welfare state is ineffective in achieving its goals, but that it is actually harmful to those whom it is, in principle at least, trying to help. That is, in Hirschman's (1991) terminology, it is attacked on 'perversity' as well as 'futility' grounds. While debate continues among academics and policy makers about the relationships between welfare expenditure, welfare provision and economic activity and growth, it is hard not to reach the conclusion that in practice government policy in the 1980s and 1990s was driven more by simple notions of 'public sector bad, private sector good' than any more complex theoretical arguments.

The second theme of policy has been the promotion of *privatization* and *marketization* (see, among much else, Hills (ed.) 1990; Johnson 1990; Le Grand and Bartlett 1993; Self 1993). What has been most noteworthy is that, with the exception of the sale of over one million council homes to their occupiers under the right to buy (see Forrest and Murie 1988), the extent of true privatization, that is, transfer of services, assets or resources from the public to the private sector, has been relatively small. This is in marked contrast with the industrial sector, where major nationalized industries such as gas, electricity and telecommunications were sold off.

Instead, policy by the end of the 1980s followed a course of promoting 'quasi-markets'. The state retained its role as financer (purchaser) of services, but its role in directly *providing* services was transferred to independent providers (Le Grand and Bartlett 1993; Glennerster and Le Grand 1995). Fifteen years of Conservative government had not led, at least by 1995, to any wholesale privatization of the welfare state, nor indeed a crisis of welfare. Indeed, it was the resilience of key aspects of the welfare state which is striking.

In health and education, what were introduced were internal markets, or market-like mechanisms, and not the transfer of institutions or personnel into the private sector. Housing policy aimed at the eventual disappearance of council housing, but by transferring the remaining rented stock to a variety of non-profit providers rather than to the true private sector. Further education was shifted out of the local authority sector to independent control with a greater role for business interests, but this was balanced by reforms in higher education which increased state influence over the universities.

The one area where something like true privatization is occurring is arguably pensions. The growth of private and occupational schemes, the cutting of the link of the basic state pension with earnings, so that relative to average incomes the basic pension was worth less in 1993 than in 1948 (Hills 1993, p. 51), and the incentives given to people to leave SERPS (state earnings-related pension scheme) and take out private pensions, have together combined to shift pensions increasingly from the public to the private sector. By the mid-1990s over half of pension income was private (Glennerster and Le Grand 1995). But in general, the effect of the 1980s reforms in the British welfare state has been to create quasi-markets rather than to privatize.

A third theme is *centralization*, the concentration of power and control in the central government at Westminster. A key feature of the Thatcher and Major governments has been the steady erosion of all alternative or intermediary loci of power, particularly the trade unions and local authorities, but including also traditional bodies such as the church, the universities and the BBC. The erosion of local authority power, has been especially marked. An entire tier of local government (the Greater London Council and the metropolitan authorities) was abolished in 1986 by central government fiat. Through tax-capping powers the Secretary of State for the Environment now effectively controls the spending and taxation of every local authority in the country. Local government taxation now accounts for only about a fifth of local spending, with more than four-fifths centrally controlled and distributed according to formulae drawn up by government ministers. Local government has effectively become local administration.

In this context, describing local authorities as 'enablers' has rather a hollow ring. In practice, what has happened is that powers and responsibilities formerly exercised by democratically-controlled bodies, or bodies on which there was some democratic representation have been transferred to unelected quangos appointed by, and responsible to, government ministers. This process began in a rather modest way with the setting up of urban development corporations with extensive planning, land-dealing and financial powers to regenerate the docklands areas of London and Merseyside (Brownill 1990; Atkinson and Moon 1994). By the 1990s, a large proportion of public spending was channelled through a plethora of unelected bodies including NHS purchasing agents and trusts, housing action trusts, housing associations, training and enterprise councils, grant-maintained schools, and so on. Government ministers could now exercise considerable patronage in appointing the members and chairmen of this 'new magistracy'.

In effect, then, Britain had moved, not towards the residual American-style welfare state feared by many at the beginning of the 1980s, but rather towards a peculiar form of corporatism, a corporatism on two legs rather than three. Partnership was stressed, but this term essentially meant a partnership between business and government - trade union participation was anathema, in contrast with the continental corporatist emphasis on 'social partners'. Instead of representation by organized labour, there was instead the vague commitment to community participation, which in practice could mean almost anything.

British social policy in the 1980s and 1990s was often dominated by radical rhetoric from government, and pronouncements of doom from many observers. In practice, it is the continuities in the system more than the changes which are most apparent. However, this may change rapidly, at least in terms of service provision over the next decade, as the quasi-market reforms of the late 1980s and early 1990s begin to bite.

Finally, in discussing the continuities and resilience in the British welfare state, quiescence should perhaps also be mentioned. Over the last 15 years, there has been a major erosion of democratic accountability, of intermediary sources of power and influence. Unemployment has risen to, and persisted at what were previously thought to be 'unacceptably high' levels. Poverty and inequality have increased. And yet, with the important exception of sporadic outbreaks of rioting in inner cities and some peripheral estates, public protest has been remarkably limited. As one factor in the equation, the British facility for muddling through should not be discounted.

6.3.2 France: Social Exclusion and 'New Poverty'

Social policy in France has traditionally been of a broadly corporatist kind, that is, reflecting occupationally-based welfare, plural service delivery and an emphasis on social integration. In the last 15 years or so, however, policy has moved in the direction of greater targeting and a stronger emphasis on redistribution. Social protection remains primarily employment related, so that benefits are in effect a substitute income related to previous earnings. This 'continental' insurance model relies on benefits being funded mainly from employer and employee contributions (Hantrais 1995).

French social policy has been characterized by a strong pro-family theme. Family policy is dominant within the French social security system, and has clear goals: to compensate parents for the costs of children and thereby to promote a high birth rate. Lewis (1992) argues that to this extent, the system is gender-neutral. In her view the system is traditionally pro-natalist, with an emphasis on good mothering, but in the 1970s and 1980s, there was an increasing preoccupation with vertical rather than horizontal redistribution, via means testing and reducing the importance of family benefits.

French family policy appears then to have moved from a pro-natalist to a more explicitly redistributive orientation. Grignon (1993), however, disputes this, arguing that there is no clear development over time. Policy consists of a mix of quasi-redistributive transfers - both lump-sum and means-tested benefits - and regressive redistribution - for example, wage supplements for civil servants.

Social provision is characterized by pluralism. For example, there are three independent funds (*caisses*) for old age, sickness and family allowances. These are co-ordinated centrally but organized regionally, and are run by elected representatives from employers and beneficiaries (Chamberlayne 1992). The French system stresses local, regional, religious, occupational and political solidarities. Social protection is a complex system, with more than 500 different social security institutions. Moreover, the state's influence on the employers and employees who run these institutions varies considerably (OECD 1994). In the housing sphere, social housing is provided by independent HLM (*habitations à loyer modéré*) organizations, which include both government-sponsored (local and regional) and independent companies. Finance for social housing as we have seen is partly provided by a salary tax on employers as well as by state direction of funds invested in the 'Livret A' savings accounts.

Post-war French social policy has hence provided a relatively generous level of insurance-based benefits, but has not until recently provided a true safety net (Collins 1990). From the mid-1970s on there has been increasing concerns about those not covered by insurance benefits - so-called 'new poverty'. These include those affected by '*précarité*', that is, dependence on fluctuating or intermittent wages, the long-term unemployed, who having exhausted unemployment benefit after 12 months effectively fall out of the system, and young workers without a contribution record (Collins 1990; Chamberlayne 1992). Prior to 1988, such individuals had to fall back on local, family, church or charitable support. In 1988, the *revenu minimum d'insertion* (RMI) was introduced. This provides a means-tested safety net, but, according to Collins (1990), is intended to be a tool of social transformation rather than a form of social assistance. It is structured as a reciprocal undertaking rather than a welfare benefit; a *contrat d'insertion* is signed by both parties, renewable at three-month intervals. The contract includes a plan of action and steps to be taken by the individual (Collins 1990). Two-thirds of the target group are childless, and most are men, 'a reminder of the pre-emption of much poverty in France by family policy' (Chamberlayne 1992, p. 313). Similarly, Collins (1990) reports that 'Many of the applicants represent, in effect, the failure of earlier youth employment programmes which in their cases have led to nothing, and there is a heavy concentration in the 25-30 age group' (Collins 1990, p. 123).

The introduction of the RMI is one aspect of the increased importance of issues related to marginalization and social exclusion. Concern has been increasingly expressed during the last twenty years about the growth of so-called new poverty, linked to increased labour-market insecurity and unemployment, and giving rise to fears about a two-speed society. At the same time, these concerns in the social policy sphere have had little impact on the conduct of economic policy, which has for ten years been a model of orthodoxy, directed towards competitive disinflation and fiscal rectitude.

Unemployment rates rose in France from 2.7 per cent in 1973 to 5.9 per cent in 1979, 10.5 per cent in 1987, and 12 per cent in 1994 (OECD 1992, 1994). Youth unemployment in 1990 was 19.3 per cent, more than twice as high as in Britain (OECD 1992). Outbreaks of rioting on social housing estates in 1981 (Willmott and Murie 1988) led to a series of urban initiatives to try to improve economic, social and environmental conditions on peripheral estates. A series of active labour-market, employment and training measures have been enacted. The latest legislation is a multi-annual law combining reduced social security contributions for low-income earners, and the introduction of schemes for young workers paying below the minimum wage (to encourage job creation); streamlining of training schemes; assistance for the unemployed to start businesses; encouragement of part-time work; and encouragement of firms to move to short-time working as an alternative to redundancies (OECD 1994). In all, a fairly familiar list of labour-market measures predicated on the orthodox view that increased labour-market 'flexibility' and the removal of structural constraints are the only routes to lower unemployment.

French government and academia were relatively uninterested in the poverty issue until comparatively recently. For Silver (1993), the French debate on exclusion and poverty must be understood in the context of French ideas of citizenship and identity. In particular, the republican tradition, and the relatively strong, centralized state involvement in the economy and society are important:

> [French] ideology emphasizes the assimilation of regional, national and religious cultures into a distinctive conception of citizenship and national civilization actively promoted by the state. Republicanism is far more intolerant of diversity in public life than American pluralism. (Silver 1993, p. 346)

Hence the terminology of *insertion* and *exclusion* 'evoking republican citizenship rather than the social democratic, Marshallian notion' (Silver 1993, p. 347). Rioting in suburban social housing estates in the 1980s, on a more modest scale than in the USA or even in Britain led to the importation, by journalists and others, of a specifically American terminology of 'ghetto' and 'underclass'. As Silver comments: 'But the American term "underclass" connotes outsiders in terms of employment, race and middle-class culture, while *exclusion* weds economic deprivation to the lack of full citizenship and not being truly "French" in a cultural sense' (Silver 1993, pp. 347-8, original emphasis).

Wacquant (1993) makes similar points in his comparative study of an American ghetto (Chicago's South Side) and a French *banlieue* (la Courneuve in north-eastern Paris). First, the French *banlieue* is a highly heterogeneous place, with a majority of native-born residents, and a highly varied immigrant population. It is thus very different from the almost 100 per cent black ghettos of the USA, where residents have virtually no contact with the 'outside' white world. In the *banlieue*, the key social division is not between immigrants and natives, but between youths and others. Racial and ethnic categories 'have little social potency' (Wacquant 1993, p. 375). Where concentrations of residents of foreign descent do exist, Wacquant argues that this results from their class position, and not from ethno-racial segmentation of the housing market.

Furthermore, the stigma experienced by *banlieue* residents is residential only, as opposed to the 'spatial-cum-racial' stigma of US ghetto dwellers. So *banlieue* adolescents regularly go to other parts of the city where they can 'pass' - as long as they hide their address. Most importantly, second-generation immigrants from North Africa are in fact fast assimilating into French society. They have largely taken on the culture and behaviour of the French. Despite higher unemployment rate and lower income levels, empirical indicators reveal an improvement in living conditions. There is no evidence of greater spatial separation of these households. In fact the reverse; access into social housing is one vector of integration by comparison with the illegal *bidonvilles* and segregated 'guest-worker estates' run by the special housing authority SONACOTRA which housed the previous generation (Wacquant 1993, p. 379). Wacquant concludes that a 'Muslim underclass' is *not* forming; problems in the *banlieue* result from crises in employment, in education and in housing, not as a result of racial animosity.

Once again, social policy developments need to be understood in the context of economic policy goals. Throughout the 1980s and 1990s, following the collapse of 'Keynesianism in one country' in the early 1980s, France has followed a policy of the *franc fort* and competitive disinflation. The control of inflation and the maintenance of a strong currency have been the targets of economic management, and unemployment has been allowed to rise, and living standards to stagnate in pursuit of that goal. It is noteworthy, that despite having a socialist president throughout this period, and a socialist government for most of it, France has pursued a more consistently tough anti-inflation policy than Britain, despite the more vociferous claims of the latter. For once, Britain has actually proved to be more pragmatic in comparison with France:

> The leader who deserves the monetarist palm is François Mitterrand. ... Mr. Mitterrand's Socialist government allowed real wages to rise by less than 6 per cent between 1983 and 1989. ... Perhaps the main policy legacy of the 1980s will

turn out to be neither 'Reaganism' nor 'Thatcherism', but 'Mitterrandism'. (*Financial Times*, 20 April 1990, quoted in Halimi, Michie and Milne 1994)

This deflationary commitment continued under the centre-right government of Edouard Balladur. While unemployment is generally acknowledged to be the most important political issue, French macroeconomic policy remains steadfast in the importance it attaches to control of public expenditure and budget deficits, both because of its Maastricht commitments, and for purely domestic counter-inflationary reasons (OECD 1994). The OECD report also notes with favour the importance attached by the French government to structural reform, and comments on the 'too high' nature of both social expenditure and French labour costs. In their view more structural reforms are needed - these will cause short-term hardship, but are the only basis for sustainable growth (OECD 1994). The likelihood is, therefore, continued high levels of unemployment and associated poverty and exclusion.

6.3.3 Germany: Unification and Diversity

The post-war Federal Republic of Germany was characterized by stability and social integration around the central consensus notion of a social-market economy. As discussed in Chapter 4, this has meant commitment to the notion that social advance was best guaranteed by sustained non-inflationary economic growth. The German social state implies a commitment to socially and occupationally stratified welfare within a pluralist and corporatist system.

The starting point for any consideration of German social policy is the extent of political consensus around the commitment to a social market economy. In the concept of the social state (*Sozialstaat*) 'the state's general commitment to providing income and employment security is complemented by an emphasis on the obligations of private associations or groups (above all employers and trade unions), families and individuals to support themselves' (Ginsburg 1992, p. 68). There is no commitment to equalizing welfare outcomes, or even to a uniform safety net. Redistribution is mainly horizontal, within occupational and social groups with relatively modest vertical redistribution. However, until relatively recently the number of poor remained low.

While the Gini coefficient for Germany is higher than for most other countries, the gap between the poor and middle-income groups is narrower, perhaps because of the success of trade unions in the 1960s and 1970s in pushing for higher increases for lower-wage earners (Ginsburg 1992; Furmaniak 1984).

Pensions and unemployment benefits reflect existing occupational and income differences, rather than being universal. For example, the short-term unemployed with a full contribution record receive 68 per cent of previous take-home pay for a year (*Arbeitslosengeld.*) Those not eligible for this benefit are means tested for *Arbeitslosenhilfe* giving 58 per cent of net pay; the means test is, however, quite severe. A third group are dependent on the much lower levels of flat-rate benefit payable through social assistance (*sozialhilfe*), while it appears that 15-25 per cent of the registered unemployed in the 1980s were not in receipt of any benefit (Ginsburg 1992, pp. 76-7).

Hence the core social benefits are relatively generous. But social assistance is both more harshly means tested and carries more stigma (Mangen 1991). Despite steep rises in the numbers dependent upon social assistance, from 0.75 million adults in 1970 to 2.4 million in 1987, organization and advocacy among claimants remains low (Ginsburg 1992).

Germany can be characterized as a relatively 'depoliticized' welfare state, with a high degree of consensus, generous benefits for those with full contribution records which replicate rather than replace existing inequalities and hierarchies, and a stigmatized social assistance sector. In terms of recent policy, Mangen (1991) argues that despite neoliberal reforms to the social security system, traditional conservative influences, particularly on family policy, remain strong.

The influence of social catholicism can be seen in the policies of the CDU-led coalition governments, such as adherence to the principle of subsidiarity, and the resolution of conflict through social partnership and the self-administration of collective social provision. The Kohl governments have taken action to constrain the growth of the welfare state, promoting more pluralism, extolling self-help, extending privatization and commercialization, increasing the consumer contribution to costs, advocating a more flexible labour market and carrying out fiscal reforms. But, Mangen argues, Kohl is a party manager, not a theorist, and the aim is budget consolidation, not a dismantling of welfare systems. Moreover, the nature of the German polity makes radical social reform on new right principles impossible: the constraints of coalition government, consensus management, co-operative federalism, the role of social insurance funds, the plurality of voluntary organizations and constitutional limits in the form of the social and labour courts are too great.

In the 1980s, however, concern grew about marginalization, that is, the 'new social question' of those who have been excluded from the benefits of the welfare state. As a result of the occupationally stratified nature of welfare, there is considerable stigma attached to social assistance.

For much of the post-war period, the number of poor was relatively small. However, in the last two decades, there has been an increase in social differentiation. First, the effects of the economic slowdown have also been felt in Germany, with increases in West German unemployment levels, even before unification. Second, with unification, Germany in effect acquired a 'regional problem' in the sense that regional differences in income, unemployment, social and environmental conditions became much more marked compared with the relatively even (by international standards) levels of regional development in the old Federal Republic. Third, in-migration by refugees and asylum seekers from a range of countries as well as the presence of 'guestworkers' already resident in West Germany, has increased the population of 'foreigners' in the country. In addition, there has been an influx of ethnic Germans from Eastern Europe and the former Soviet Union.

The stratified nature of welfare arrangements will tend anyway to reinforce social distinctions among, for example, pensioners and the unemployed. But it is in relation to ethnic minorities that concerns are usually expressed about social exclusion. So-called 'guestworkers' have been present in the Federal Republic since the 1950s. After 1973, active recruitment ended. More recently, according to Ginsburg (1992) the term '*gastarbeiter*' has been replaced popularly with '*Auslander*' (foreigner) which has become pejorative, in a similar way to 'immigrant' in the UK. As a term it is applied exclusively to non-whites, who number about 4.5 million (7.5 per cent of the population), including 1.5 million Turks. Most live in ethnically segregated inner cities, in private rented tenements

It has been a fundamental policy principle that the Federal Republic is not and should not become a country of immigration. Only a tiny proportion of foreign workers have become naturalized German citizens. Children of foreigners remain foreigners, and the barriers to naturalization and citizenship are much higher than in other European countries. Nationality is by *jus sang* and not *jus soli*. The 1990 Immigration Law made right of abode easier for long-settled foreigners, but dual citizenship is impossible.

Economic and social policy have been closely linked in post-war Germany:

According to a by-now legendary dictum, for Erhard the 'best social policy is an effective economic policy'. But his understanding of the social dimension was a rejection of a robust redistributive role for the social state, since a strategic societal policy (*Gesellschaftspolitik*) as opposed to a narrower welfare policy (*Sozialpolitik*) would be more likely to support the generation of economic growth that would render redistribution superfluous. (Mangen 1991, p. 108)

The social policy regime was thus to a large degree predicated upon economic success and the maintenance of full employment. In the last few years, Germany has lost its image of being a low-inflation, low-unemployment country. Unemployment both east and west has risen considerably. In western Germany, unemployment is expected to peak in 1994 at 3 million or 9.5 per cent of the labour force, while in eastern Germany unemployment stabilized in 1992 at about 14 per cent. However, to the latter figure can be added a level of disguised unemployment through training schemes, job creation and subsidies to core industries. Unemployment in the east would be higher still without the fall in the size of the labour force through emigration, early retirement and the fall in female participation rates, and the estimated 400,000 east German residents who commute to jobs in the west (OECD 1993). Future development of social policy in Germany will depend in part on the success of economic policy in reducing unemployment and economic disruption.

6.4 BIFURCATION IN CONTEXT: HOUSING, URBAN CHANGE AND ECONOMIC RESTRUCTURING

The development of housing policies in the last two decades is linked not only to changes in the welfare states of each of the three countries, but also to more general processes of urban change and economic restructuring. For example, policies favouring owner-occupation have tended to reinforce trends towards suburbanization, given the location of much owner-occupied housing in the suburbs. At the same time positive policies of employment decentralization have led to the exodus of skilled workers, and to the unskilled and unemployed becoming trapped in the inner city or on peripheral social housing estates.

Indeed, housing policies have sometimes been advocated as instruments of urban economic development. In the OECD's view, housing policy can facilitate growth by speeding up structural adjustment and increasing labour flexibility (OECD 1988). In earlier, Keynesian times, the construction sector was used as an instrument for the maintenance of full employment. Housing construction and housing renewal projects could be an important source of both direct and indirect job creation. However, the extent to which such employment creation actually benefits disadvantaged urban residents is at least debatable, raising issues about job additionality and displacement.

More recently, in line with the shift from a Keynesian to a more market-orientated approach, the job-creation aspects of housing policy have become less important while housing's role in attracting inward capital investment into urban areas has been given greater attention. The upgrading of urban housing, planned gentrification, and shifts in the tenure pattern have become important aspects of the way in which post-industrial cities compete for highly mobile capital. At a fundamental level, the very fabric of cities is largely defined in terms of their economic and residential structures.

Hence, in order to understand how an orthodoxy emerged around so-called holistic approaches to housing problems, we need to look also at what has rapidly become the dominant policy response to economic restructuring. In order to understand housing policy, we need therefore to look at how broader policies which seek to cope with the consequences of economic restructuring - these include urban policy, regional policy and labour-market policies - have developed over the last 20 years.

The type of urban policies which had emerged by the late 1980s and early 1990s in many European countries, reflected a concern in particular with urban economic development and employment, as well as with housing, neighbourhood stabilization and environmental quality. These urban policies emerged as a response to well-established and widespread processes of suburbanization and decentralization - that is, the movement of both population and jobs out of cities. Problems of urban decline affect larger cities in particular - there is often a mismatch between the current size of a city (a product mainly of historical factors) and the functions which the city performs in the national and global urban system. As the OECD puts it: 'Many cities which grew to pre-eminence in the early twentieth century have a population size in the national settlement hierarchy which their current functional status would not seem to justify (OECD 1987, p. 18).

In this context of urban decline, the key role of urban policy is seen as being the revitalization of urban economies. Such policies should have the characteristic of being 'adaptive' - that is, they should be designed in order to facilitate or promote the adaptation of urban economies to a changed national and international economic environment (OECD 1987; Cheshire and

Hay 1989). Adaptive or enabling policies are contrasted with earlier, so-called defensive policies. For example, Cheshire et al., in a study for the European Commission, put forward one way of classifying policies into those 'preventing change' and those 'promoting adaptation' (Cheshire et al. 1986). Moreover, the suggestion is that policies in many European countries have steadily improved, that is, moved on from the purely defensive and ultimately self-defeating policies of the 1970s to the more flexible market-orientated approach of the 1980s and 1990s.

In the OECD's view, future economic growth will be based on the diffusion of new technologies. The role of urban policies is, therefore, to bring about, 'the necessary institutional transformation in OECD countries that could facilitate this process' (OECD 1987, p. 19). The goals of urban policies are therefore to strengthen the comparative position of urban economies in order to increase employment and the participation of disadvantaged groups and minorities; and to improve the physical environment. Urban problems are seen as symptoms of adjustment to changes in the functions and the supply-side conditions of particular cities interacting with the adaptive capacity of the local economy and social structure (Cheshire 1990).

Hence, the *causes* of urban problems are seen to lie in decentralizing demographic and economic processes, and the *role* of policy is defined in terms of revitalizing urban economies by facilitating adaptation to the changed economic environment. By the 1990s, urban policy had become focused more on issues of urban economic development. Policies, whether pursued by national or local governments, were to be adaptive rather than defensive, meaning a strong orientation towards the market. The role of policy is to facilitate adaptation to world market conditions, not to modify or even to challenge the premises on which the notion of a global marketplace is constructed. European cities thus become competitors with each other within a new international spatial division of labour; urban policy becomes dominated by urban entrepreneurialism (Parkinson 1989). Planners and other public officials become active agents in the process of economic restructuring, by seeking to attract industry and jobs through offering attractive packages to employers (Fainstein 1990).

Moreover, it is not only the economic, but also the residential structure of cities which must be made attractive in order to ensure that the city does not slip down the international hierarchy. Several studies have shown that it is the occupational rather than the industrial structure of cities that is important (OECD 1987). Prosperous cities have higher proportions of professional and

white-collar occupations. The residential base thus becomes an asset of
greater of lesser worth for the post-industrial city, just as the manufacturing
base was for the industrial city. Moreover, such an approach can be justified
on equity as well as efficiency grounds. For example, Dangschat quotes the
Mayor of Hamburg in 1983, arguing that 'it is the best protection for the
socially weak, if Hamburg can be more attractive for the better-offs'
(Dangschat 1990).

A similar view is taken by the European Commission regarding the goals
of structural funds expenditure. Hence, in the Delors Report on Economic
and Monetary Union we find the following view of regional policy:

> The principal objective of regional policies should not be to subsidize incomes and
> simply offset inequalities in standards of living, but to help to equalize production
> conditions through investment programmes in such areas as physical infrastructure,
> communications, transportation and education so that large scale movements of
> labour do not become the major adjustment factor. (Quoted in Tsoukalis 1993, p.
> 246)

Similarly, Begg and Mayes (1991) distinguish policies of structural
intervention from policies of inter-regional transfers, the latter having the
danger that they may in fact sustain the clientilist culture and create
dependency. According to Martin and Tyler (1992) successful regions are
characterized by their 'flexibility' in adapting to change. Flexibility in this
context has several attributes; flexibility in the labour market; flexibility in
organizational response; in enterprise development; and in capital-market
response (provision of venture capital). Regional policies should, therefore,
seek to develop and support such flexibility.

What about the leading social and economic problem of the 1990s in
Europe: unemployment? Regional and urban policies often aim, in principle
at least, at creating or keeping jobs in areas which have high levels of
unemployment and whose economic structure, geographical location, or
other circumstances suggest are vulnerable to further job losses and unlikely
to attract much in the way of new jobs in a free market. Labour-market
policies are similarly designed to help unemployed individuals back into
work, or in some cases, prevent individuals currently employed from losing
their jobs. But is this just rhetoric or a serious attempt at reducing
unemployment?

Aiming to do something about concentrations of unemployment might
mean one of three things:

1.   reducing the level of unemployment overall;
2.   spreading a given level of unemployment more evenly across different areas and sections of the population;
3.   ameliorating the conditions of the unemployed.

Urban and regional policies as well as active labour-market policies are sometimes discussed as if they were designed to achieve (1), a reduction in unemployment overall. But such a belief conflicts with the core dominant belief on the role of macroeconomic policy espoused both by member-state governments and by the EU, the economic orthodoxy that has been universal since the collapse of France's 'Keynesianism in one country' in 1983. Governments by and large accept the primacy of the control of inflation among the various goals that policy might have. Traditional Keynesian demand-side policies to boost output and employment and thereby reduce unemployment are considered to be ineffective if not actually perverse; 'real' growth and jobs result from private investment and private activity which require, above all, stable prices.

Hence the level of unemployment is in effect set nationally, or even supra-nationally via the ERM, and particularist policies cannot influence it except through better matching of unemployed people to vacancies. This could be via providing better information about job opportunities to local unemployed people; through training and re-training programmes; by locational policies that attract firms into high-unemployment areas; or through encouraging changes in attitudes towards work by the unemployed (including preparedness to take lower wages).

Apart from some possible improvement in labour-market matching, then, urban policy cannot have an impact on national levels of unemployment, unless governments were to adopt a much more relaxed view about inflation. This has led some analysts to conclude that the only effective solution must lie with national macroeconomic policies rather than with urban and regional policies.

However, policies can affect the *location* of jobs, and hence the distribution of unemployment. Urban and regional policies can attract jobs into a specific location (or retain existing jobs there) but only at the price of a contraction of employment somewhere else. Training programmes can enable long-term unemployed or other disadvantaged groups to compete more effectively but against other unemployed people. Given a credible government commitment to a particular fiscal and monetary stance, these policies are essentially a zero-sum game. The point is clearly made by the authors of a study of labour-market policies and unemployment in the OECD:

> For a given level of aggregate demand in the economy it has to be asked whether job creation measures or employment subsidies can increase the total number of jobs. If the total number of jobs does not increase, the justification for shifting the work available from one line of activity to another, or from one individual to another, seems unclear. If the number of jobs does increase, it might be expected to affect pressure of demand in the labour market and thus jeopardize the objective of controlling inflation. (Jackman et al. 1990, p. 9)

However, at the urban or regional level, a case *can* be made out for 'shifting the work available' from one group to another. This might be in order to break up concentrations of unemployment, with their attendant negative externalities; or to spread job opportunities around more fairly; or to reduce the ratio of long-term unemployed within the unemployment total. These are all very important policy goals, with significant and substantive effects on the welfare of particular households. More generally, much urban policy can be seen in terms of an offset to the anti-urban bias of government programmes and expenditure. But the point remains that this is not the same as 'reducing unemployment' in a national sense. Training, counselling and work-placement measures can only be effective where there is a relatively high ratio of vacancies to unemployed. Wage subsidies may create job opportunities for the long-term unemployed, but in doing so 'substitute the target group for other (non-subsidized) candidates, impact on the wages of existing employees and cause displacement of jobs in other companies through the product market' (Tarling et al. 1992, p. 137). In their review of policy responses to long-term unemployment in the European Community, Tarling et al. (1992) found that enterprise creation, including by co-ops, was the most effect measure in terms of relatively low displacement, that is, the ability to create jobs rather than just redistribute existing ones.

An alternative, ameliorative rationale for urban policies remains. That is, while such policies may not have any effect on the level of unemployment nationally or even locally, they can improve the living conditions of unemployed people. This might be through housing improvements and the provision of communal, cultural and sporting facilities; or through enabling unemployed people to undertake voluntary or community work; or through training and personal development programmes designed to keep the unemployed in contact with 'work discipline' - and more positively to prepare themselves to take advantage of future opportunities arising from an economic upturn.

Although the rhetoric surrounding policy suggests that reducing unemployment - aim (1) - is the goal, in practice redistributing it is usually the best that can be hoped for. Much of the time not even this is achieved - the amelioration of current conditions rather than their removal is what is being aimed at. Alongside this has been the growing tendency of governments and bodies such as the EU and the OECD to stress solutions to problems of inequality which are 'bottom up', community led or 'holistic'. The creed of this approach is that the range of problems affecting a local area needs to be tackled through several agencies working together.

The emphasis is on *local* solutions to local problems: the involvement of the local 'community' (rarely defined) and the local business sector is seen as being crucial to the success of urban regeneration, housing and local economic development programmes. This 'bootstraps' strategy has become the conventional wisdom with regard to local economic development in a remarkably short space of time, and is a paradigm shared by the political left, right and centre (Eisenschitz and Gough 1993).

The role of extra-local factors - such as national and international economic restructuring or national macroeconomic policies - is played down. But structural factors will be decisive. If national governments across the EU, together with supranational institutions such as a future European Central Bank, consistently pursue deflationary policies which ensure high unemployment, then particularist policies will have little effect. The OECD, for example, incessantly stresses the need for 'structural reforms' and 'flexibility' with an almost religious fervour. For example:

> Unemployment, which is high and rising in many countries, may not decline much in the coming recovery ... there would seem to be little scope for unemployment rates to come down much without stoking inflation, unless significant further progress is made with structural reforms to improve the functioning of labour markets. (OECD 1991b)

So unless workers become more mobile and/or accept lower wages, continuing high levels of unemployment will be necessary to keep EU governments on track for the counter-inflationary convergence to which they are now politically committed. The doctrine that there is 'no alternative' to market forces coupled with the repeated assertions that labour markets require structural reform, urban policies should be 'adaptive' and regional policy should not try to resist the sectoral consequences of world-wide restructuring of economic activity and the division of labour, in effect requires local communities to bootstrap themselves out of the cycle of economic decline and deprivation into which national and international forces have pushed them.

Where does this leave housing policy? Certainly, activist policies, such as the post-war British New Towns programme, which aimed to move workers to the location of new economic growth are rejected. Instead the emphasis is on community regeneration and local economic development, with the rehabilitation or even demolition of existing social housing, often a key ingredient. The rationale for how housing investment can act as a catalyst for sustained economic development, or why the elusive goal of national economic growth can best be attempted by concentrating resources on those communities and geographical areas least likely to provide fertile ground for self-sustaining endogenous growth, is never explained. In practice, many of these programmes are essentially ameliorative (a worthwhile objective) while being cloaked in a rhetoric of growth and development.

We can now see how the bifurcation of housing policy is consistent with a more general trend in which responsibilities for social outcomes have been progressively decentralized, from national states to local communities, while responsibility for economic management has been pushed (or pulled) upwards to the supranational EU level, and also 'outward' to the realm of market forces. The bifurcation, or 'splitting apart' of housing policy necessarily follows from housing's dual nature as the object of both economic and social policy. So, markets, rather than governments, have taken on the role of determining levels of output and investment, and of bringing supply and demand into balance. But national governments have also to some extent reduced their responsibilities for social aspects of housing policy, transferring duties (and in some cases resources) to local or neighbourhood level.

6.5 CONCLUSIONS

In this chapter we have briefly surveyed the evidence on rising inequality and polarization in Europe as a whole, and in Britain, France and Germany in particular. We have also briefly examined the response of welfare policies to this growth in inequality, and we have looked at the connections between bifurcation in housing and the broader process of urban economic restructuring.

Not surprisingly, in surveying developments in the welfare states of France and Germany we find both similarities and differences compared with Britain. The overall impression is one in which similar concerns are raised and in which neoliberal approaches have a significant impact. But these factors are expressed within a very different set of institutions and practices, an essentially different welfare-state regime. Paradoxically, the greater pluralism in the continental systems - the range of social security funds, health insurance funds, social housing companies - make radical changes in the direction of greater privatization less likely. This is reinforced by the less centralized nature of policy: in Germany the division of powers between Federal, state and local government being enshrined in the basic law, while in France an extensive programme of decentralization was carried out in the early 1980s.

But underlying these differences we find strong similarities in terms of policy makers' views about the role of the state, about the ineffectiveness of much public policy, about the importance of market forces, about the correct policy responses to economic restructuring, and perhaps most important of all, about the implicit resignation to greater inequality and polarization as phenomena which governments may deplore but in practice can do little to affect.

The more detailed examination of the development of policy responses to the urban effects of economic restructuring in the last section bears this out. Everywhere, there is a retreat from the *comprehensive* responsibility of the national state to achieve specific outcomes in welfare. Responsibilities for welfare now rest with a combination of national governments, local communities and the European Union, as well as, of course, 'the market'.

It is important to place the discussion of housing policies within this broader context. By doing so, we can avoid the fallacy of the pseudo-medical approach to policy analysis, discussed in Chapter 1, and begin to understand the reasons both for the similarities in the general direction of housing policies in the three countries, and the continuing differences. What we have found is that there are important similarities in terms of the effects of economic restructuring and the growth of inequality and social polarization. This has led to increased policy concerns about marginalization and social exclusion. But the ability of social policy to respond to such concerns has been constrained in each country by the subordination of social policy to economic policy of an orthodox kind, and by the belief that the state's role is primarily to facilitate and support market forces, including in particular promoting more flexible labour markets.

At the same time it would be quite wrong to analyse the situations in Britain, France and Germany as being simply three national representations of a general process. In each country, the underlying issues and conflicts are mediated through a unique set of institutions, an inherited set of historical practices and a specific national politics.

Having placed housing policies in a broader context we are now better able to evaluate them in a genuinely comparative way, and in particular to assess whether the development of policy over the last two decades should be described as a process of policy convergence, or in some other way. This is the task of the final chapter.

7. Policy Convergence or Policy Collapse?

7.1 INTRODUCTION

In drawing conclusions from a study of housing policies in three countries, one is faced with two immediate and related problems. First, one has to assess the relative importance of the similarities and differences between the three countries studied. What do these similarities and differences tell us about the causes both of system change and policy change? Second, how do these empirical findings relate to the theoretical literature: do the findings confirm or refute the theoretical hypotheses, and does theory help or hinder us in trying to make sense of the findings?

7.2 THE CONVERGENCE DEBATE

The focus of many comparative housing policy studies is primarily empirical, with theory kept to a minimum. For example, in one of the earliest comparative studies, McGuire (1981) identified four policy 'cycles': first, acute shortage and an emphasis on stimulating production; second, an objective of increasing the size of units; third, a focus on higher quality; and fourth, reduction in the state burden by switching from indiscriminate to targeted subsidies. A decade later Boelhouwer and van der Heijden (1992) in their seven-country study identified four policy 'stages' in the period 1970-90. These are: a quantitative stage; a qualitative stage; an emphasis on distributive issues; and finally the re-emergence of housing shortages. Boelhouwer and van der Heijden's typology is more flexible than McGuire's; stages do not necessarily coincide for all countries and some stages can occur simultaneously in the same country.

The concept of policy 'cycles' is not a particularly useful one. By suggesting a process of circulation and repetition it entirely misses the idea of a *dynamic* change from one phase of policy to the next. It suggests a 'natural' progression from one set of problems to the next, ignoring the complex interplay between structural change, political action and policy change, which is a main concern in this book. Much of this literature rests on an implicit pseudo-medical explanatory model, as discussed in Chapter 1.

Boelhouwer and van der Heijden's typology is useful as a descriptive tool, but does not take us very far in terms of providing an explanation as to why successive stages of policy should occur at all, let alone occur at different times in different countries. They do, however, correctly emphasize the (often implicit) role that convergence theories have played in comparative housing research: 'Despite ... criticisms, convergence theory forms the theoretical framework of much social scientific research, including most (comparative) housing research' (Boelhouwer and van der Heijden 1992, p. 5). These authors follow Schmidt (1989) in tracing this influence back to the work of Donnison (1967). The core idea is that similarity of economic and demographic developments in different countries, will mean that housing policies will converge, despite differences in politics, ideology and institutional arrangements.

This approach to the comparative study of housing policies can hence be seen as one example of what Wilensky et al, (1987) identified as the dominant approach to welfare-state research, that is, the explanation of rising welfare-state expenditures as the consequence of economic development and socioeconomic convergence across countries. This strand of research is close to what Esping-Andersen calls the 'systems/structuralist' approach: industrialization makes social policy both necessary - because pre-industrial modes of social organization are destroyed - and possible - through the rise of modern bureaucracy. Hence, 'this approach is inclined to emphasize cross-national similarities rather than differences; being industrialized or capitalist over-determines cultural variations or differences in power relations, (Esping-Andersen 1990, p. 12). Esping-Andersen, of course, is concerned to emphasize the differences rather than the similarities between countries, using the key concept of welfare-state regime (see Chapter 1).

Many comparative studies of housing policies in Europe make use of the concept of policy convergence. A good example is the work of Ghékiere (1991, 1992). Ghékiere argues for 'certain types' of convergence in the housing policies of the EU12 in the 1980s; specifically, that there is a 'convergence model', relevant to a growing number of countries which transcends the national context, and even the political colour of the government in power (Ghékiere 1992, p. 205). He argues that though there are important differences, particularly between the countries where there has been a sharp break with the previous model - by which he includes the UK, Spain, Ireland and the Netherlands - and those where there has been some continuity and some continuing adherence to the principle of social economy (especially France and Germany), the key change is from the 'long boom' model of massive state intervention, through state building programmes and rent control, and the post-1975 model.

He defines this latter convergence model as being ideologically driven by the doctrine of the minimal state, imported from the USA, welcomed and developed in the 'Anglo-Saxon' countries (presumably the UK) but progressively adopted in other European countries, and 'even' within the EU organizations. The model comprises disengagement of the state from housing, abolition or liberalization of rent control, and the determination of investment levels by private rather than public activity. The Anglo-Saxon model is posited on the hypothesis that because housing need and supply are globally in balance, disequilibria (that is, unmet needs) persist only because of rigidities in the market, not because of inadequate supply. Hence the main regulatory role should fall to the market, with the state's role being limited to the correction of dysfunctions. The model typically is implemented through a shift to targeted support, decentralization of housing policy and the dismantling of specific systems of actors and circuits of financing (*banalisation*).

Ghékiere admits that this model is 'rather caricatured' (p. 219) and cannot be strictly applied to each of the (then) twelve member states of the EU, but argues that the convergence model guides the direction of policy. Its application '*pure et dure*' is restricted to the UK, Ireland and the Netherlands, countries with 'liberal' or 'ultraliberal' governments. Policy in Germany, Denmark and France, by contrast is characterized by the 'continual adaptation' of the instruments of intervention, so there has not been such a break with previous policies. That is, Ghékiere argues that these countries have more flexible housing policy mechanisms, as opposed to the more rigid and hence antiquated systems elsewhere.

The policy convergence case is unconvincing. Ghékiere draws too great a distinction between Anglo-Saxon radicals and Rhineland pragmatists. Housing policy in Britain after 1979 had many continuities with earlier periods - increased control by central government, bipartisan support for owner-occupation, the shift towards means testing, mechanisms to raise social and private rents, and so on. Ghékiere also claims that in Britain, social rented housing was financed by 'direct state loans, rarely repaid', and hence the costs of the system rapidly became prohibitive, while in Germany and France, the system of public loans was progressively diversified. In fact, local authority loans in Britain have always been raised directly or indirectly (via the Public Works Loans Board) from the market, and do of course get repaid over time, the loan charges falling on the Housing Revenue Account. Indeed, it is precisely the low debt encumbrance of many smaller British local authorities as these loans were paid off that made stock transfers attractive as a form of privatization from the mid-1980s on. At the same time, as shown in Lefebvre et al. (1991) among others, the French system of financing social housing has encountered considerable difficulties caused by disintermediation reducing the funds available from Livret A accounts. Similarly, as Harloe (1995) has pointed out, it is 'corporatist' Germany that, together with Britain, has gone furthest in privatizing its social rented stock.

Ghékiere claims that 12 years of ultra liberal policy in Britain has 'degraded' the UK situation and multiplied homelessness and exclusion through reduced supply. While the trend in British housing policy is not disputed, it is important to point out that even by the mid-1990s, Britain had a much larger social sector than either Germany or France, and that in Britain, unlike the other two countries, there is a legal right of access to housing for certain groups of homeless households. Homelessness may appear to be a greater problem in Britain than in France or Germany precisely because of the existence of this legally enforceable right to housing for some groups. Statistics on priority homelessness in Britain measure a channel of access into social rented housing rather than the level of social exclusion. Of course, this is not to deny that homelessness, including street homelessness, is a problem in Britain, or to deny that it has worsened over the last 20 years. It is simply to point out that the data for accurate inter-country comparisons do not yet exist (Bayley 1994).

Furthermore, as discussed in Chapter 3 above, it was in France rather than in Britain that 'Anglo-Saxon' monetary orthodoxy was applied most consistently through the 1980s and 1990s. Britain, despite the hard-line rhetoric, has swung wildly between hairshirt 'sado-monetarism' and binges of debased Keynesianism in the form of tax cuts and 'dashes for growth'. Clearly, there *are* important differences between Britain on the one hand and

France and Germany on the other - in terms of ideology, of institutions, and of practice - but these differences require a more sophisticated formulation to capture them

More generally, the convergence debate does need to be approached carefully. Apparent similarities do not imply convergence. At the heart of the debate is a process by which various social, economic and political trends, common to more than one country, are mediated through a set of national institutions, policy traditions, history and culture which are unique to individual countries. The result of this is a complex pattern which requires careful analysis.

It is the apparent similarities between housing policies in different countries - for example, the supposed disengagement of the state, the switch from producer to consumer subsidies - which leads commentators such as Ghékiere to speak of convergence in European housing policies. But the term convergence - at least in its strong form - entails more than mere similarity. It conveys the idea of a causal process by which the housing systems of different countries *necessarily* become more alike over time. Indeed the concept of convergence is grounded in the sociological literature on the theory of industrialism; it implies the view that industrialization is the motor of social change, and that all industrial societies will converge towards a similar form of mixed economy with substantial state intervention (Harloe and Martens 1983). Convergence theory implied that the logic of industrialism would lead not to class conflict, but to elite leadership and mass response. Pluralistic industrialism would generate convergence, as there were in effect no ideological choices left. But in practice, the pattern has been one of divergence, rather than convergence (Goldthorpe 1984).

As shown in Chapter 6, the evidence on convergence in economic indicators between member states or between regions in the EU, is, at the very least, inconclusive. Moreover, there are good reasons to believe that further economic integration is more likely to produce greater divergence rather than convergence in living standards throughout the European Union. The Maastricht Treaty and the whole process of economic and monetary union is predicated on the idea that 15 or more EU economies can and will converge to the point where they can be painlessly joined together. But, as we have seen in the four years since the Treaty was signed, the attempt at such forced economic convergence has given rise to powerful countervailing political forces, both within the EU and within individual member states.

Clearly, there are important forces - both economic and political - which act in the direction of greater convergence between the housing policies of

European countries. But accounts which stress only these forces are necessarily partial. We should, therefore, reject convergence theory as an overarching, linear, uni-directional explanation of trends in housing policies.

Nevertheless, we can identify important common *themes* in policy development in the recent period. These include:

* a greater role for markets in the production, allocation and financing of housing;
* the promotion and encouragement of owner-occupation;
* a switch from new building to renovation;
* an emphasis on the cost-effectiveness of policy measures;
* greater market orientation and private sector ethos of social housing agencies;
* at the same time, wider responsibilities of social housing agencies to house the poor and cater for a range of disadvantaged and special needs groups;
* targeting of social housing subsidies as part of a widespread trend in social policy towards selectivity;
* deregulation of housing finance markets;
* an emphasis on 'holistic' solutions to problems of poor housing and concentrated poverty.

We can identify broad policy trends, but these do not amount to a process of convergence. Moreover, these broad trends are mediated through the specific institutions, politics and histories of each country. The importance of these differences should not be underestimated. This can be illustrated with an example: rent-pooling in Britain. For specific historical and political reasons (Daunton 1987) there was an established social housing stock in Britain prior to 1939, owned by the local authorities. This specific historical circumstance allowed the use of rent-pooling and hence cross-subsidy within the stock as a way of keeping down the rents of new social units, an option that was not available elsewhere in Europe. Hence this particular policy development can only be understood by reference to specific historical and political factors. But once in existence, the use of rent-pooling as a device had important consequences for the development of social housing in Britain (Malpass 1990) including, arguably, a weaker incentive to maintain the stock because of the lack of a direct link between an individual tenant's rent and the service received (Emms 1990).

The same point could be demonstrated using examples from other countries. The important conclusion is that historical circumstances, political forces or institutional structures in part determine the shape of specific policies. These policies in their turn then impact on the institutions, agents and households within the housing system, setting parameters for further changes to the system. This is what is meant by saying that policy development is path dependent.

7.3 THE COLLAPSE OF HOUSING POLICY

Having rejected policy convergence as an overarching explanatory concept, is there anything we can put in its place? As an alternative formulation to policy convergence, we could construct a narrative of housing policy development which emphasizes the weakening, or even collapse, of housing policy in the three countries studied. The starting point for this is that, as traditionally understood, housing policy was about estimating housing needs, setting quantitative output targets, boosting housebuilding, especially in recessions, raising the average physical condition of the stock, removing substandard housing, and pursuing a goal of a decent home for every household.[1] It was these sorts of considerations that dominated discussions of housing policy in the three decades after 1945, and indeed the debate on the 'Housing Question' for a half-century or more prior to that.

The ending of the crude shortage of housing units in many European countries led to a weakened perception of housing as a national issue. Housing began to be seen more as a range of local, sectional and special needs issues. Policy has shifted from mass solutions to individual solutions.

The interests of the majority of the population are largely served by the state intervening mainly to ensure continuity and reasonable conditions in the market. This means providing a legal framework for the execution of contracts; ensuring a supply of finance; supplying output to some degree, especially counter-cyclically; providing a land-use planning framework; maintaining affordability through subsidies, especially to owner-occupiers; and, perhaps most importantly, ensuring steady economic growth and *relatively* full employment.

Other aspects of housing policy, for example, homelessness, social housing provision, means-tested housing allowances, are provided to a minority of the population, a minority which is increasingly segregated or at least differentiated from the majority in terms of its location, its ethnic group or its household type. Whatever the formal appearance, such policies and their associated expenditures are consented to by the majority not as a form of collective provision, but rather as an expression of altruism (helping the poor); or as an insurance payment against riot, theft or social disorder; or as socially necessary expenditure (because low paid but essential workers need to live somewhere). This fragmentation or bifurcation is much more pronounced with regard to housing than it is in regard to other social policies such as health or education, both because of the nature of housing, which has many of the characteristics of a private good (Barr 1987, pp. 408-10) and also because of the fact that housing was never provided in Western Europe as a universalist social service.

At the same time, the state has tried to reduce its own share of housing costs, and thereby to bring about an increase in the share borne by households themselves. Several factors are relevant here. With economic growth, real incomes rise and households can bear a larger proportion of costs without hardship. At the same time, central and local governments facing 'fiscal crisis' through the continual growth in assumed responsibilities and hence expenditures, have sought to pull back from commitments. But rising average prosperity has been accompanied by falling real incomes for some, and increases in both poverty and inequality. Although the state has attempted to reduce its share of housing costs, in practice this has been difficult to implement, as cuts in producer subsidies lead to greater take-up of means-tested allowances, and economic restructuring raises unemployment and hence benefit payments.

Alongside this, there has been a trend towards devolution and decentralization. Again, this is a complex process. It is clear that central governments have become more aware of the boundaries of their own competence and abilities.   But the actions of central government in redefining a narrower role for itself has both negative and positive consequences for local areas.   Decentralization can be a means of encouraging pluralism and sharing power, or it can simply be a way of offloading responsibilities by devolving responsibility but not power or resources (Johnson 1987).

The decentralization of responsibility is common to Britain, France and Germany. But in terms of political and institutional relationships, Britain is very different from the other two countries. In Britain, local authorities are viewed by central government as a problem, rather than as a resource (Goodchild and Truscott 1988). In Britain, despite greater centralization, the government appears able to avoid responsibility for overall conditions in the housing market. In Germany in the mid-1980s public disquiet over soaring rents and homelessness translated into sufficient political pressure on the housing minister to cause a change of direction, and the announcement of the 'million homes' programme. In Britain, rising homelessness, mortgage repossessions and dismal output levels provoke no such reaction. Britain seems in this regard to be a country of extremes. From an almost total reliance on the local authorities as providers of new housing, policy has swung towards the almost complete marginalization of local authorities within the policy-making system.

We can see, then, that housing policy in the traditional sense has virtually collapsed. It has bifurcated, that is, split apart, leaving behind two separate but related sets of policy issues. On the one hand there is a set of issues which relate to concentrations of poverty, associated with economic restructuring and social disintegration. These are not fundamentally bricks-and-mortar issues, or even about housing management and housing finance. They are increasingly about social dysfunction, about the collapse of communities, about the impacts of mass unemployment and poverty on everyday life.

At the same time, we have a second set of issues which are far removed from this grim picture, but equally distant from the earlier concerns of output targets and physical standards. These issues revolve mainly around the continuing expansion of owner-occupation as a visible sign of economic and social success, both for the individual household and for society as a whole, including maintaining the value of the asset to the households which have purchased it. The key development is the normalization of property ownership as a route to social stability.

Despite the rhetoric about the fight against social exclusion, the reality is that the European political economy is now founded in practice on the acceptance at a more or less permanent level, of a continuing divide between the haves and have-nots in each country. In housing policy, this underlying belief finds expression in the retreat of national governments from responsibility for achieving more equal housing outcomes. As the divide grows, policy bifurcates between on the one hand measures to maintain market stability for the majority, either in terms of mass owner-occupation or a more balanced private renting/owner-occupation split, and on the other hand, measures to alleviate some of the worst excesses for the poor, while transferring responsibility from national to local, or even community level. The rhetoric of so-called holistic solutions supposedly integrating housing, employment and welfare aspects has been accompanied by the state withdrawing from its responsibility for full employment and reducing its welfare commitment. The emphasis on empowerment, localism and bootstraps approaches needs to be seen in this light.

Contemporary debates about housing resonate with echoes from pre-1914 debate on the housing question, just as the contemporary debate on the urban underclass is marked by conscious and unconscious parallels with Victorian discussion of the social residuum (Macnicol 1987)[2]. It is almost as if the debate has resumed at the point reached prior to the establishment of the post-war welfare states. Increasingly, it is not the economic restructuring and neoliberalism of the 1980s and 1990s that appears to be a deviation from trend, but rather the three decades of welfare-state optimism after 1945.

Against this background we can then see the collapse - or at least the bifurcation - of housing policy as part and parcel of the way in which both economy and society have changed since the end of the long boom. That is, we see in housing the reflection of the broader pattern of welfare division and polarization.

7.4   EVALUATION: HOUSING POLICY AS WELFARE DIVISION

Comparative housing studies must accommodate both the common patterns of social and economic change and also specific national circumstances. Harloe (1995) in his major study of social housing in six countries (Britain, France, Germany, Netherlands, Denmark and the USA) argues that in comparative studies of housing policy, one must account for both similarities and differences across countries - a position I fully support. Harloe quotes Gourevitch (1986) with approval: '[e]ach country is affected by these twin factors: the force of epochs, which cuts across the particularities of circumstance, and the force of national trajectories, which expresses the features specific to each nation's history' (Gourevitch 1986, p. 217). Harloe goes on to attack the three-fold typology of Esping-Anderson which classifies welfare states as Anglo-Saxon, corporatist or social-democratic, and criticizes the concept of 'welfare state regime' itself. He concludes: 'the analysis of the dynamics of structures of housing provision is not helped by any fixed categorization of regime types, especially as these have not been constructed with empirical reference to the history of housing markets and policies' (Harloe 1995, p. 534).

What Harloe appears to be saying is that these categories, developed by reference to other aspects of social policy, are not useful in studying housing markets and policies comparatively. While agreeing with Harloe's specification of the problem, I disagree with his rejection of the principle of applying welfare typologies to the study of housing. Although strict typologies of welfare-state regimes tend to break down when confronted with the complexity and hybridity of actually existing systems, the broad distinction between the Anglo-Saxon British welfare state and the corporatist systems of France and Germany is meaningful. This distinction, established in the literature at the level either of general analysis of the welfare state or specifically in relation to social insurance, has been found to be of some relevance to the study of housing policies, as Chapters 2, 3 and 4 have demonstrated.

Britain, in comparison with France and Germany has: a greater commitment to, indeed obsession with, owner-occupation; a weak private rented sector; unusual dominance of local authority ownership of rented housing; and particularly severe pauperization and means-tested dependence in the social sector. Additionally, there is a greater concern with housing policy as a redistributive tool rather than a reflection of the status order; far greater centralization of policy with a minor role for sub-national government in policy formulation; greater mistrust of the state as an active agency in implementing change; a more deregulated and *laissez-faire* environment; and since the 1960s a rejection of national output targets. If we make use of the question Esping-Andersen posed with regard to social insurance, the choice for British housing policy of 'whether to allow the market or the state to furnish adequacy and satisfy middle-class aspirations' was answered with a clear decision in favour of the market.

How can we reconcile both the similarities and differences between Anglo-Saxon and corporatist policy regimes? Convergence arguments often seem to take one of two opposed forms. In the first version, Europe is seen as converging to the Anglo-Saxon model. Britain is Airstrip One, the unsinkable aircraft carrier to which American free-market ideologies are flown for re-export to regional markets. As with Japanese cars and Korean hi-fis, Britain is the point of entry through which foreign state-of-the-art ideology gains access to previously sheltered European markets. As free-market liberal ideology becomes ever stronger, both corporatist welfare states and even the saintly European Union succumb.

In the alternative version, the process is reversed. Britain is an aberration - an atavistic nation-state of a kind which has become obsolescent elsewhere in Western Europe, and which has been kept alive only through the continuing effects of the powerful and unique political phenomenon known as Thatcherism. However, Britain's institutions desperately require modernizing, and this process will inevitably take Britain closer to the norm of the modern European welfare state, which is essentially the traditional Rhineland corporatist state - somewhat modified and more market friendly, but clearly recognizable through its emphasis on consensus, on modernization and on partnership.

The evidence that I have presented in this book shows that neither of these versions can be sustained. First, as Harloe shows, housing has always been an anomalous and ambiguous component of the welfare state. The majority of citizens in all Western European countries as well as in the USA have been housed by private sector activity, with only a minority in the social sector. Indeed, apart from the Netherlands, the largest social sector in Europe is found not in any of the corporatist or social-democratic countries, but in Britain. While the promotion of owner-occupation and the deregulation of finance markets have proceeded much further in Britain than elsewhere, the differences seem to be those of degree, not those of kind.

Second, as we have seen, some aspects of the French and German housing systems reflect a more thoroughgoing liberal ideology than in Britain. The course of French housing policy in the last decade has been strongly influenced by the strict adherence of the French state to the principles of monetary and fiscal orthodoxy. These principles are often closely associated with the British state under Thatcher and Major, but in practice were often honoured more in the breach than in the observance. Similarly it was in Germany, not in Britain, that the entire social rented stock was in effect privatized in the mid-1980s, and a consideration of German housing policy more generally shows a close concern with market processes and a clear vision of state activity supporting and not replacing market forces.

So the notion of a linear 'liberal to corporatist' continuum with Britain at one pole and France and Germany at the other is not accurate. The study of housing policy in Britain, France and Germany reveals a complex pattern which cannot be reduced to a simple formula. There are economic, political and social forces which are common to all three countries (as well as to many others), but these forces are mediated through very different institutions and political structures. Moreover, the effect of these institutions and structures is more than just to speed up or slow down the pace of change and adjustment - they leave a profound impression on both policy and its implementation. It is here that the concept of path dependence is useful - countries become locked into particular patterns of policy development at an early stage, for reasons that may be historical, deliberately chosen, or the product of accident. Once locked in, this pattern then constrains future development.

All explanations of comparative policy development therefore involve some combination of common structural forces on the one hand, and different institutional and political mechanisms on the other. So, while Esping-Andersen, for example, emphasizes the latter, Harloe puts more weight on the former. Ultimately, the exact proportions in the mixture are perhaps only a matter of taste; I am not concerned here to prolong further the debate on structure and agency, but simply to reaffirm that any adequate causal explanation requires the presence of both components.

Whatever the relative contributions of structure and agency which best explains the current state of housing policy in Britain, France and Germany, the general *direction* of policy is clear, in all three of the countries studied. Housing policy in the sense in which the term was understood at the zenith of the post-war welfare state has collapsed or is collapsing, leaving behind a bifurcated or polarized set of policies towards housing which both reflect the division of modern European societies into a relatively contented majority and an impoverished minority, and by and large promote the acceptance of this state of affairs.

7.5 UNDERLYING CAUSES

Contrary to much wishful thinking on the left and centre-left, the European dimension does not offer an alternative vision to this, but largely reflects and reinforces what has become the consensus among policy makers: that primacy must be given to the free play of market forces; that government is mainly the problem not the solution; that little can be done about growing economic inequality; that mass unemployment and poverty are probably an inevitable part of the political and economic landscape. Furthermore, there seems to be relatively little prospect of any radical change to this position. Not only do the majority of politicians and senior officials subscribe to this limited and pessimistic vision of government's role, but it is a view increasingly shared by electorates also.

Paul Krugman has argued that the key economic variables which affect people's standard of living are productivity, income distribution and unemployment. Other variables such as inflation and the budget deficit have only indirect effects (Krugman 1990). Moreover, of these productivity is the most important: 'Productivity isn't everything, but in the long run it is almost everything. A country's ability to improve its standard of living over time depends almost entirely on its ability to raise its output per worker, (Krugman 1990, p. 9). For reasons that are unclear, despite being much debated, productivity growth in the USA and Western Europe slowed after 1973. The ending of the long boom continues to define the era in which we are living - in Krugman's phrase, the age of diminished expectations. He is referring to the expectations of individual households about their future levels of economic welfare, but the phrase can equally well be applied to collective expectations about the ability of welfare states to provide full employment, social protection, and high standards of public and private welfare. The stuttering of the great Keynesian economic machines has thrown into jeopardy not just the post-war consensus on collective government management of the economy, but also the continuous growth in the welfare state which was predicated on just such economic management.

More specifically in Europe, there has been the inexorable rise and persistence of unemployment. Unemployment in the twelve countries which now comprise the European Union was not only far lower in the early 1970s (below 4 per cent) but also below the level of unemployment in the USA (although still above Japanese levels). Unemployment rose steadily throughout the 1970s, and in the 1980s and 1990s has remained considerably above levels in the United States, and far above those in Japan. Explanations abound for this phenomenon. For free-marketeers the culprit is Europe's regulated labour markets, compared with the more liberalized US system. As evidence, they point to the much lower rates of job creation in Europe, and the consequent lower employment rates. That is, Europe's growth in unemployment has largely been caused not by demographic factors (increases in the labour force) so much as from an inability to create enough jobs. For interventionists, the reasons are more directly to do with government policy (Nolan 1994). A decade or more of deflationary policies, in which the control of inflation was prioritized over full employment, has left Europe's economies working at well below capacity, and with a consequently large volume of demand-deficient unemployment (see Michie and Wilkinson 1994). The solution is not yet more market liberalization, but rather active policies of demand management to boost output and employment. These policies now look even further away with the institutionalization of deflationary policies in the mechanisms of the ERM and the Maastricht Treaty. Bean (1992) argues that European unemployment is high for a combination of both classical and Keynesian reasons. But depressingly, he concludes that we are not much further on than ten years ago in understanding why.

Whatever the causes of the surge in unemployment, there can be little doubt that it is now the major socioeconomic issue, particularly in the three countries in our study - Britain, France and Germany. On standardized unemployment rates, unemployment rose in Britain from 3.6 per cent in 1971 to 8.7 per cent in 1991, in France from 2.7 per cent to 9.5 per cent, and in Germany from 0.9 per cent to 4.3 per cent. By 1993-94, figures were 7.3 per cent in West Germany (15.1 per cent in the East), 12.0 per cent in France and 10.2 per cent in Britain.

These economic developments have put similar pressures on social policies in the three countries in two ways. First, the slowdown in economic growth, coinciding with large, sometimes explosive growth in welfare expenditures has raised the issue of 'can the welfare state be afforded?' to the top of the political agenda. As Rose (1986) pointed out, it is not the growth in public expenditure *per se* which is crucial, but rather the 'front-end load', that is, the proportion of economic growth absorbed by public expenditure. In the seven OECD countries studied by Rose, this increased from 28 per cent (1952-60) to 47 per cent (1961-72) to 147 per cent (1973-82).

Second, the increase in unemployment, together with other factors such as the growth in the numbers of single-parent families and the widening distribution of income, has led to increased numbers of poor people, and consequently greater demands on social protection systems and other forms of social welfare. To this might be added changes in the demographic structure, with increased numbers of elderly relative to working-age population, although many of the more apocalyptic claims about the consequences of an ageing population can be discounted.

Together, then, these economic developments create similar pressures on social policies in our three countries and elsewhere. Moreover, the concentration of problems among a minority of the population, and the growing gulf between those living standards remain tolerable or better, and those whose real position worsens, will by its very nature weaken support for universal welfare programmes. Hence there is a strong interconnection between these economic factors - changes in the material basis of households' lives - and the more directly political or ideological factors discussed below.

In addition, there has been a shift in political attitudes among policy makers and politicians, and possibly also among voters. It would be difficult as well as time-consuming to tease out the complex relationships between structural economic changes and changes in ideas and political values in the 1970s and 1980s. But it is clear that there was a widespread shift to the right, away from planning and towards the market, away from government intervention and towards market liberalization. Self (1993) identifies the important role of public choice theory in the construction of the new ideology:

> Mainstream public choice theories have been fused with market theories and converted into a powerful new ideology which has become politically dominant over the last two decades. This new ideology has overthrown or undercut the previous dominant ideology often described as the Keynesian welfare-state. ... Unfortunately there is as yet no good name for this new composite ideology. 'Government by the market' suggesting the dominance of a market-based view of the role of politics and government, perhaps adequately conveys its meaning. (Self 1993, p. 56)

As Self points out, the new ideology shares with the Keynesian welfare-state one it replaced the characteristic of being a combination of economic and political thought. While the Keynesian welfare-state view emphasized market failure and the need for government intervention to ensure both economic growth and equitable social arrangements, the new ideology reverses this, emphasizing government failure and the scope for markets to achieve efficiency and equity goals. Importantly, this *is* an ideology, that is, in Self's words it 'comprises a cohesive set of beliefs and values, of positive and normative assumptions about the nature of the world ... An effective ideology will mobilize political supporters to share the general beliefs and goals of a party, interest group or politician' (Self 1993, pp. 54-5).

A secondary question is the degree to which this change in core economic beliefs and social philosophy is simply an elite phenomenon, or whether it is shared by the majority of the population also. Radical right governments in Britain were elected on minority shares of the vote, the Conservatives achieving a remarkably consistent 41-42 per cent in the elections of 1979, 1983, 1987 and 1992. France was governed by socialist governments for much of this period, while Germany's Federal government remained a coalition which represented social-Catholic as well as neoliberal elements. At the very least this suggests that there was not a widespread, fundamental shift towards more right-wing, neoliberal values among electorates in the 1980s and 1990s.

Furthermore, in Britain at least there is considerable survey evidence that the welfare state continued to be extremely popular with voters in the 1980s, and that voters expressed willingness to pay higher taxes to support the welfare state (see Taylor-Gooby 1991b, Ch. 5 for a discussion). In 1983, 32 per cent of the British population supported increased taxes and spending on health, education and social benefits, compared with only 9 per cent who wished both taxes and spending to be reduced. By 1989 the figures were 56 per cent and 3 per cent.

Nevertheless, voters continued to return governments that favoured tax cuts over increased spending. The explanation for this paradox may lie in the relatively low priority voters give to the welfare issue as a determinant of how they vote, or it may simply be evidence of the gap between voters' theoretical beliefs and their practical concerns.

Whatever the degree of genuine ideological change among either elites or masses, and whatever the strengths or shortcomings in the new market ideology, the essential point for our argument here is that at the very least, these political developments in the last two decades represent a considerable loss of faith in the post-war Keynesian social-democratic project. The reduction in economic momentum, the chronic problem of inflation and the re-emergence of mass unemployment, above all the seeming inability of traditional policy mechanisms - or indeed *any* policy mechanism - to have much impact on these problems has led to citizens having much weaker beliefs in government's ability to do very much to ensure economic growth and improve social conditions. This represents a widespread and significant development in the political economy of the Western European countries. Of course, there are significant differences in how these issues were played out in Britain, France and Germany, and the actual institutional and policy environments had significant effects in terms of how severe the consequences were and who bore them. But the common experiences of disillusionment should not be ignored. This is the age of diminished expectations not just about individual economic advancement but also about the effectiveness of government.

7.6 CONCLUSIONS

In drawing conclusions from this research, two caveats are necessary. First, my research has concentrated on only three countries. Generalization from such a narrow base is necessarily problematic, but I believe that a detailed understanding of the housing policies of a small number of countries yields more insights than a superficial examination of a larger number.

Second, one must, of course, guard against idealizing policy in some earlier epoch. Clearly, there was no stage in which housing policy was ever truly comprehensive - housing policy in different historical periods in each of the three countries studies reveals particular emphases linked to the policy and economic concerns of the time.

The central argument of this book has been that in the three countries studied, the development of housing policies can best be understood in terms of a process of bifurcation as both reflection and reinforcement of broad structural and policy trends. Ultimately, the complexities of the interactions between system change and policy change, and between common structural forces and nationally specific institutions and practices, make it unrealistic to propose a single, simple explanation for policy development in the three countries. But as a description of the process, policy collapse is preferable to policy convergence. The phrase captures the key aspect examined in this book: the fragmentation of housing policy as a tool for a more equal and more integrated society. This should be seen as both cause and effect of the trend towards greater inequality and polarization in European countries, which I have briefly referred to here and is more adequately analysed elsewhere. Moreover, there seems increasingly wide acceptance that while such trends are to be deplored, there is little that governments can do to affect these processes. Indeed, we seem even to accept the fact that we understand very little about why (as opposed to how) such inequality and polarization has increased in the last twenty years.

Furthermore, the capacity of national governments to effect a radical change of direction, even if they had the will to do so, is being eroded. Policy is increasingly being made at other levels: economic powers pass upward to supranational institutions, while decentralization in many countries (although not Britain) means that the tools of social intervention pass downwards to regions and communities. At all levels, the increased role of markets reduces the scope for policy intervention. So while there will continue to be debate among elites, between political parties, and among the public too, about the *specifics* of housing policy in each country -where the limit of owner-occupation is, the balance between means-tested and general support, what the most effective ways of targeting diminishing resources are, and so on - there seems little scope for changing the broad limits which have been imposed.

Yet underlying this the goals of a truly holistic - that is, universal - housing policy remain the same: a decent home for all, the improvement of the housing stock, a reduction in inequality. But to achieve this would require not just linking certain aspects of housing to other social issues (what is meant by holistic in practice) but where necessary challenging the economic orthodoxy that limits the scope and function of social policy in general.

This would mean recognizing housing as a social investment; looking at the housing system as a whole; prioritizing need; promoting fairness, investment and quality rather than tenure specific goals; linking housing to the debate about inequality and polarization; and seeking the solution to current housing problems in their root causes of unemployment, family breakdown and political unresponsiveness. Only in this way might the bifurcation of housing policy be reversed and the two paths brought together.

NOTES

1.   The definition of 'household' is itself problematic, of course. In particular, the post-war period has seen a shift in the commonly accepted definition from being essentially synonymous with 'family' to something much broader.
2.   By pointing this out, I do not seek to deny the existence of the 'real problem' by showing historical parallels.   This is a curious form of argument anyway, as if the force of a contemporary problem were somehow reduced by showing that things were even worse in some previous age.

References

Abrahamson, R. (1992) 'Welfare Pluralism: Towards a New Consensus for a European Social Policy?', in Hantrais, L. et al., *The Mixed Economy of Welfare*, Cross-National Research Papers No.6, Loughborough University.

Atkinson, A.B. (1991) 'Poverty, statistics and progress in Europe', London School of Economics ST/ICERD Welfare State Programme Discussion Paper WSP/60.

Atkinson, A.B. (1993) 'What is Happening to the Distribution of Income in the UK?', London School of Economics ST/ICERD Welfare State Programme Discussion Paper WSP/87.

Atkinson, R. and Moon, G. (1994) *Urban Policy in Britain: The City, the State and the Market*, Basingstoke: Macmillan.

Audit Commission (1992) *Developing Local Authority Housing Strategies*, London: HMSO.

Ball, M., Harloe, M. and Martens, M. (1988) *Housing and Social Change in Europe and the USA*, London: Routledge.

Bank of England (1992a) 'House prices, arrears and possessions', *Quarterly Bulletin*, May, 173-9.

Bank of England (1992b) 'Negative equity in the housing market', *Quarterly Bulletin*, August, 266-8.

Barlow, J. and Duncan, S. (1994) *Success and Failure in Housing Provision. European Systems Compared*, Oxford: Pergamon.

Barr, N. (1987) *Economics of the Welfare State*, London: Weidenfeld & Nicholson.

Bayley, R. (1994) 'A right to housing, but not to a house', *Inside Housing*, 1 July.

Bean, C. (1992) 'European Unemployment: A Survey', London School of Economics Centre for Economic Performance Discussion Paper No. 71, March.

Begg, I. and Mayes, D. (1991) 'Social and Economic Cohesion Among the Regions of Europe in the 1990s', *National Institute Economic Review*, November, 63-74.

Begg, I. and Mayes, D. (1993) 'Cohesion, Convergence and Economic and Monetary Union Europe', *Regional Studies*, 27 (2), 149-65.

Benit, C. (1994) 'La Diffusion de l'Accession à la propriété en Europe', Unpublished dissertation, l'IAURIF and Universités Paris I and Paris VIII.

Bentham, G. (1986) 'Socio-tenurial polarization in the United Kingdom, 1953-83: Income evidence', *Urban Studies*, 2, 157-62.

Blanc, M. (1991) 'Du logement insalubre à l'habitat social devalorisé. Les minorités ethniques en Allemagne, France et Grande-Bretagne', *Les Annales de la Recherche Urbaine*, No. 49.

Blanc, M. (1993) 'Housing segregation and the poor: new trends in French social rented housing', *Housing Studies*, 8, 207-14.

Boelhouwer, P. and van der Heijden, H, (1992) *Housing Systems in Europe, Part 1* Delft: Delft University Press.

Borkenstein, H.J. (1993) 'Ausgabenschwerpunkte im Haushalt 1993 des Bundesbauministeriums', *BundesBauBlatt*, Heft, 2 February, 84-92.

Bouw (1988) '1992' Special, No. 43, 14 October.

Bramley, G. (1989) *Meeting Housing Needs*, Bristol: Association of District Councils/School of Advanced Urban Studies.

Bramley, G. (1990) *Bridging the Affordability Gap*, Bristol: School of Advanced Urban Studies.

Bramley, G. (1991) *Bridging the Affordability Gap in 1990*, London: Association of District Councils/House Builders' Federations.

Britton, A. (1993) 'Two routes to full employment', *National Institute Economic* Review, 2, 5-11.

Brownill, S. (1990) *Developing London's Docklands: Another Great Planning Disaster*, Liverpool: Paul Chapman.

Bundesministerium für Arbeit und Sozialordnung (1993) *Sozialbericht 1993*.

Buskase, H. (1992) 'Wohnen in den neuen Bundeslandern - Erblasten und Perspektiven', *Der langfristige Kredit*, 21 and 22 November, 734-6.

Calcoen, F. (1992) 'Le droit au logement: de l'affirmation à la concretisation. Le cas de la France', Paper to the 5th International Housing Research Conference, Montreal, Canada.

Castles, S. (1984) *Here for Good: Western Europe's New Ethnic Minorities*, London: Pluto Press.

Central Statistical Office (1991) *Social Trends No. 21*, London: HMSO.

Central Statistical Office (1995) *Social Trends 1995*, London: HMSO.

Chamberlayne, P. (1992) 'Income maintenance and institutional forms: a comparison of France, West Germany, Italy and Britain 1945-1990', *Policy and Politics*, 20 (4), 299-318.

Cheshire, P. (1990) 'Explaining the recent performance of the European Community's major urban regions', *Urban Studies* 27 (3), 311-33.

Cheshire, P. and Hay, D. (1989) *Urban Problems in Western Europe: An Economic Analysis*, London: Unwin Hyman.

Cheshire, P., Hay, D. and Carbonaro, G. (1986) *Regional Policy and Urban Decline, the Community's Role in Tackling Urban Decline and Problems of Urban Growth*, Luxembourg: European Communities.

Cingolani, M. (1993) 'Disparités Regionales de Produit par Tête dans la Communauté Européenne', *European Investment Bank Papers*, 19, March.

Clapham, D. and MacLennan, D. (1983) 'Residualisation of public housing: a non-issue', *Housing Review*, January-February, 9-10.

Cole, I. and Furbey, R. (1994) *The Eclipse of Council Housing*, London: Routledge

Collier, J (1994) 'Regional Disparities, the Single Market and European Monetary Union' in Michie, J. and Grieve Smith, J. *Unemployment in Europe*, London: Academic Press.

Collins, M. (1990) 'A guaranteed minimum income in France?', *Social Policy and Administration*, 24 (2), 120-24.

Comby, J. (1992) 'Origine et portée de la loi d'orientation pour la ville', *L'Obervateur de l'immobilier, revue trimestrielle du Crédit Foncier de France*, 21, 38-41.

Commission of the European Communities (1993) *Employment in Europe*, Luxembourg: European Commission.

Cooper, S. (1985) *Public Housing and Private Property*, Aldershot: Gower.

Coulter, F.A.E., Cowell, F.A. and Jenkins, S.P. (1993) 'Family Fortunes in the 1970s and 1980s', in Blundell, R., Preston, I. and Walker, I. (eds), *The Measurement of Household Welfare*, Cambridge: Cambridge University Press.

Council of Mortgage Lenders (1990) *Housing Finance in Europe*, London: Council of Mortgage Lenders.

Crook, T. and Kemp, P. (1991) *The Business Expansion Scheme and Rented Housing*, York: Joseph Rowntree Foundation.

Cross, M. (1993) 'Generating the "new poverty": a European Comparison', in Simpson, R. and Walker, R. *Europe: For Richer or Poorer?*, London: CPAG.

Dangschat, J. (1990) 'Economic improvement divides the city - the case of Hamburg', Paper to Conference on International Housing, Paris, June.

Dangschat, J. (1993) 'Berlin and the German system of cities', *Urban Studies*, 30 (6), 1025-51.

Daunton, M. (1987) *A Property-owning Democracy?*, London: Faber.

David, P.A. (1985) 'Clio and the Economics of Qwerty', *American Economic Review*, 75, 332-7.

David, P.A. (1986) 'Understanding the Necessity of Qwerty: The Necessity of History', in Parker, W.N. (ed.), *Economic History and the Modern Economist*, London: Basil Blackwell, pp. 30-49.

Davies, H., Joshi, H. and Clarke, L. (1993) 'Is it cash the deprived are short of?', Paper to Conference on Research on the 1991 Census, University of Newcastle-upon-Tyne, September.

Department of the Environment (1977) *Housing Policy: A Consultative Document*, Cmnd 6851, London: HMSO.

Department of the Environment (1987) *Housing: The Government's Proposals*, Cm 214, London: HMSO.

Department of the Environment (1991) *Household Projections 1989-2011*, London: HMSO.

Department of the Environment (1995) 'Households in England, their housing tenure and the housing stock 1991-2001' (mimeo), Department of the Environment.

Department of Social Security (1993a) *Households Below Average Income: A Statistical Analysis 1979-1990/91*, London: HMSO.

Department of Social Security (1993b) *The Growth of Social Security*, London: HMSO.

Deutsche Institut für Wirtschaftsforschung (DIW) (1995) 'Wohnungsbau 1995 weiter auf hohem Niveau', in DIW Wochenbericht 5.

Dick, E. (1993) 'Mietenreform und Wohngeldsondergesetz in den neuen Bundeslandern', *BundesBauBlatt*, Heft, 4 April, 242-52.

Donnison, D. (1967) *The Government of Housing*, Harmondsworth: Penguin Books.

Dorling, D., Gentle, C. and Cornford, J. (1992) 'Housing Crisis: Disaster or Opportunity', CURDS Working Paper No. 96, University of Newcastle.

Drake, M. (1991) *Housing Associations and 1992*, London: NFHA.

Durance, A. (1992) *Le financement de logement*, Paris: Masson.

Duvigneau, H.J. and Schonefeldt, L. (1989) *Social Housing Policy, Federal Republic of Germany*, Brussels: COFACE.

Eisenschitz, A. and Gough, J. (1993) *The Politics of Local Economic Policy*, Basingstoke: Macmillan.

Emms, P. (1990) *Social housing - a European Dilemma*, Bristol: SAUS.

English, J. (1982) 'Must Council housing become welfare housing?', *Housing Review*, September-October, 154-5 and November-December, 212-13.

Ermisch, J. (1991) 'European integration and external constraints on social policy: is a Social Charter necessary?', *National Institute Economic Review*, May, 93-105.

Esping-Andersen, G. (1990) *The Three Worlds of Welfare Capitalism*, Cambridge: Polity Press.

Esping-Andersen, G. and Korpi, W. (1984) 'Social Policy as Class Politics in Post-war Capitalism: Scandinavia, Austria and Germany', in Goldthorpe, J.H. (ed.), *Order and Conflict in Contemporary Capitalism*, Oxford: Clarendon Press.

Eurostat (1991) *National Accounts ESA Aggregates 1970-1989*, Luxembourg: Commission of the European Communities.

Fainstein, S. (1990) 'Urban economic development and the transformation of planning in the United States and Great Britain', Working Paper No. 7, Center for Urban Policy Research, Rutgers University, New Jersey, USA.

Fainstein, S. (1994) *The City Builders*, Oxford: Basil Blackwell.

Flamand, J.P. (1989) *Loger le Peuple*, Paris: la Découverte.

Ford, J. (1994) 'The Consequences of mortgage areas and possessions in a depressed housing market', Joseph Rowntree Foundation Housing Research Findings, No. 125.

Forrest, R. and Murie, A. (1983) 'Residualization and council housing: aspects of the changing social relations of housing tenure', *Journal of Social Policy* 12 (4), 453-68.

Forrest, R. and Murie, A. (1988) *Selling the Welfare State: The Privatization of Public Housing*, London: Routledge.

Forrest, R., Murie, A. and Williams, P. (1990) *Home Ownership: Differentiation and Fragmentation*, London: Hyman.

Fribourg, A.M. (1992) Personal interview.

Froger, J. (1992) 'La mise en oeuvre du droit au logement dans le parc locatif privé', Paper to 5th International Housing Research Conference, Montreal.

Furmaniak, K. (1984) 'West Germany: Poverty, Unemployment and Social Insurance', in Walker, R., Lawson, R. and Townsend, P. (eds), *Responses to Poverty*, London: Heinemann.

Gardiner, K. (1993) 'A Survey of Income Inequality over the Last Twenty Years - How Does the U.K. Compare?', London School of Economics ST/ICERD Welfare State Programme Discussion Paper WSP/100.

Geindre, F. (1989) *L'Attribution des Logements Sociaux*, Paris: Ministere de l'Equipement et du Logement, Rapport au ministre.

Ghékiere, L. (1991) *Marches et Politiques du Logement dans la CEE*, Paris: Documentation Française.

Ghékiere L. (1992) *Les Politiques du Logement dans l'Europe de Demain*, Paris: Documentation Francaise.

Giddens, A. (1984) *The Constitution of Society*, Cambridge: Polity Press.

Ginsburg, N. (1992) *Divisions of Welfare*, London: Sage.

Glennerster, H. and Le Grand, J. (1995) 'The Development of Quasi-markets in Welfare Provision', *International Journal of Health Services*, 25 (2), 203-18.

Goldthorpe, J. (1984) 'The End of Convergence: Corporatist and Dualist Tendencies in Modern Western Societies', in Goldthorpe, J. (ed.), *Order and Conflict in Contemporary Capitalism*, Oxford: Oxford University Press.

Goodchild, B. and Truscott, R. (1988) 'Decentralization in France: an assessment of its application to housing and urban policy', *Urban Law and Policy*, 9, 295-318.

Gotting, U. (1994) 'Destruction, adjustment and innovation: social policy transformation in Eastern and Central Europe', *Journal of European Social Policy*, 4 (3), 181-200.

Gourevitch, P. (1986) *Politics in Hard Times: Corporative Responses to International Economic Crisis*, Ithaca and London: Cornell University Press.

Green, A. (1994) 'The Changing Spatial Distribution and Segregation of Poverty and Wealth', Paper to JRF Programme on Income and Wealth, Workshop 3-4 February.

Grignon, M. (1993) 'Conceptualising French Family Policy: The Social Actors', in Hantrais, L. and Mangen, S., *The Policy-making Process and the Social Actors*, Cross-National Research Papers 3rd series, Loughborough University.

Guibert, L. (1992) 'Point de vue sur le dispositif', *L'Observateur de l'Immoblier, Revue Trimestrielle du Credit Foncier de France*, 21, 42-45.

Gude, S. (1991) 'Discrimination problems in the housing market' in Norton, A. and Novy, K. *Low Income Housing in Britain and Germany*, London: Anglo-German Foundation.

Haffner, M. (1991) 'Fiscal treatment of owner-occupiers in the EU: a description', Paper to conference on Housing Policy as a Strategy for Change,' Oslo, Norway.

Halimi, S., Michie, J. and Milne, S. (1994) 'The Mitterrand Experience', in Michie, J. and Grieve Smith, J. *Unemployment in Europe*, London: Academic Press.

Hamm, H. (1993a) 'Wohnungsbautätigkeit 1992: Wohnungsbauexpansion als Motor der Wirtschaftsentwicklung', *BundesBauBlatt*, Heft, 7 July, 498-509.

Hamm, H. (1993b) 'Der soziale Wohnungsbau im Jahre 1992', *BundesBauBlatt*, Heft, 5 May, 340-48.

Hamnett, C. (1984) 'Housing the two nations: socio-tenurial polarization in England and Wales 1961-1981', *Urban Studies*, 43, 389-409.

Hantrais, L. (1995) *Social Policy in the European Union*, London: Macmillan.

Harloe, M. (1995) *The People's Home?*, Oxford: Basil Blackwell.

Harloe, M. and Martens, M. (1983) 'Comparative housing research', *Journal of Social Policy*, 13, 255-77.

Hass-Klau, C. (1986) 'Berlin: "Soft" Urban Renewal in Kreuzberg', *Built Environment*, 12 (3), 165-75.

Heald, D. (1983) *Public Expenditure*, Oxford: Martin Robertson.

Hepworth, N. P. (1984) *The Finance of Local Government*, London: George Allen & Unwin.

Heinz, W. (1991) 'The role of local authorities in meeting housing need', in Norton, A. and Novy, K., *Low Income Housing in Britain and Germany*, London: Anglo-German Foundation.

Hills, J. (ed.) (1990) *The State of Welfare: The Welfare State in Britain Since 1974*, Oxford: Clarendon Press.

Hills, J. (1993) *The Future of Welfare: a Guide to the Debate*, York: Joseph Rowntree Foundation.

Hills, J. (1995) *Inquiry into Income and Wealth Vol 2: A Summary of the Evidence*, York: Joseph Rowntree Foundation.

Hills, J., Hubert, F., Tomann, H. and Whitehead, C. (1990) 'Shifting subsidy from bricks and mortar to people', *Housing Studies*, 5, 147-67.

Hirschman, A.O. (1991) *The Rhetoric of Reaction: Perversity, Futility, Jeopardy*, Cambridge, Mass.: Belknap Press.

Holmans, A.E. (1991) 'House-prices, land-price, the housing market and housing purchase debt in Britain and other countries' (mimeo), Department of the Environment.

Holmans, A.E. (1993) 'Sales of houses and flats by local authorities to sitting tenants: the dwellings sold, the circumstances of buyers and sources of finance', in Department of the Environment, *Housing in England*, London: HMSO, Chapter 10.

Hubert, F. (1992) 'Risks and Incentives in German Social Housing', Free University of Berlin (mimeo).

Hubert, F. (1993) 'Germany's Housing Policy at the Crossroads', Free University of Berlin, Institut für Wirtschaftspolitik und Wirtschaftsgeschichte, Discussion Paper, November.

Hubert, F. (1994) 'Private Rented Housing in Germany', Report to Scottish Homes, December 1994, Berlin: Free University of Berlin.

Jackman, R., Pissarides, C. and Saviour, S. (1990) 'Labour Market Policies and Unemployment in the OECD', London School of Economics, Centre for Economic Performance, Discussion Paper No. 11.

Jenkins, S.P. (1991) 'Income inequality and living standards: Changes in the 1970s and the 1980s', *Fiscal Studies*, 12, February, 1-28.

Jenkins, S.P. (forthcoming) 'Accounting for Inequality Trends: Decomposition Analysis for the UK 1971-1986', *Economica*.

Johnson, N. (1987) *The Welfare State in Transition: The Theory and Practice of Welfare Pluralism*, London: Harvester Wheatsheaf.

Johnson, N. (1990) *Reconstructing the Welfare State*, Hemel Hempstead: Harvester Wheatsheaf.

Johnson, P. and Webb, S. (1993) 'Explaining the Growth in UK Income Inequality: 1979-1988', *Economic Journal*, 103, 429-45.

Katseli, L. (1989) 'The political economy of macroeconomic policy in Europe', in Guerrieri, P. and Padoan, P.C. (eds), *The Political Economy of European Integration*, Hemel Hempstead: Harvester Wheatsheaf.

Kleinman, M.P. (1988) 'The changing role of council housing in England: a study of supply, access and allocation, 1976-1985', unpublished Ph.D. thesis, University of London.

Kleinman, M.P. (1991) 'Social housing in the 1980s and 1990s: past experience and future trends', University of Cambridge Department of Land Economy Discussion Paper No. 32.

Kleinman, M. (1992) *Policy Responses to Changing Housing Markets; Towards a European Housing Policy?*, LSE Welfare State Programme Discussion Paper WSP/73, London School of Economics.

Kleinman, M. (1993) 'Large scale transfers of council housing to new landlords: is British social housing becoming more "European"?', *Housing Studies*, 8 (3), 163-78.

Kleinman, M., Whitehead, C. and Morrison, N. (1994) 'Housing needs, housing demand and housing output in the 1990s', in Cross, D. and Whitehead, C.' *Redevelopment and Planning 1994*, Cambridge: Department of Land Economy, University of Cambridge.

Kohli, J. (1993) 'Wohnungspolitik und Wohnungswirtschaft in den neuen Ländern', Geographische Rundschau, 3 March, 140-45.

Kreibich, V. (1991) 'Housing needs now and in the 1990s', in Norton, A. and Novy, K., *Low Income Housing in Britain and Germany*, London: Anglo-German Foundation.

Krugman, P. (1990) *The Age of Diminished Expectations*, Cambridge, Mass.: MIT Press.

Krugman, P. (1991) *Geography and Trade*, Cambridge, Mass.: MIT Press.

Kuznets, S. (1955) 'Economic Growth and Income Inequality', American Economic Review, 45, 1-28.

Lacoste, G. (1990) 'Logement Scenario pour 2015', *Les cahiers de l'IAURIF*, No. 93, June.

Langeveld, A. and de Vries, D. (1990) 'Op naar een Europese bouwregelgering', (Towards a European Building Regulation), *Corporatie Magazine*, 1 (4), 21-3.

Lefebvre, B. (1993) 'Housing in France: the consequences of ten years of deregulation', in Turner, B. and Whitehead, C. (eds), *Housing Finance in the 1990s*, Gavle, Sweden: National Swedish Institute for Building Research.

Lefebvre, B., Mouillart, M. and Occhipinti, S. (1991) *Politique du logement: 50 ans pour un échec*, L'Harmattan: Paris.

Le Grand, J. and Winter, D. (1987) 'The Middle Classes and the Welfare State', *Journal of Public Policy*, 6 (4), 399-430.

Le Grand, J. and Bartlett, W. (1993) *Quasi-markets and Social Policy*, London: Macmillan.

Leibfried, S. (1993) 'Towards a European Welfare State?', in Jones, C. (ed.), *New Perspectives on the Welfare State in Europe*, London: Routledge.

Lever, W. (1993) 'Competition within the European Urban System', Urban Studies, 30 (6), 935-48.

Lewis, J. (1992) 'Gender and the Developments of Welfare Regimes', *Journal of European Social Policy*, 2 (3), 159-73.

Louvot, C. (1989) 'La croissance du nombre de ménages soutiendra la construction neuve jusqu'au milieu des années 90', *Economie et Statistique*, No. 225, October, 19-29.

Louvot, C. (1992) 'De la location à la propriété: le parc de logements se redistribue', *Economie et Statistique*, No. 251, February.

Louvot, C. and Renaudat, J.P. (1990) *Le parc de logements et son occupation: mouvements annuels entre 1982 et 1988*, Paris: INSEE.

Lundqvist, L. (1992) *Dislodging the Welfare State? Housing and privatisation in four European states*, Delft: Delft University Press.

Macnicol, J. (1987) 'In Pursuit of the Underclass', *Journal of Social Policy*, 16 (3), 293-18.

Malpass, P. (1983) 'Residualization and the restructuring of housing tenure', *Housing Review*, March/April, 44-5.

Malpass, P. (1990) *Reshaping Housing Policy*, London: Routledge.

Malpass, P. (1995) 'Unravelling Housing Policy in Britain', University of West of England (mimeo).

Malpass, P. and Murie, A. (1994), *Housing Policyand Practice: Third Edition*, Basingstoke: Macmillan.

Mangen, S. (1991) 'Social Policy, the Radical Right and the German Welfare State',in Glennerster, H. and Midgley, J., *The Radical Right and the Welfare State*, Hemel Hempstead: Harvester Wheatsheaf.

Martin, R. and Tyler, P. (1992) 'The nature of British regional problems in the context of European integration', in Mansley, N. et al., *Cambridge Economic Review*, Cambridge: PACEU/Department of Land Economy, University of Cambridge.

Massot, A. (1990) 'Logements Parisiens: Pourquoi la Hausse?', Les Cahiers de l'IAURIF, September.

Matznetter, W. (1993) 'Housing and the European Communities', Paper to Conference on European Network for Housing Research, Budapest, September.

McCrone, G. and Stephens, M. (1995) *Housing Policy in Britain and Europe*, London: UCL Press.

McGuire, C. (1981) *International Housing Policies*, Lexington: Lexington Books.

Merlin, P. (1988) 'L'évolution du parc de logements 1945-1986', *Travaux et documents (INED)*, 120, 203-21.

Michie, J. and Wilkinson, F. (1994) 'The Growth of Unemployment in the 1980s', in Michie, J. and Grieve Smith, J., *Unemployment in Europe*, London: Academic Press.

Mishra, R. (1990) *The Welfare State in Capitalist Society*, Hemel Hempstead: Harvester Wheatsheaf.

Monk, S. and Kleinman, M. (1989) 'Housing', in Brown, P. and Sparks, R., *Beyond Thatcherism*, Milton Keynes: Open University Press.

Mouillart, M. (1992) 'Quels sont les Besoins en Logement?', *L'Observateur de l'Immobilier, Revue Trimestrielle du Crédit Foncier de France*, 20, 28-35.

Muellbauer, J. (1994) 'Anglo-German differences in housing market fluctuations: the role of institutions and macroeconomic policy', *Economic Modelling*, 11 (2), 238-49.

National Housing Forum (1989) *Housing Needs in the 1990s*, London: National Housing Forum.

Nevin, E. (1990) *The Economics of Europe*, London: Macmillan.

Nolan, P. (1994) 'Labour Market Institutions, Industrial Restructuring and Unemployment in Europe', in Michie, J. and Grieve Smith, J., *Unemployment in Europe*, London: Academic Press.

O'Donnell, R. (1992) 'Policy Requirements for Regional Balance in Economic and Monetary Union', in Hannequat, A., *Economic and Social Cohesion in Europe*, London: Routledge.

OECD (1987) *Revitalising Urban Economies*, Paris: OECD.

OECD (1988) *Urban Housing Finance*, Paris: OECD.

OECD (1990) 'Housing policies and social integration in cities - issues paper', OECD Group on Urban Affairs 17th session, Paris: OECD.

OECD (1991a) 'Project group on housing, social integration and livable environments in cities - draft terms of reference', OECD Group on Urban Affairs, Paris: OECD.

OECD (1991b) *Economic Outlook July 1991*, Paris: OECD.

OECD (1992) *Economic Surveys - France 1991/1992*, Paris: OECD.

OECD (1993) *Economic Surveys - Germany 1993*, Paris: OECD.

OECD (1994) *Economic Surveys - France 1994*, Paris: OECD.

O'Higgins, M. and Jenkins, S.P. (1989) 'Poverty in Europe, Estimates for 1975, 1980 and 1985', paper presented at the seminar on Poverty Statistics in the European Community, Nordwijk, Netherlands.

Osenberg, H. (1993) 'Rehousing the homeless: new model projects in Germany, East and West', Paper to Conference on International Housing,'Transformation in the East, Transition from the West', Budapest, Hungary, September.

Oxley, M. (1991) 'The Aims and Methods of Comparative Housing Research' *Scandinavian Housing & Planning Research*, 8 (2), 67-77.

Oxley, M. and Smith, J. (1993) 'Private Rented Housing in the European Community', European Housing Research Working Paper No. 3, De Montfort University, Milton Keynes.

Padoa-Schioppa, T. (ed.) (1987) *Efficiency, Stability and Equity*, Oxford: Oxford University Press.

Parkinson, M. (1989) 'The Thatcher government's urban policy 1979-1989: a review', *Town Planning Review*, 60 (4), 421-40.

Pearsall, J. (1984) 'France', in Wynn, M. (ed.), *Housing in Europe*, London: Croom Helm.

Pfaller, A., Gough, I. and Therborn, G. (eds) (1991) *Can the Welfare State Compete?* A Comparative Study of Five Advanced Capitalist Countries, London: Macmillan.

Potter, P. and Drevermann, M. (1988) 'Home Ownership, Foreclosure and Compulsory Auction in the Federal Republic of Germany', *Housing Studies*, 3 (2), 94-104.

Power, A. (1993) *Hovels to High-Rise*, London: Routledge.

Priemus, H. (1991) 'Unification of the European building market: possible consequences for the Dutch construction industry', *Netherlands Journal of Housing and the Built Environment*, 6 (1), 35-45.

Priemus, H., Kleinman, M.P., Maclennan, D. and Turner, B. (1993) *European Monetary, Economic and Political Union: Consequences for National Housing Policies*, Delft: Delft University Press.

Priemus, H., Kleinman, M. P., Maclennan, D. and Turner, B. (1994) 'Maastricht Treaty: Consequences for national housing policies', *Housing Studies*, 9 (2), 163-82.

Pryke, M. and Whitehead, C. (1991) 'An Overview of Recent Change in the Provision of Private Finance for Social Housing', Discussion Paper No. 28, Department of Land Economy Property Research Unit, University of Cambridge.

Robinson, R. and O'Sullivan, T. (1983) 'Housing Tenure Polarization: Some Empirical Evidence', *Housing Review*, July/August, 116-17.

Robinson, R., O'Sullivan, T. and Le Grand, J. (1985) 'Inequality and Housing', *Urban Studies*, 22, 249-56.

Room, G. and Berghman, J. (1990)'*New Poverty' in the European Community*, London: Macmillan.

Rose, R. (1986) 'Common Goals but Different Role: The State's Contribution to the Welfare Mix', in Shiratori, R. (eds.), (1986) *The Welfare State East and West*, New York: Oxford University Press.

Saunders, P. (1990) *A Nation of Home Owners*, London: Unwin Hyman.

Schmidt, S. (1989) 'Convergence theory, labour movements and corporatism: the case of housing', *Scandinavian Housing and Planning Research*, 6, 83-101.

Schuler-Wallner, G. and Wullkopf, U. (1991) *Housing Shortage and Homelessness* in the Federal Republic of Germany, Darmstadt: Institut Wohnen und Unwelt.

Schulte, B. (1993) 'Guaranteed minimum resources and the European Community', in Simpson, R. and Walker, R., *Europe: For Richer or Poorer?*, London: CPAG.

Self, P. (1993) *Government by the Market?*, London: Macmillan.

Silver, H. (1993) 'National conceptions of the new urban poverty: social structural change in Britain, France and the United States', *International Journal of Urban and Regional Research*, 17 (3), 336-54.

Simon, G.L. (1990) 'Trends and prospects on the threshold of the internal market', *Social Europe*, No. 3.

Smith, D. (1987) *The Rise and Fall of Monetarism*, Harmondsworth: Penguin.

Spicker, P. (1991) 'The principle of subsidiarity and the social policy of the European Community', *Journal of European Social Policy*, 1 (1), 3-14.

Stark, D. (1992) 'The great transformation? Social change in eastern Europe', *Contemporary Sociology*, 21, 299-304.

Taffin, C. (1992) Personal communication.

Taisne, C. (1990) 'Le 1 per cent et le logement social', *Les Cahiers de l'IAURIF*, September.

Tarling, R., Gray, A., Hirst, A. and McEvoy, K. (1992) 'Policy responses to long-term unemployment in the European Community - the ERGO programme', in Mansley, N. et al., *Cambridge Economic Review*, Cambridge: PACEC/Department of Land Economy, University of Cambridge.

Taylor-Gooby, P. (1991a) 'Welfare state regimes and welfare citizenship', *Journal of European Social Policy*, 1 (2), 93-105.

Taylor-Gooby, P. (1991b) *Social Change, Social Welfare and Social Science*, Hemel Hempstead: Harvester Wheatsheaf.

Titmuss, R. (1963) *Essays on the Welfare State*, 2nd edition, London: Allen & Unwin.

Tomann, H. (1990) 'Housing in Germany', in Maclennan, D. and Williams, R., *Affordable Housing in Europe*, York: Joseph Rowntree Foundation.

Tomann, H. (1993) 'Developments in German housing finance' in Turner, B. and Whitehead, C. (eds), *Housing Finance in the 1990s, Research Report SB53*, Gavle, Sweden: The National Swedish Institute for Building Research.

Tsoukalis, L. (1993) *The New European Economy*, Oxford: Oxford University Press.

Turner, B., Hegedus, J. and Tosics, I. (1992) *The Reform of Housing in Eastern Europe and the Soviet Union*, London: Routledge.

Ulbrich (1993) 'Wohnungsversorgung in der Bundesrepublik Deutschland', *Aus Politik und Zeitgeschichte*, B 8-9/93, 19, February, S. 22.

van Vliet, W. (1990) *International Handbook of Housing Policies and Practices*, New York: Greenwood Press.

Wacquant, L.J.D. (1993) 'Urban outcasts: stigma and division in the black American ghetto and the French urban periphery', *International Journal of Urban and Regional Research*, 17 (3), 366-83.

Ward, C. (1985) *When We Build Again*, London: Pluto.

Whitehead, C., Cross, D., Kleinman, M. and Connolly, V. (1992) *Housing the National: Choice, Access and Priorities Volume II*, London: Royal Institution of Chartered Surveyors.

Whitehead, C.M.E. and Kleinman, M.P. (1986) *Private Rented Housing in the 1980s and 1990s*, Cambridge: Granta Editions.

Whitehead, C.M.E. and Kleinman, M. P. (1992) *A Review of Housing Needs Assessment*, London: Housing Corporation.

Whitehead, C., Kleinman, M. and Chattrabhuti, A. (1994) *The Private Rented Housing Market: A Review of Current Trends and Future Prospects*, London: Council of Mortgage Lenders.

Wilcox, S. (1994) *Housing Finance Review (1994/95)*, York: Joseph Rowntree Foundation.

Wilcox, S. with Bramley, G., Ferguson, A., Perry, J. and Woods, C. (1993) *Local Housing Companies: New Opportunities for Council Housing*, York: Joseph Rowntree Foundation.

Wilderer, H. (1993) 'Der deutsche Wohnungsmarkt - nicht nur in Ballungszentren ein Problemfall ohne Ende', *Der langfristige Kredit*, 8 April, 221-4.

Wilensky, H.L., Luebbent, H.L., Hahn, G.M., et al., (1987) *Comparative Policy Research*, Berlin: Gower.

Willmott, P. and Murie, A. (1988), *Polarization and Social Housing*, London: Policy Studies Institute.

Woodward, R. (1991) 'Mobilising Opposition: The Campaign against Housing Action Trusts in Tower Hamlets', *Housing Studies*, 6 (1), 44-56.

Index